JOURNAL FOR THE STUDY OF THE NEW TESTAMENT SUPPLEMENT SERIES
200

Executive Editor
Stanley E. Porter

Sheffield Academic Press

Doing Things with Words in the First Christian Century

F. Gerald Downing

Journal for the Study of the New Testament
Supplement Series 200

Copyright © 2000 Sheffield Academic Press

Published by
Sheffield Academic Press Ltd
Mansion House
19 Kingfield Road
Sheffield S11 9AS
England

http://www.shef-ac-press.co.uk

Typeset by Sheffield Academic Press
and
Printed on acid-free paper in Great Britain
by Antony Rowe Ltd,
Chippenham, Wiltshire

British Library Cataloguing in Publication Data

A catalogue record for this book is available
from the British Library

ISBN 1-84127-151-9

CONTENTS

ACKNOWLEDGMENTS

Seven of these pieces have appeared in other publications, mostly in the last decade; one will appear elsewhere around the same time as this volume appears. Three chapters, drafted in the last eighteen months, appear here for the first time. I wish to express my thanks to Editors and Presses for permission to reprint the following.

'*A bas les aristos*: The Relevance of Higher Literature for the Understanding of the Earliest Christian Writings', *NovT* 30.3 (1988), pp. 212-30.

'Words as Deeds and Deeds as Words', *BibInt* 3.2 (1995), pp. 129-43.

'Word-processing in the First Century: The Social Production and Performance of Q', *JSNT* 64 (1996), pp. 29-48.

'A Genre for Q and a Socio-cultural Context for Q: Comparing Sets of Similarities with Sets of Differences', *JSNT* 55 (1994), pp. 3-26.

'Markan Intercalations in Cultural Context', in G. Brooke (ed.), *Narrativity and the Bible* (Leuven: Peeters, forthcoming).

'Compositional Conventions and the Synoptic Problem', *JBL* 107.1 (1988), pp. 69-85.

'A Paradigm Perplex: Luke, Matthew and Mark', *NTS* 38 (1992), pp. 15-36.

'Theophilus' First Reading of Luke–Acts', in C.M. Tuckett (ed.), *Luke's Literary Achievement* (JSNTSup, 116; Sheffield: Sheffield Academic Press, 1995), pp. 91-109.

Most of these studies have been shared early on in their time with the Ehrhardt Biblical Seminar in the Department of Religions and Theology in the University of Manchester, the kindness and help of whose members I also acknowledge.

Some small revisions have been made (in style of punctuation, bibliographical details, etc.) and in some of the introductions and conclusions.

ABBREVIATIONS

AB	Anchor Bible
ABRL	Anchor Bible Reference Library
AC	*L'antiquité classique*
AHES	*Archive for History of Exact Sciences*
AJP	*American Journal of Philology*
ANF	Ante-Nicene Fathers
ANRW	Hildegaard Temporini and Wolfgang Haase (eds.), *Aufstieg und Niedergang der römischen Welt: Geschichte und Kultur Roms im Spiegel der neueren Forschung* (Berlin: W. de Gruyter, 1972–)
AristSocSup	Aristotelian Society Supplement
ASNS	*Annali della Scuole Normale Superiore*
BETL	Bibliotheca ephemeridum theologicarum lovaniensium
BHT	Beiträge zur historischen Theologie
Bib	*Biblica*
BibInt	*Biblical Interpretation: A Journal of Contemporary Approaches*
BibRes	*Biblical Research*
BibSem	Biblical Seminar
BIS	Biblical Interpretation Series
BNTC	Black's New Testament Commentaries
BSP	Bochumer Studien zur Philosophie
BTB	*Biblical Theology Bulletin*
CBQ	*Catholic Biblical Quarterly*
CCWJC	Cambridge Commentaries on Writings of the Jewish and Christian World 200 BC to AD 200
CNT	Commentaire du Nouveau Testament
CQ	*Classical Quarterly*
CS	Classical Studies
CurTM	*Currents in Theology and Mission*
EKKNT	Evangelisch-Katholischer Kommentar zum Neuen Testament
EPRO	Études préliminaires aux religions orientales dans l'empire romain
ExpTim	*Expository Times*
FRLANT	Forschungen zur Religion und Literatur des Alten und Neuen Testaments

FzB	Forschung zur Bibel
GR	*Greece and Rome*
GRR	*Graeco-Roman Religion*
GTA	Göttingen theologische Arbeiten
HCS	Hellenistic Culture and Society
HTR	*Harvard Theological Review*
HTS	Harvard Theological Studies
IBS	*Irish Biblical Studies*
ICC	International Critical Commentary
IDB	George Arthur Buttrick (ed.), *The Interpreter's Dictionary of the Bible* (4 vols.; Nashville: Abingdon Press, 1962).
Int	*Interpretation*
JAC	*Jahrbuch für Antike und Christentum*
JAP	*Journal of Applied Philosophy*
JBL	*Journal of Biblical Literature*
JEH	*Journal of Ecclesiastical History*
JHC	*Journal of Higher Criticism*
JHS	*Journal of Hellenic Studies*
JJS	*Journal of Jewish Studies*
JQR	*Jewish Quarterly Review*
JR	*Journal of Religion*
JRH	*Journal of Religious History*
JRS	*Journal of Roman Studies*
JSJ	*Journal for the Study of Judaism*
JSNT	*Journal for the Study of the New Testament*
JSNTSup	*Journal for the Study of the New Testament*, Supplement Series
JSOT	*Journal for the Study of the Old Testament*
JSOTSup	*Journal for the Study of the Old Testament*, Supplement Series
JTS NS	*Journal of Theological Studies* (New Series)
JVG	N.T. Wright, *Jesus and the Victory of God* (London: SPCK, 1996)
KEK	Kritische-exegetische Kommentar
LCL	Loeb Classical Library
LCM	*Liverpool Classical Monthly*
ModC	*Modern Churchman* (now *Modern Believing*)
NCB	New Century Bible
Neot	*Neotestamentica*
NovT	*Novum Testamentum*
NovTSup	*Novum Testamentum*, Supplements
NPNF	Nicene and Post-Nicene Fathers
NTD	Das Neue Testament Deutsch

NTOA	Novum Testamentum et orbis antiquus
NTPG	N.T. Wright, *The New Testament and the People of God* (London: SPCK, 1992)
NTS	*New Testament Studies*
OTP	James Charlesworth (ed.), *Old Testament Pseudepigrapha* (2 vols.; London: Darton, Longman & Todd, 1983)
PA	Philosophia Antiqua
PG	J.-P. Migne (ed.), *Patrologia cursus completa...Series graeca* (166 vols.; Paris: Petit-Montrouge, 1857–83)
PhilQ	*Philosophical Quarterly*
PL	J.-P. Migne (ed.), *Patrologia cursus completa...Series prima* [latina] (221 vols.; Paris: J.-P. Migne, 1844–65)
PRS	*Perspectives in Religious Studies*
RAC	*Reallexikon für Antike und Christentum*
RNT	Regensburger Neues Testament
RPA	*Revue de philosophie ancienne*
RQ	*Restoration Quarterly*
RTP	*Revue de théologie et de philosophie*
SBB	Stuttgarter biblische Beiträge
SBLDS	SBL Dissertation Series
SBLSBS	SBL Sources for Biblical Study
SBLSP	SBL Seminar Papers
SBLTT	SBL Texts and Translations
SBS	Stuttgarter Bibelstudien
SBT	Studies in Biblical Theology
SHTC	Studies in the History of Christian Thought
SJP	*Southern Journal of Philosophy*
SNTS	Society for New Testament Study/Studiorum Novi Testamenti Societas
SNTSMS	Society of New Testament Studies Monograph Series
SJT	*Scottish Journal of Theology*
StudPhilAnn	*Studia Philonica Annual*
SWR	Studies in Women and Religion
TAPA	*Transactions of the American Philological Association*
TDNT	Gerhard Kittel and Gerhard Friedrich (eds.), *Theological Dictionary of the New Testament* (trans. Geoffrey W. Bromiley; 10 vols.; Grand Rapids: Eerdmans, 1964–)
TJT	*Toronto Journal of Theology*
TU	*Texte und Untersuchungen*
TWNT	*Theologisches Wörterbuch zum Neuen Testament*
TynBul	*Tyndale Bulletin*
TZ	*Theologische Zeitschrift*
VC	*Vigiliae christianae*
WBC	Word Biblical Commentary

WMANT	Wissenschaftliche Monographien zum Alten und Neuen Testament
WUNT	Wissenschaftliche Untersuchungen zum Neuen Testament
YCS	Yale Classical Studies
ZNW	*Zeitschrift für die neutestamentliche Wissenschaft*
ZTK	*Zeitschrift für Theologie und Kirche*

INTRODUCTION

It is possible to be aware of gaining a great deal from leading and from less eminent scholars—and still remain dissatisfied. For it is disconcerting when otherwise perceptive writers on Christian origins drop in occasional illustrations from that wider culture which most early Greek-speaking Christians breathed, without explaining why just these disparate oddments have been chosen (either as similar or as distinctive) when so much else has been omitted. So, one can read a massive study on one of the gospels and be reminded of the importance of what the original audience would take for granted—and yet this study may include in any detail no more than a dozen allusions to ideas and events in the world around. Or an exegete of the New Testament, arguing the case for there having been diversity among early Christians, will still set them against a backdrop of stereotyped and uniform Stoics, Epicureans, Platonists, Pythagoreans and Cynics.

Distinctions are drawn between 'narrative' and 'teaching' in the traditions ascribed to Jesus (often in favour of the enhanced reliability of one over against the other), a distinction that the texts themselves explicitly rebut, and that much philosophy of language, action and mind refutes. Again, ancient authors are imagined writing as we might, shut away in bookish quiet, free from disturbance, exercising our individual creative abilities (and gaining academic recognition for our individual contributions), rather than in the social interplay ancient authors themselves describe. Literary genres from antiquity are discerned, perhaps even with the help of the ideal constructs outlined by theoreticians of the day, and these forms are then imposed on the earliest Christian writings as though laid down by law; without note of how much interplay in practice there is even among the supposedly distinct kinds of texts produced by the theoreticians themselves; and without apparent realization of how speeches of all kinds, and romances, histories, lives, epics, satires, have features (including structural features) in common across supposed genres.

Various solutions continue to be put forward to explain the literary interrelationships of the synoptic Gospels, Matthew, Mark and Luke, some of these without any basis in the known or discoverable conventions and practicalities of literary composition at the time. Individual texts are analysed to discern detailed intentions (whether of author, editor, or of 'the text itself') and the text may then be declared integral or composite, all without reference to the ways contemporaries understood words—explained meaning and reference—and sought to effect coherent communication.

In short, even where there is attention to the non-Christian and not-specifically Jewish context of the early Christian movement(s), it is often either too narrow or too shallow—or both. Yet with quite a swift immersion in our more readily available Greek and Latin literary remains, it is here suggested, much more of the full richness of that ancient 'intertexture'[1] emerges, an intertexture that can then readily be seen so often to be missing in studies with which we are presented; and then, too, the positive and the negative contextual generalizations that are on occasion proposed (whether apparently neutral, favourable or hostile to some Christian orthodoxy or other received opinion) will readily prompt counter-instances.

Of course it is risky to offer the critical judgments just outlined. But if they spur others to demonstrate that the ancient world and early Christianity(-ies) are still more richly and more complexly and still less definably interlinked, so much the better. And if on the other hand it were all shown to have been simpler and clearer than is argued below, at least the work that follows may have helped prompt that clarification.

The dependence on others of what follows, and my gratitude to those others (over and above any criticism) will be obvious, and acknowledged. This volume represents in part some of the work of the last 25 years or more, work that had this aim from the start, of pointing out the greater richness, complexity—and openness—of the integral context of early Graeco-Roman Christianity than most allow. Some chapters have appeared in print previously, others arise out of very recent research and have been written for this volume. Their themes are now to be

---

1.   On 'intertexture' see V.K. Robbins, *The Tapestry of Early Christian Discourse: Rhetoric, Society and Ideology* (London: Routledge, 1996); and *idem*, *Exploring the Texture of Texts: A Guide to Socio-Rhetorical Interpretation* (Valley Forge, PA: Trinity Press International, 1996).

summarized, together with the threads that are meant to hold them together as a cumulative and coordinated argument.

'*A bas les aristos*' notes that the writings of Roman and provincial aristocrats from a wide time-span are used at least on occasion by many students of Christian origins, but without the propriety of this practice being questioned, or criteria of relevance being proposed. It is then argued that these are indeed valid contextual sources for our researches into the early Christian communities, for it was very much an oral and public society, and there were many settings in which the work of wealthy literati would be made directly or indirectly available to a wider audience. Theatres, courts, streets, temple porticos, markets, as well as homes where slaves and others would be present offered ample opportunities for what we have inherited as 'literature' to permeate 'downwards' (*à bas les aristos*!) to include even the illiterate, but also to allow popular audiences to make their responses known. And writers on education at least make it clear how far popular thought reached at any rate the children of the most exclusive families, through their domestic slaves. (One temporal qualification is, however, suggested, a fairly arbitrary self-limitation to data from two to three generations at most before and after the period being considered. Culture was not static, and was known not to be. We should not range indefinitely in time, at least not without quite precise and argued warrants.) Further and more detailed illustrations of aspects of the power of popular culture are offered in the later chapters on aspects of 'Q' and Mark and Luke.

A concentration on orality, on speech, has, however, tended to lead to some false dichotomies: between speaking and writing, and between speaking and doing, between words and deeds. 'Words as Deeds and Deeds as Words' sets out to redress the latter imbalance. A sharp disjunction between 'sayings' and 'facts' was proposed some time ago by E.P. Sanders, classifying some narratives of actions of Jesus as reliable 'facts', and all accounts of sayings as so open to later recasting as to have no initial historical plausibility.[2] The distinction goes back in fact at least to early 'form criticism'. By contrast, in reality, as people in the ancient world knew, and as modern philosophers have reminded us,

2. E.P. Sanders, *Jesus and Judaism* (London: SCM Press, 1985), pp. 13-18 and ch. 4; for a recent argument the other way, W. Arnal, 'Major Episodes in the Biography of Jesus: An Assessment of the Historicity of the Narrative Tradition', *TJT* 13.2 (1997), pp. 201-226.

speaking is an action, and may be very effective (while a wordless deed may be an 'empty gesture'). But it is also the case that 'actions' are only performed, perceived, reported in a social context, they and the reporting of them are as much shaped by agents' and reporters' intentions, perceptions and (re-)interpretations as any speeches and accounts of speech are. This conclusion is further illustrated and supported by comparing accounts of healings with accounts of utterances ('apothegms' or *'chreiai'*), with the aid of various standard analyses.

Whether it is words about speech or words about other activities, it is still with words that we have to do in most of the sources available to us: words as written down. 'Words and Meanings' asks, Can we tell how these writers may have thought words in general work, how they may have expected them to work (logically, and in practice), how they may have learned to use them? In particular, Can we tell how precise and narrow or how broad and flexible they expected the sense and reference of their words to be? Exegetes will often claim that some different phrasing in Matthew, Mark and Luke betokens some theologically significant disagreement; or they will discern breaks in the logic of some sequence in one of the Gospels (or in 'Q', the supposed lost common source used by Matthew and Luke in additon to their use of Mark), and suggest secondary, editorial interference. It is here argued that in ordinary communication (if not in philosophical dialectic) words were taken to be exchangeable names (labels—quite readily exchangeable labels, for the most part) for things or for ideas (or for 'meanings') perceived in a very reified ('thingy') way. So the words themselves are not expected to be precise (just 'good Greek' or 'allowable Latin' names/labels). Furthermore, the same 'labels' could be used for different 'meanings'. Ancient school books show us this, ancient writers tell us this, ancient theoretical linguists accept the word-name model instinctively and explicitly. We may well ourselves explain the way words work rather differently, and demand greater lexicographical nicety; but we have no warrant for expecting in our sources a greater precision than ancient usage expected. On its own, a fresh phrase, a fresh additional phrase, is as likely—indeed, more likely—to betoken freshness in a competent author rather than a fresh author or 'a different meaning', however unsatisfactory that may appear to us.

As well as tending to impose our own tacit understanding of language onto ancient wordsmiths, and however ready we are in other contexts to allow that 'the past is another country, they do things differently there',[3] we expect ancient authors to have written as individuals, the product must have been all their own work, expressing their own individuality. 'Word-processing in the Ancient World' argues that this expectation is false. When writers do tell us how they operate, it is much more socially, the setting is much more like a seminar than a quiet study; we have no accounts of literary production on 'a desk in a scholar's study lined with texts'.[4] This has a particular bearing on our understanding of the composition of 'Q' as the charter of an early Christian community—and a fortiori very unlikely to be the product of successive individuals disagreeing 'editorially' with their individual predecessors, and in successive 'editions' imposing different 'meanings' (in this picking up again the theme of the previous chapter).[5]

In all but one of the remaining chapters I consider individual works in the light of some of the conclusions already reached, and of further corollaries still to be elaborated. I move first to 'Q' itself, agreed by many (but not universally) to be the oldest of our records claiming to relate directly to Jesus, 'Q' seen as the now-lost source used by Luke and Matthew independently of each other in augmenting and enriching Mark. A few years back Richard Burridge presented a detailed but flexible account of the sorts of ways in which people in the ancient world wrote the 'Life' of another person, including among the variants, the Life of a teacher, a philosopher. Burridge himself explicitly excluded

---

3.   On any supposed 'culture gap' see, for instance, F.G. Downing, 'Intepretation and the Culture Gap', *SJT* 40 (1987), pp. 161-71; repr. in *idem, Making Sense in (and of) The First Christian Century* (JSNTSup, 197; Sheffield: Sheffield Academic Press, 2000), the companion volume to this.

4.   B.L. Mack, *A Myth of Innocence: Mark and Christian Origins* (Philadelphia: Fortress Press, 1988), pp. 322-23. It could have been meant as a joke; but the context indicates that this is the model deployed.

5.   I have just received John S. Kloppenborg Verbin's very fine *Excavating Q: The History and Setting of the Sayings Gospel* (Edinburgh: T. & T. Clark, 2000), and must note the persuasive restatement of a structure for Q in terms of recurrent themes of judgment, of the rejection of God's prophets, and of allusions to the story of Lot. My sketch of the shared composition of Q would now have to include this structure. Yet I still cannot see how it could have been imposed later, for, disappointingly, although the author accepts in some measure some of the arguments of this present chapter, my challenge here is not met. The scattered Galilaean Q people's shared (Greek) written foundational traditions are still subjected to a significant restructuring that responds to late 60s CE tensions, making their confident radical life style in effect into an interim ethic, with no attempt to show how this might have been negotiated among them.

'Q' from consideration, but in 'A Genre for Q and a Socio-cultural Context for Q', his scheme is outlined, and it is argued that the reconstructed document Q as usually understood fits Burridge's flexible pattern well, as the Life of a Cynic philosopher (even though other distinguishable genres also include elements in common with all kinds of Lives). The Life of a (Cynic) philosopher would have afforded the closest (but not the sole valid) analogy for Greek speakers encountering Q, and the most likely (adaptable) model for its composition.

Burridge is quite certain that Mark is a clear example of the genre 'Life'. But, as I have just allowed, other genres also share some of the same significant features, if not so many, and they warrant careful attention if we are to understand aspects of Mark less frequent or quite unrepresented in Lives available to us. One such trait prominent in Mark is the device of 'intercalation', the 'sandwiching' of one narrative within another. After considering various works—histories, Lives and plays in particular—we find the closest analogies are afforded in the popular romances. The early Christians were open to a very wide range of influences in their cultural world.

Pervasive throughout those further influences was Rome itself with its imperial ideology. In general terms this embracing factor has of course been widely recognized in New Testament studies, most elaborately in interpreting the Apocalypse of John, but also in such details in the Gospels as an apparent concern (and an increasing concern) from Mark through to John, to exculpate Pilate (and ease the obvious conflict with imperial authority). My seventh chapter, on the other hand, notes in Mark's story of Jesus how many apparent and positive similarities there are with elements in the story of Romulus. Should we not allow, as one strand among others in Mark, that he is actually presenting Jesus as a 'Rival to Romulus'? It seems unlikely that so many resonances would have been lost on hearers; and once noted, their retention must have been deliberate (and so, indeed, may well have been intended from the start).

It has been my contention over the years that our grand conclusions must be tentative; but that the wider our web, the more connections it includes, the firmer we may judge the result. In the foregoing the 'Q hypothesis' has been accepted, while the fact that it is disputed has been allowed. Those who urge other solutions have yet to show that they match the ways in which any authors at the time used literary sources, accepting words and phrases, paraphrasing, rearranging, excising, elaborating. 'Compositional Conventions and the Synoptic Problem' demonstrates some ancient authors' fairly easily achieved results, and argues that Matthew and Luke independently of each other using Mark and Q match what we may discern among their near contemporaries; whereas other proposals (Mark conflated the other two; or Matthew augmented Mark and then Luke unpicked and reassembled the result; or vice versa) suggest very complex and quite unprecedented procedures. 'A Paradigm Perplex' examines one such alternative solution (that of Michael Goulder) in more detail, with particular attention to the practical, physical problems of writing words in one scroll while consulting two others and attempting to refer back and forth among them.

Some of the arguments in these last two chapters depend in part, and explicitly, on journal contributions that are not included here, but which have been reprinted elsewhere. One is 'Towards the Rehabilitation of Q' (1965),[6] which included some passages from Matthew, Mark and Luke carefully tabulated side by side to illustrate the complexity of alternatives to the Q solution; and the other appeared in two parts as 'Redaction Criticism: Josephus' *Antiquities* and the Synoptic Gospels', I and II (1980), examining in extensive detail Josephus' retelling of the Scriptures, including stretches where he is conflating two sources.[7] It is perhaps worth noting that Michael Goulder's response to 'A Paradigm Perplex' (his 'Luke's Compositional Options')[8] accused the former piece of ignoring issues that were in fact referred to in the footnotes and had been already discussed in some detail in the above pair of articles to which an attentive reader's attention was repeatedly called.

'Theophilus' First Reading of Luke–Acts' then collects together and further illustrates the major theme of this volume, the many and diverse ways in which various early Christians display their integration in the wider culture of their time and place, the topic with which we began. We touch again on orality, on various literary genres, on social mix and

---

6. F.G. Downing, 'Towards the Rehabilitation of Q,' *NTS* 11 (1965), pp. 169-81; repr. A.J. Bellinzoni (ed.) *The Two-Source Hypothesis: A Critical Appraisal* (Macon GA: Mercer University Press, 1985), pp. 269-86 (together with a response to some rejoinders).

7. F.G. Downing, 'Redaction Criticism: Josephus' *Antiquities* and the Synoptic Gospels', I, *JSNT* 8 (1980), pp. 46-65, and II, *JSNT* 9 (1980), pp. 29-48; repr. S.E. Porter and C.A. Evans (eds.), *New Testament Interpretation and Methods* (BibSem, 45; Sheffield: Sheffield Academic Press, 1997), pp. 161-99.

8. M.D. Goulder, 'Luke's Compositional Options', *NTS* 39 (1993) pp. 150-52.

implicit social attitudes, on respect for antiquity, respectable religion and responses to Roman authority, and on romance and other entertainment. (I note one retraction of a previous conclusion: it is here argued that Luke would *not* in all probability have expected his work to be read by outsiders.[9] It remains the case that he would most likely have expected it to reassure fellow Christians in their contacts with respectable 'pagans'.)

The question of degrees of certainty has been raised from time to time. The final chapter, 'Shifting Sands', responds to scholars who for all their scepticism assure us they can tell us 'what Jesus *really* said and did' (or really neither said nor did). A reconstruction that appears encompassing and coherent allows for a fair degree of internal certainty—but no more than that. The fact that some accounts (as from Jesus, or some later followers) are secure in my reconstruction does not mean that they must be in someone else's; that they are refused to Jesus in another's detailed sketch does not in itself force me to omit them in mine.[10] The more encompassing and the more coherent the reconstruction the more persuasive and the more secure, of course; but no reconstruction is going to be all-encompassing, and none has appeared so full and so self-consistent as to persuade even a majority or render rivals otiose.

There is a very brief 'Concluding Unscientific Postscript', to which a reader wondering about the present writer's context, faith (and likely ideological infections) may turn before reading further.

9.   I suggested this in passing in two pieces, 'Ethical Pagan Theism and the Speeches in Acts', *NTS* 27 (1981), pp. 544-63; and 'Common Ground with Paganism in Luke and in Josephus', *NTS* 28 (1982), pp. 546-59. The main thrust of the exposition—the extent of 'common ground'—remains, I would aver, clearly demonstrated.

10.   I was proposing this in some detail in my *The Church and Jesus* (SBT 2.10; London: SCM Press, 1968) and updated it in my 'The Social Contexts of Jesus the Teacher: Construction or Reconstruction?', *NTS* 33 (1987), pp. 439-51; and have expanded that argument and updated it further in my 'The Jewish Cynic Jesus', in A. Schmidt and M. Labahn (eds.), *Jesus, Mark and Q: The Teaching of Jesus and its Earliest Records* (JSNTSup; Sheffield: Sheffield Academic Press, forthcoming).

Chapter 1

A BAS LES ARISTOS*

Introduction

The narrative of Luke–Acts presupposes in audience and author alike, a conviction that life in the contemporary Roman world is lived in a continuum. Although not everyone speaks Greek as their first language, ideas and life-style can be shared from one region to another, and among people of very differing social status. There is not just a common language (*koine* Greek), but a common universe of discourse, a common intertexture. A great many common threads appear in their shared thoughts and reflections. People may well disagree with one another; but they understand each other.

I am not here concerned to argue whether things happened as Luke indicates. What I want to discuss is whether his presupposition of a common culture widely shared (if with different levels of sophistication) can be held to be valid. At the same time I shall be considering the closely connected issue of whether our major 'pagan' literary remains, emanating, broadly speaking, from aristocratic circles, may be used—with whatever specifiable care and qualification—to illuminate our understanding of the early Christians (and not just Luke's picture of them). Do our non-Christian, 'aristocratic' remains afford us usable insights into a variegated common culture that was the intellectual world where those who produced our New Testament documents were at home? Or do these aristocratic writings come in effect from 'another world', contemporary and coterminous with but distinct from and irrelevant for the social setting of the early Christians? It is the former

* Repr. from *NovT* 30.3 (1988), with kind permission. There this was subtitled, 'The Relevance of Higher Literature for the Understanding of the Earliest Christian Writings'. My thanks for help with this paper also go to the Seminar on Luke–Acts in the Graeco-Roman World, chaired by L. Alexander, at the British New Testament Conference, Durham, 1987.

conclusion that I mean to urge: hence my title, '*A bas les aristos*'.

I have found doubts expressed in occasional asides as to the propriety of such use of aristocratic material to illustrate common beliefs and attitudes among the early Christians. But I have not been able to discover any comprehensive discussion of the issues involved.[1]

Most accounts of the world of the first Christians in fact simply use without more ado the surviving writings of provincial and Roman aristocrats, and other literary figures from their milieu, and are fairly generous in the time-span over which they permit themselves to range. So we find Virgil and Cicero, as well as Seneca, Juvenal, Epictetus, the Plinys, Quintilian, Plutarch, Dio Chrysostom, and also Philo and Josephus; and we find Tacitus, Dio Cassius, Lucian, Aristides; but we also find Homer and Herodotus, Plato and Aristotle, the tragedians, Zeno, Epicurus and Lucretius, from earlier times, together with Celsus in Origen, Philostratus, Porphyry, Julian and so on, from much later.[2]

The question of propriety has nonetheless to be raised, despite the widespread agreement in practice. Is this scholarly hospitality to the aristocrats appropriate? The question itself splits into three issues (though they remain linked): that of place, that of date and that of social level. It is with the latter that I am here chiefly concerned, but must address the others briefly.

Geography

A number of modern writers consulted argue cogently that some data from around the first century have a geographically restricted relevance. For instance, conditions in Egypt as evidenced in the papyri are often quite clearly different from those in Syria or in Asia (which may have more in common with each other). Italy and Greece may differ considerably; so, too, Gaul, Spain, North Africa.[3] I have noted in pass-

---

1.   At the 1987 SNTS meeting in Göttingen I consulted a number of eminent colleagues, who seemed to accept the relevance of the issue, but could recall no previous discussion of it, other than the few that follow here.

2.   For my own interest I made a list of ancient authors and then checked that against writings of current and recent scholars on the New Testament and related studies. Philo, Philostratus, Plutarch, Cicero, Apuleius, Lucian, Dio Chrysostom and Josephus were the ones who put in an least one appearance in most books; K. Berger, H.C. Kee, H. Koester, R. MacMullen and C.H. Talbert were among the most hospitable from among 14 authors and a score of books.

3.   There are useful detailed studies in *ANRW*, II.3-10.

ing, for example, the suggestion that in Gaul you might find cultural centres in the countryside, well away from any settled town; whereas for the east, temples and other public buildings seem always to be urban.[4] Urban centres as such are much more nearly standardized (as, e.g., Dio presupposes),[5] but here again one really needs to know something of the proportion of citizens to resident non-citizens, and of various groups among them; and of the relationships of townspeople and peasants in the countryside around. Yet, while laws and rights may differ in detail from city to city, there may even more significantly be a common reliance on legal process as such: witness both Dio and the papyri.[6]

I do not intend arguing the issue of geographical distinctiveness in any detail. The documentary materials I am here concerned with seem to have little specifically local flavour to them. I would, rather, accept entirely Helmut Koester on 'the international character of cultural life'. Whether you came from Spain, Gaul, Libya, Pontus, from Antioch, Alexandria or Rome, you would include a very similar list of authors to listen to or to read; and that would be so, even if you had an extensive literature in your native Latin, say (with help from Cicero, if need be, and other popularizing translators after him). There was a common syllabus ahead of Josephus when circumstances demanded that he turn his attention this way.[7]

4.   R. MacMullen, *Paganism in the Roman Empire* (New Haven: Yale University Press, 1981), p. 18.

5.   Dio Chrysostom (of Prusa), *Discourses* 32; 33; 49.9; 80.21, in *Dio Chrysostom, Discourses* (trans. J.W. Cohoon; LCL; London: Heinemann; Cambridge, MA: Harvard University Press, 1932–).

6.   A.S. Hunt and C.C. Edgar (trans.), *Select papyri* I, II (LCL; London: Heinemann; Cambridge, MA: Harvard University Press, 1932); and G.H.R. Horsley, *New Documents Illustrating Early Christianity*, I–VIII (Macquarie: Ancient History Documentary Research Centre, 1981–).

7.   H. Koester, *Introduction to the New Testament* (2 vols.; ET; Berlin: W. de Gruyter, 1982), I, pp. 97-101; Josephus, *Apion* 1.1-56; and, on education in the ancient world, e.g., Dio, *Discourse* 18; Ps-Plutarch, *De liberis educandis*; and H. Marrou, *A History of Education in Antiquity* (ET; London: Sheed & Ward, 1956); M.L. Clarke, *Higher Education in the Ancient World* (London: Routledge, 1971); and S.F. Bonner, *Education in Ancient Rome* (London: Methuen, 1977).

Chronology

On dating, the situation among contemporary scholars seems rather less satisfactory. I note that Ramsey MacMullen exercises more self-denial here than do most of our New Testament specialists. He refuses, for instance, the Corpus Hermeticum, even in a survey covering the second century; and he expresses similar reservations elsewhere.[8] It would seem preferable to keep (if arbitrarily) to a moving bracket of around two centuries, six generations, with our focus of attention on the middle two. If we can reinforce or illustrate, from earlier or later data, conclusions formed from within the bracketed period, well and good, if not strictly necessary. But there seems no good reason to go beyond this already generous boundary in order to fill in a gap, importing something for which evidence nearer in time is lacking. We ought not to take the risk.

Such restraint is not entirely arbitrary. Though E.R. Dodds' *Pagan and Christian in an Age of Anxiety* has been subject to some adverse criticism of late,[9] Dodds is not alone, I think, in detecting a marked change in attitudes after Marcus Aurelius. One may compare G.W. Bowerstock's more recent study of the Sophists (and perhaps Jacob Neusner on Rabbinics).[10] But it is not only today's scholars who note significant alterations in attitudes and institutions. Writers at the time also suppose they are seeing changes: compare Plutarch on the decreasing use of oracles, Pliny the Younger on the decline in religious observance (which he blamed on the Christian movement), Seneca on fashion and technology, Pliny the Elder on medical practice, Trajan on the new mood of the age, Lucian on archaizing pedantry.[11] It may be

---

8.   R. MacMullen, *Paganism*, p. 174 and n. 36; *idem, Roman Social Relations, 50 BC to AD 284* (New Haven: Yale University Press, 1974), p. vii.

9.   E.R. Dodds, *Pagan and Christian in an Age of Anxiety* (Cambridge: Cambridge University Press, 1965); and the comment from MacMullen, *Paganism*, p. 176, n. 55.

10.   G.W. Bowerstock, *Greek Sophists in the Roman Empire* (Oxford: Clarendon Press, 1969); J. Neusner, *Midrash in Context* (Philadelphia: Fortress Press, 1983).

11.   Plutarch, *De defectu oraculorum*, 394D–409D; Pliny the Younger, *Letters* 10.96; Trajan, in Pliny the Younger, *Letters* 10.97; Seneca, *Epistulae morales* 90.21-22; Pliny the Elder, *Natural History* 29.2; Lucian, *How to Write History*. Many more instances are available.

possible to argue on the basis of interpreted data that one should be stricter still; but till that is done, to concentrate on the third and fourth generations of any given sequence of six seems relatively safe without being absurdly parsimonious.

Society

The major question remaining is, as announced, that of whether our supposedly aristocratic sources provide us with any reliable information at all about what was going on among the people who formed the bottom 95 per cent or so of the social pyramid.[12] What I hope to argue, as, again, I trust my title indicates, is that these sources are quite certainly relevant. Stories, ideas, attitudes moved down. And, furthermore, there was some feedback, so that our sources preserve some genuine responses to what lowlier people were thinking and feeling and saying.

Although the question of the social setting of evidence adduced is occasionally noted in the literature (and has arisen in formal as well as informal discussion of work of my own), there seems to be, as noted already, no comprehensive discussion of the issues at all. There is occasionally a distinction drawn between *Hoch-* and *Kleinliteratur*; more rarely attention is drawn to a middle ground of *Fachprose*; and rather more often the question of the social composition of early Christian congregations is raised. These will be briefly reviewed. But there is still more importantly the issue of the oral and public nature of contemporary culture—even if its literary crystallizations should in fact be shown themselves to have had a restricted circulation and target audience.

On *Hoch-* and *Kleinliteratur* I have been able to find very little critical discussion at all, despite occasional references in passing.[13] In the Introduction to his 1987 study of 'Q', John S. Kloppenborg traces the distinction back to Franz Overbeck and the latter's attention to the formal differences between early Christian writing on the one hand, and

---

12. R. MacMullen, *Roman Social Relations*, p. 4; E.A. Judge, *The Social Pattern of Christian Groups in the First Century* (London: Tyndale Press, 1960), pp. 16-17; 52-54.

13. C.H. Talbert, *What is a Gospel?* (Philadelphia: Fortress, 1977), pp. 3-4; P.L. Shuler, *A Genre for the Gospels* (Philadephia: Fortress Press, 1982), pp. 6-15; K.L. Schmidt, 'Die Stellung der Evangelien in der allgemeinen Literaturgeschichte', in H. Schmidt (ed.), *EUXARISTHRION: Studien zur Religion und Literatur des Alten und Neuen Testaments* (Göttingen: Vandenhoeck & Ruprecht, 1923), pp. 50-134.

both late classical and Christian patristic literature on the other.

The early Christian material appears in this account simply as a quite distinct oral (and corporate) production. Kloppenborg argues here and in his book as a whole that on the contrary, and despite the valid distinctions that have been made, there are a number of surviving documents that provide a continuum of 'more or less sophisticated literary forms'.[14] The basis for that case was urged, of course, many years back by C.W. Votaw, though without reference to Overbeck, or any discussion of the latter's analyses.[15] K.L. Schmidt is also often referred to in this connection, but he seems to have presupposed the distinction rather than reviewed the arguments in its favour.[16]

Votaw's case on Gospel genre was taken up and argued more recently by C.H. Talbert and P.L. Shuler, and more recently still, by R.A. Burridge.[17] Although I do not find that Talbert and Shuler have successfully argued for the distinctive genres they have proposed (on which see the critique in Burridge), they, and Burridge even more so, have adduced a large number of similarities between facets of the Gospels and other writing of the time; and I have myself argued that such motifs, individually and in clusters, are more significant still.[18] These

14. J.S. Kloppenborg, *The Formation of Q* (Philadelphia: Fortress Press, 1987), pp. 3-8; quoting from p. 8.

15. C.W. Votaw, *The Gospels and Contemporary Biographies in the Greco-Roman World* (repr. Philadelphia: Fortress Press, 1970 [1915]).

16. K.L. Schmidt, 'Die Stellung'; cf. R. Bultmann, *History of the Synoptic Tradition* (ET; Oxford: Basil Blackwell, 1972), p. 372; A.D. Nock, *Essays on Religion in the Ancient World* (ed. Z. Stuart, London: Oxford University Press, 1972); despite his 'Early Gentile Christianity and its Hellenistic Background', I, pp. 40-133, and 'Christianity and Classical Culture', II, pp. 676-81, Nock does not directly address the issue of *Hoch-* or *Kleinliteratur*; nor does E. Norden, *Agnostos Theos* (repr. Stuttgart: Teubner, 1956 [1912]), on 'hellenistischer-römischer Literatur', pp. 87-95, nor on the *'genos'* of the *prooimium*, pp. 213-27, while using a list of sources for comparison as generous as any I have met, with no hint of controversy on this issue.

17. Talbert, *What is a Gospel?*, pp. 3-5; Shuler, *A Genre for the Gospels*, pp. 6-15; R.A. Burridge, *What are the Gospels? A Comparison with Graeco-Roman Biography* (SNTSMS, 70; Cambridge: Cambridge University Press, 1992).

18. F.G. Downing, 'Contemporary Analogies to the Gospels and Acts: Genres or Motifs?', in C.M. Tuckett (ed.), *Synoptic Studies: The Ampleforth Conference of 1982 and 1983* (JSNTSup, 7; Sheffield: JSOT Press, 1984), pp. 51-65; and Downing, 'Ears to Hear', in A.E. Harvey (ed.), *Alternative Approaches to New Testament Study* (London: SPCK, 1985), pp. 97-121. On the issues of the genre(s) of the Gos-

motifs just do occur across the board, and strongly suggest that there is no gulf between aristocratic culture and the milieux of the first Christians. The same sort of conclusion seems to emerge from Klaus Berger's 1984 systematic general survey, 'Hellenistische Gattungen im Neuen Testament',[19] where a full range of illustrative sources is used without any apology. But one may compare H.D. Betz's study of Galatians, M.M. Mitchell's study of 'political' language in Paul; and J.L. White and others on New Testament letters.[20] There clearly are differences in vocabulary (and not just its range) and in grammatical style. Even Josephus, aiming upwards, found himself laughed at for his 'schoolboy' efforts.[21] But that is a difference at the most superficial and least significant level. When we come to contents and kinds of content, then closely comparable material abounds.

However, on the issue of language and of style as such, there are some supporting comments from James W. Voelz, in his 'The Language of the New Testament':[22] 'in the last 50 years, however, there has been general agreement that the literary aspects of NT Greek have been overly minimized'. There are now, he concludes, no simple 'Deissmanites'. In a diagram he urges a wide 'middle area' of language accessible both to the masses and the literati.

Alongside this we may then place the known range of *Fachprose*, technical writing in fields such as medicine and architecture, 'literate but not literary'.[23] There is no need to suppose that someone used to this material would restrict his or her attention to it. Lucian mentions in

pels, see now, of course, R.A. Burridge, *What are the Gospels?*; and ch. 5, below.

19. K. Berger, 'Hellenistischer Gattungen im Neuen Testament', *ANRW* II.25.2 (1984), pp. 1031-1462; the same findings applied in detail to the New Testament, in *idem*, *Formgeschichte des Neuen Testaments* (Heidelberg: Quelle & Meyer, 1984).

20. H.D. Betz, *Galatians* (Hermeneia; Philadelphia: Fortress Press, 1979); M.M. Mitchell, *Paul and the Rhetoric of Reconciliation: An Exegetical Investigation of the Language and Composition of I Corinthians* (Tübingen: J.C.B. Mohr; Louisville, KY: Westminster/John Knox Press, 1992); J.L. White, *Light from Ancient Letters* (Philadelphia: Fortress Press, 1986).

21. Josephus, *Apion* 1.53.

22. J.W. Voelz, 'The Language of the New Testament', *ANRW* II.25.2 (1984), pp. 920-51 (928, 935).

23. L. Alexander, 'Luke's Preface in the Context of Greek Preface Writing', *NovT* 38.1 (1986), pp. 48-74, citing p. 61; and *eadem*, *The Preface to Luke's Gospel* (SNTSMS, 78; Cambridge: Cambridge University Press, 1993); and Lucian, *How to Write History*, 16.

passing an army surgeon who felt drawn to write an account of a campaign he shared in, however little Lucian himself thought of the result. Further down the literary ladder we have the *Life of Aesop, Secundus the Silent Philosopher*, the *Life of Alexander* and the *Philogelos*. In literary production, however uneven the results, there seems little evidence of a chasm or gulf between the aristocratic authors and the rest.

When Luke presents early Christians naturally able to converse with a wide range of people he seems to be reflecting what the wider evidence suggests to contemporary scholars; and on this we may compare also work on Acts itself by P.W. van der Horst.[24] In this light the question of the social levels of the early Christians may lose some of its urgency, but it remains relevant. Even if we do not take the local churches in general as far up the lower echelons as E.A. Judge does (drawing perhaps too much of his evidence from Acts), there has emerged a current consensus that accords the Pauline churches at least a social mix that would include the local urban aristocracy, the masters of sizable houses and households.[25] Of course, even if that be accepted, we do not know for sure that other Christian groups included a similar range of people: for instance, the early Jesus tradition as evidenced in the synoptic gospels may have been carried by more narrowly plebeian communities. But, again, this evidence as a whole does suggest that there is no call to presuppose a socially based cultural gulf, unless and

24. P.W. van der Horst, 'Hellenistic Parallels to the Acts of the Apostles', *ZNW* 74 (1983), pp. 17-26; and, with the same title, *JSNT* 25 (1985), 49-60; but also other contributions to the *Corpus Hellenisticum Novi Testamenti* project: *idem, Aelius Aristides and the New Testament* (Leiden: E.J. Brill, 1980); 'Macrobius and the New Testament', *NovT* 15 (1973), pp. 220-32, and further contributions in that journal; and *idem, Hellenism–Judaism–Christianity* (Kampen: Kok, 1994); also of interest, G. Mussies, *Dio Chrysostom and the New Testament* (Leiden: E.J. Brill, 1972); and H.D. Betz (ed.), *Plutarch's Ethical Writings and Early Christian Literature* (Leiden: E.J. Brill, 1972); and *idem* (ed.) *Plutarch's Theological Writings and Early Christian Literature* (Leiden: E.J. Brill, 1975). In all these studies the writers simply go ahead and make their comparisons without apology; and I note H.D. Betz, *Plutarch's Ethical Writings*, p. 3, 'The various levels [sc., of morality] do not exclude one another'; similarly pp. 7-8.

25. Judge, *Social Pattern*; with the concurrence of, for example, G. Theissen, *The Social Setting of Pauline Christianity* (ET; Philadelphia: Fortress Press, 1982); W.A. Meeks, *The First Urban Christians* (New Haven: Yale University Press, 1983). But on this now see the critique of J. Meggitt, *Paul, Poverty and Survival* (Edinburgh: T. & T. Clark, 1998).

until there is further pressing evidence. In this connection I note with interest Richard L. Rohrbaugh's arguments against over-clear distinctions between the ideas and attitudes of groups in a given society, as distinguished by us, and proposing instead, 'overlapping memberships and complex standards of value'.[26]

In the very few references I have found to this issue in the secondary literature I have noted only some very brief and quite rare explicit initial caution, on using our 'aristocratic' data for telling us what 'the poor' thought—especially the rural poor. Ramsey MacMullen does so on more than one occasion, and is followed in this by Abraham J. Malherbe.[27] With care, they both allow, however, it is entirely acceptable (though neither specifies the care demanded). What I want to discuss in the remainder of this paper is some of the evidence that persuades me that such cautious optimism is justified.

The Public Character of Cultural and Intellectual Life

A convenient introduction is afforded by Helmut Koester's 'The Public Character of Cultural and Intellectual Life',[28] listing the performance of plays and poetry in theatres and lecture halls and other auditoria, but especially emphasizing the public colonades as places where lectures and discussions took place. Koester concludes, 'The prerogative of the commonwealth [community] over the private sphere is striking'.[29] His general picture can readily be supported from incidental remarks in the writings of Dio Chrysostom of Prusa. Often quoted or alluded to is Dio's description of the plebeian Cynics in Alexandria:

> There are, as well, quite a few Cynic philosophers, so-called, in your city...people whose ideals are genuine enough, but whose bellies need filling... They gather at street-corners and in alley-ways and at temple gates and con youngsters and sailors and crowds made up of that sort.[30]

26. R.L. Rohrbaugh, '"Social Location of Thought" as a Heuristic Construct in New Testament Study', *JSNT* 30 (1987), pp. 103-19, citing p. 108, where Rohrbaugh is quoting J. Boon.

27. MacMullen, *Roman Social Relations*, p. 26; and *idem*, 'Peasants during the Principate', *ANRW* II.1, p. 254; A.J. Malherbe, *Social Aspects of Early Christianity* (Philadelphia: Fortress Press, 2nd edn, 1983), pp. 17-20.

28. Koester, *Introduction*, pp. 93-97.

29. Koester, *Introduction*, p. 95; and, e.g., Dio, *Discourse* 32.68.

30. Dio, *Discourse* 32.9.

In the theatre in Alexandria, Dio would expect to see not just free citizens, but at least visitors from all parts of the Empire, as well as from beyond its borders, in a list reminiscent of Acts 2: Greeks and Italians, people from Syria, Libya, Cilicia, Ethopians and Arabs, as well as Bactrians, Scythians, Persians, and even a few Indians, alongside the Alexandrians with their wives and women.[31] Elsewhere he can also imagine a stranger attending a meeting of the popular assembly in Prusa.[32]

In another *Discourse*, Dio depicts two men (sic) 'debating at their ease at home', rather than 'before the judges or in the market place';[33] But they have a large crowd of followers with them. One of them, who is not a freeman, wins the argument. There is, however, no indication in Dio that the context of the discussion is any different from what it would have been in the other settings (even if we might choose to suppose the tone and register might not have been quite the same). Much the same conclusion emerges from Dio's easy comparison between talk at a symposium and in a crowd assembled for some formal games.[34]

There is certainly not a lot of difference discernible in the kinds of arguments and illustration—and language—between discourses of Dio's apparently delivered in the emperor's court, and those of the assemblies of free citizens he addressed in Alexandria, Rhodes, Corinth, Tarsus, Nicea, his home town of Prusa, and so on; and then those where he stood in Cynic garb and spoke to whomsoever gathered round to listen.[35] Dio himself says quite explicitly that he was used to delivering to people in general (*anthrōpoi*) what he has previously spoken to their superiors, 'popular assemblies, kings or dictators'.[36] He does not hide the fact that he is going to reuse addresses for a number of audiences. He admits that not everyone will understand a quite sophisticated argument against trying to reconstruct the historical Trojan War out of

31. Dio, *Discourse* 32.40; cf. Acts 2.9-11.

32. Dio, *Discourse* 53.1.

33. Dio, *Discourse* 15.1; compare—and contrast—E.A. Judge, 'The Early Christians as a Scholastic Community', *JRH* 1 (1960), pp. 4-15; and 'St. Paul the Sophist', *JRH* 3 (1963), pp. 125-37; and 'St. Paul and Classical Society', *JAC* 15 (1972), pp. 19-36.

34. Dio, *Discourse* 27.1-6; cf. *Discourse* 26.

35. Compare Dio, *Discourses* 1–3 with 32–50, and, e.g., 4–10.

36. Dio, *Discourse* 57.10-12.

Homer, but he expects it to be discussed.[37] In his home town, he claims, almost everyone knows his speeches, reporting them to one another, 'with improvements', he notes, wryly. They are as popular as song-sheets.[38] Again, in Prusa, defending himself against accusations of profiteering during a grain shortage, Dio addresses fellow citizens who include at least some who were poor enough and desperate enough to have taken part in a short-lived riot the night before.[39]

The situation he presupposes, then, is one where very similar material can be used—and succesfully, it seems—for audiences from a wide range of places and social contexts; and one in which what is said to a fairly select group is almost certain to be disseminated much more widely. I want only to cite a few more of the indications he affords of the sorts of people who would have listened to his and others' more or less cultured speeches, Cynic or or Stoic or more general, of the kinds that have been preserved for us.

I think we may take it that Dio's pictures of Diogenes's Corinth, as an example, are not historically researched: rather do they mirror Dio's own day.[40] At the Isthmian Games a mixed crowd would expect intellectual entertainment from Sophists, individuals reading their own prose and poetry, lawyers settling cases out of court, along with jugglers and athletes—and Cynics like Diogenes of old, or Dio himself. People would drift from one focus to the next.[41] In Tarsus, and probably elsewhere, people would gather round physicians, exploring human anatomy.[42] The wealthy as well as the humble and poor might well approach to discuss some issue with a Cynic or some other accessible philosopher.[43] In his own 'Olympic Discourse' (at the Games of 97 CE), Dio assumes that he will compete successfuly for an audience from among people who come for the whole range of the other distractions listed.[44] Elsewhere Dio appeals to the example of Socrates, talking everywhere and to everyone, in the gymnasia, the Lyceum, in workshops and in the

---

37. Dio, *Discourse* 11.6; cf. 12.1.
38. Dio, *Discourse* 42.4.
39. Dio, *Discourse* 46.
40. Compare J. Murphy-O'Connor, *Saint Paul's Corinth* (Wilmington, DE: Michael Glazier, 1983), pp. 94-96.
41. Dio, *Discourse* 8.9; and cf. *Discourse* 27, referred to above.
42. Dio, *Discourse* 33.6.
43. Dio, *Discourse* 9.8; cf. 13.12; and 32.
44. Dio, *Discourse* 12.1-5, 13; 27, yet again; 72.2, 11, 13, 16.

market place; or of the Cynic who despises the council chambers, theatres and assemblies, and summons an assembly all of his own. (It is in open-fronted workshops that Ronald Hock placed Paul's initial contact with potential converts, on the analogy of the Cynic model, Simon the Cobbler.)[45] In Borysthenes a population speaking a very poor Greek nonetheless gathered to listen to Dio—senior and distinguished men, with a large crowd in attendance, in the court of the Temple of Zeus, their usual meeting place—and these people knew their Homer.[46] (The picture in Acts 17 of Paul on the Athenian Areopagus, and of people rushing into the theatre in Ephesus, would have seemed entirely plausible to other first-century hearers.)

The impression so far gained of a very pervasive oral culture sharing much common content with the refined literature of the aristocracy is further supported by our other sources. Although there may be evidence for a shift from literary production designed for oral performance early in our period, yet even that production itself remains oral (as I have myself shown elsewhere, citing Josephus, Pliny the Younger, Quintilian and Dio).[47] Style may differ, but there is still no difference in kind between the high literary and other verbal communication. High, middling and low-brow talk about many of the same things using—or at least comprehending—many of the same words and constructions.

Lucian, in the middle of the second century CE, affords just such evidence in general in his own writing, but particularly in his portrayal of Cynics, 'bawling out...the standard street-corner stuff about virtue', but wrapped up in references to the classical myths.[48] The traditional stories Lucian preserves of a much more admired Cynic (or near-Cynic), Demonax, have him in touch with senators and governors and children and young men and women and others in the market place, with crowds readily gathering to listen in on some witty exchange. Lucian expects

---

45. Dio, *Discourse* 12.14; 54.3; 80.2; and note R.F. Hock, *The Social Context of Paul's Ministry* (Philadelphia: Fortress Press, 1980); and now, also, F.G. Downing, *Cynics, Paul and the Pauline Churches* (London: Routledge, 1998), esp. ch. 6, 'Paul the Teacher and Pastor', pp. 174-203.

46. Dio, *Discourse* 36, e.g. 36.17, 26.

47. K. Quinn, 'The Poet and his Audience in the Augustan Age', *ANRW* II.30.1 (1982), pp. 75-180; cf. Downing, 'Ears to Hear'; and chs. 4 and 5, below.

48. Lucian, *Peregrinus* 3–4, *et passim*, in *Lucian* (trans. A.M. Harmon; LCL; London: Heinemann; Cambridge, MA: Harvard University Press, 1913–); and *The Runaways*; *Philosophies for Sale*; and Ps.-Lucian, *The Cynic*.

his account of Demonax to appeal to 'people of culture' (*aristois*), and eulogises Demonax's erudition and his 'Attic grace'.[49] The *chreiai* Lucian includes from Demonax he presents very much in their popular condensed forms, closely akin to the much more extensive Cynic *chreiai* collected some centuries later by Diogenes Laertius, attributed to Diogenes himself in the main, but with some for Antisthenes, Crates, Hipparchia and others. As Dio remarks, 'the mass of ordinary people still remember the sayings of Diogenes', (even if the attribution of many of them is suspect).[50] Cynic material preserved in popular form then determines in large measure the literary appearance of these 'classical' Cynic sayings when they appear in 'aristocratic writers' from our period (for instance, in Cicero and in Plutarch), as well as in the school books, the *progymnasmata*.[51]

The administration of justice afforded another related setting where the eminent and the ordinary and the very few between might meet. Many of our aristocratic literary figures will have trained to plead in the courts. Quintilian tells us something of what that would entail: 'We must often express our views before an ignorant audience (*apud imperitos*), and quite ordinary people in particular (*populumque praecipue*), of whom most are uneducated (*indocti*)...'[52] Not every judge is learned (*eruditus*): you may find a simple soldier or a countryman.[53] The courts, anyway, are public, and you must understand your total audience if you

---

49. Lucian, *Demonax* 2, 6.

50. Dio, *Discourse* 72.11.

51. Despite the insistence above on limiting the time-span from which we draw our data, I would agree with common practice and on this basis accept Diogenes Laertius, *Lives of Eminent Philosophers*, as a collection of traditional materials relevant to the first century CE, for we find much of the matter there already evidenced in earlier writers, not least in the *progymnasmata*, the school books, on which see R.F. Hock and E.N. O'Neil (trans. and eds.), *The Chreia in Ancient Rhetoric. I. The Progymnasmata* (Atlanta: Scholars Press, 1986); on the spread of Cynic *chreiai* in other sources, cf. L. Paquet, *Les cyniques grecs: Fragments et témoinages* (Ottawa: Les Presses de l'Université d'Ottowa, 2nd edn, 1988); and cf. F.G. Downing, *Jesus and the Threat of Freedom* (London: SCM Press, 1987); *Christ and the Cynics* (JSOT Manuals, 4; Sheffield: JSOT Press, 1988), and *Cynics and Christian Origins* (Edinburgh: T. & T. Clark, 1992); and *Cynics, Paul and the Pauline Churches*.

52. Quintilian, *Institutes* 3.8.2; cf. 5.7.31; in *Quintilian* (trans. H.E. Butler; LCL: London: Heinemann; Cambridge, MA: Harvard University Press, 1920–).

53. Quintilian, *Institutes* 11.1.45.

are to win its sympathy.[54] A decision can be effectively swayed by the applause drawn from the crowd.[55]

But the education for this career involves a thorough knowledge of poets, historians and philosophers, and not just other orators.[56] Dio has a yet more literary list. His brief picture of court sessions as popular entertainment is even livelier than Quintilian's.[57] Pliny the Younger, as another example, tries to give an account of the distinctive atmosphere of a centumviral (financial) court hearing: 'the bench of magistrates (*iudices*), the throng of advocates, the suspense before the verdict, the reputations of the various speakers, the divided enthusiasm of the public'.[58] Pliny does complain, though, in an earlier letter, of people hired to attend court and applaud the advocate who paid them, though they might need a signal to remind them when to respond.[59] Pliny was a pupil of Quintilian's, with the same approved education, but also claiming a similar concern to move a mixed audience, popular and patrician, with the same stock in trade, for seven hours—but still without having to pay for his applause.[60] Again, in Philo's Alexandria the law courts were a place for public entertainment in just the same way, as also seems clear for the rest of the cities of the Empire as a whole.[61]

Luke also presupposes precisely this kind of situation (Acts 16.22; 17.7; 18.17): a large crowd is present when the courts are in session, and the crowd's response may well sway the decision. We may also note again H.D. Betz on Galatians: the recipients are expected to be able to appreciate an argument in complex conventional form (even if not as precisely so as Betz concludes), similar to if not identical with Quintilian's recipe for a legal argument. Then again, the Corinthian Christians seem to have found it natural to continue using the public courts (1 Cor. 6). We have here another area where there are clear

54. Quintilian, *Institutes* 3.8.7, 11.
55. Quintilian, *Institutes* 8.3.3; 11.3.131; 12.5.6; 12.9.4.
56. Quintilian, *Institutes* 10.1; cf. 1.8-9.
57. Dio, *Discourse* 18.
58. Pliny the Younger, *Letters* 2.19.2, in *Pliny: Letters and Panegyricus* (2 vols.; trans. B. Radice; LCL; London: Heinemann; Cambridge MA: Harvard University Press, 1969).
59. Pliny the Younger, *Letters* 2.14.4.
60. Pliny the Younger, *Letters* 4.16; 4.19.
61. Philo, *Abr.* 20, in *Philo* (trans. F.H. Colson and G.H. Whittaker; LCL; London: Heinemann; Cambridge, MA: Harvard University Press, 1929–); cf. Dio, *Discourse* 31.68, again.

indications of aristocratic learning being offered to ordinary people in a setting where their response to what they hear is made very obvious, and seems to be noted.

Similar again, as Quintilian has shown, is the political arena. L.L. Welborn and more elaborately M.M. Mitchell, for instance, have been able to argue that Paul and by implication the Corinthian Christians, too, are fully used to the rhetoric of urban politics.[62]

The theatre constitutes another important setting, though it seems difficult to ascertain in detail what would have been the most popular pieces presented. In an aside Philo says,

> A short while ago, when some players were acting a tragedy and recited these words of Euripides,
>
> > The name of Freedom is worth all the world; if one have little,
> > let him think it much—
>
> I saw the whole audience so carried away with enthusiasm that they stood bolt upright, raising their voices above the actors.[63]

Philo may of course simply be quoting the account of the incident from someone else; but he takes it for granted that a Jew (not a full citizen of Alexandria, whatever his community's claims) could attend a production of Euripides.[64] Luke, as we have already noted, only takes us into a theatre for a protest meeting; but Dio does much the same in Euboea.[65]

The cost of such performances is borne by wealthy patrons, the seats are free (even if the best ones are reserved for the eminent).[66] Common people and senators attend the same entertainments. 'I listen to comedies, watch farces, read lyric poetry, and appreciate Sotadic ["blue"] verse...' 'I am human', wrote Pliny the Younger, complacently.[67] So far as I am aware such texts as we have of the plays commonly presented comprise a small selection of the fifth-century Greeks and sec-

---

62. Quintilian, *Institutes* 3.4.5; L.L. Welborn, 'On the Discord in Corinth: 1 Corinthians 1–4 and Ancient Politics', *JBL* 106.1 (1987), pp. 85-11; and cf. also M.M. Mitchell, *Paul and the Politics of Reconciliation*.

63. Philo, *Omn. Prob. Lib.* 141 from Euripides, *Augē* (Strobaeus).

64. Cf. Philo, *Agr.* 35; *Ebr.* 177.

65. Dio, *Discourse* 7.23.

66. Epictetus, *Dissertations* 2.4.9; cf. Suetonius, *Claudius* 25.4; Dio, *Discourse* 32.41-42. Public space comprised a large part of the area of a town (MacMullen, *Roman Social Relations*, p. 63) and a very great number of people were expected to make use of such provision.

67. Pliny the Younger, *Letters* 5.3.2.

ond-century Romans (Aeschylus, Sophocles, Euripides; Plautus and Terence with some fragments from Menander). Koester concludes that for this period mime may have been more important, and for that we have, of course, only some titles.[68] Perhaps Petronius and Juvenal, Lucian and Apuleius, too, give us an indication of their character. Recent scholars have, I think properly, fought shy of taking the exaggerated caricatures in Petronius and Juvenal as any more representative of real life (rather than popular taste) in the first century than are *Dallas* or *Chateauvallon* or *Brookside* for our day.[69] With careful analysis, however, such material could still be informative; but I have not been aware of any sensitive study based on it. J.P.V.D. Balsdon, in his *Life and Leisure in Ancient Rome* notes the lack of any thorough treatment of the 'spirtuality' conveyed.[70] There is, however, again a firm indication of a shared oral culture, but in this case, rather less on which to base an assessment of its content.

Acts, clearly, has nothing to say about dramas. It does, however, suggest the importance and relevance of the lecture hall, and, even more, of the wealthy home, as settings for early Christian communication; and, as noted, one can draw some support for the latter from Paul's letters. My only question here is whether this suggests, at least for some strands of early Christianity, any kind of socio-cultural exclusiveness. I have already pointed out that Dio can give an imaginary discussion this latter kind of setting; but he has to make the point overtly: so, presumably, neither content nor style on their own will differentiate it from public discourse.[71]

Our main source for this kind of scholarly lecturing and perhaps seminar is Epictetus, who, as Stanley Stowers points out, has specifically given up the outdoor approach to passers-by.[72] Despite Epictetus's

68. Koester, *Introduction* §3.4b, pp. 123-27.

69. Contrast J. Carcopino, *Daily Life in Ancient Rome* (ET; Harmondsworth: Penguin Books, 1956 [1941]), readily using Juvenal etc.; but note W.R. Halliday, *The Pagan Background of Early Christianity* (London: Hodder & Stoughton, 1925), much more cautious.

70. J.P.V.D. Balsdon, *Life and Leisure in Ancient Rome* (London: Bodley Head; New York: McGraw–Hill, 1969), p. 12.

71. Dio, *Discourse* 15.1; see n. 33, above, and the relevant main text.

72. S.K. Stowers, 'Social Status, Public Speaking and Private Teaching: The Circumstances of Paul's Preaching Activity', *NovT* 26.1 (1984), pp. 59-82, citing p. 79; cf. Epictetus, *Dissertations* 2.12; 1.1.27; 1.7.32; 1.9.29, etc. ('seminars' with Musonius Rufus). However, on the term 'diatribe', see now the critical assessment

lowly status as a freedman, it is often insisted that he is only addressing young men of equestrian if not patrician rank. After all, he appealed strongly to the Emperor Marcus Aurelius in the next century. There are certainly indications that some of his hearers were wealthy. The discussion with the father of a sick child takes for granted a staff of household servants. Other discussions picture people dancing attendance on the emperor, and hoping for high office. Epictetus does not expect his listeners to include cobblers or carpenters.[73] Yet when Epictetus is considering whether or not a philosopher should marry, he pictures him having to help with care for a newborn baby and himself get older children off to school; and compare, 'Ought we not, as we dig and plough and eat, offer hymns of praise to God?'[74] He himself (as slave still, or freedman) had been a pupil of Musonius, who commended agricultural labour (and marriage, too) for anyone concerned to make progress in philosophy. Pupil and teacher could talk while they worked.[75]

So much, then, for teaching in a private setting, more or less formal. There remains the setting of a leisurely meal, more or less informal; it is not clear how far a 'symposium' as such would have been thought distinctive. When Dio describes one, it sounds very like Paul's impression of the way the Supper of the Lord was being conducted in Corinth:

> Some attend for the sake of drinking and devote themselves to that…saying and doing unpleasant and indecorous things…the naturally loquacious, feeling they have got their table-companions for an audience recite stupid and tedious speeches, while others are singing in tune and out of it—almost more annoying than the quarrelsome and abusive… others bore people to death by their uncongenial manner, refusing to share a drink, or the conversation…[76]

There is a similar account in Plutarch.[77]

---

by P.P. Fuentes González, 'Le genre littéraire: La question de la "diatribe"', ch. 6 of his *Les Diatribes de Télès* (Histoire des doctrines de l'antiquité classique, 23; Paris: Vrin, 1998), pp. 44-78.

73. Epictetus, *Dissertations* 1.11; 1.19; 2.14.
74. Epictetus, *Dissertations* 3.22.70-72; 1.16.16.
75. Musonius Rufus 11 and 14.
76. Dio, *Discourse* 27.2-3.
77. Plutarch, *Quaestiones Conviviales* 2.10, 11, in *Plutarch's Moralia* (trans. F.C. Babbit, W.C. Hembold, P.H. de Lacy *et al.*; LCL; London: Heinemann; Cambridge, MA: Harvard University Press, 1928–), IX (trans. E.L. Minar Jr, F.H. Sandbach and W.C. Hembold); pointed out to me by Stephen Barton, in conversation.

Another contemporary account of a meal, this time from Pliny, has been popularized by Theissen, followed by Meeks: here it is quite clear that the guests are by no means the social equals of the host. Pliny discusses the etiquette of dining with social inferiors;[78] and, as Theissen, again followed by Meeks, points out, the problems posed are also aired in Martial and in Juvenal, and, we might add, Petronius. But however tactful, careful, spendthrift or inegalitarian the fare, patron and clients would recline and eat and talk, the conversation ranging widely, as in Petronius's *Satyricon*, at Trimalchio's table (or among Athenaeus's *Deipnosophists*, or at Lucian's *Carousal*, next century). As with Trimalchio, the host would be likely to initiate and very likely dominate the conversation. But there were such contexts for social intercourse among people from very different stations in life. Seneca may have been a little unusual in dining with his slaves—even if only when he had no other company. He says he is following older custom.[79] And even in much stricter households slaves could not but overhear mealtime conversations (in fact Seneca says some were specifically enjoined to do just that). When Pliny the Younger upbraids a friend for reneging on his acceptance of an invitation to a meal, he says, 'You would have heard a comic play, a reader or singer, or all three if I had felt generous...a feast of fun, laughter and learning...'[80] And slaves would have been there to serve and to perform, and to hear; and, surely, to talk about it all afterwards.

In this kind of setting there is certainly again a further opportunity for some of the lower orders to be passive recipients of aristocratic communication, receiving cultural stimulus to pass in turn to others less privileged. But there is also a real opportunity for explicit feedback (more than providing applause in a law court), and even for original input. It is very important in considering our issue to realize that the massive staffs of the exclusive households from which our 'aristocratic' writings come will also have provided multiple channels for communication at least downwards—and quite likely upwards, too.

Whether free and educated women are present is not so clear. Juvenal in Rome expects them to be, and to engage in scholarly conversation—and does not approve. Dio's *Discourse* 61, a literary discussion with a

78. Pliny the Younger, *Letters* 2.6; cf. G. Theissen, *Social Setting*, pp. 156-57; Meeks, *First Urban Christians*, p. 68.

79. Seneca, *Epistulae Morales* 47.2-5, 15-16.

80. Pliny the Younger, *Letters* 1.15; again, pointed out to me by Stephen Barton.

well-read woman who holds her own, may well be relevant. Plutarch imagines the Dinner of the Seven Wise Men to have included Eumetis, the young daughter of Cleobulus, admired for her intelligence. She sits for the meal, while an older woman, Melissa, reclines with her partner. Eumetis joins in the mealtime conversation, but is silent when the serious talk begins in the Symposium proper. Luke certainly seems to suppose that women will be present at Christian meetings, even if Mary, sitting silent and docile at Jesus' feet, is their model.[81]

While still with wealthy households, it is also worth noting that Calpurnia, the young wife of Pliny the Younger would listen (but behind a screen) as he read his current work to male friends; and he claims to have valued her appreciation. He also notes how he valued the contribution of his secretary, Encolpius, 'the one who is our joy for work or play...who else will read and appreciate my efforts?'[82]

Returning then to dining rooms, the meals of voluntary associations, *thiasoi*, taking place in their own rooms or in temples, afforded yet another setting where people of sometimes similar but sometimes quite varied backgrounds could meet and talk; so, too, would public feasts by donors, again in temple premises. (Already in the previous century Cicero thought of the cult of Cybele as a setting for good conversation helped along by good food.)[83] And Luke presents a very similar picture in both volumes: a meal is an occasion for sometimes very varied people to meet and talk.

In considering input 'from below' we must not overlook the importance in wealthy households of the slaves in charge of young children,

81. Juvenal, *Satire* 6.434-41; Plutarch, *Septem sapientium convivium*, *Moralia* 148C–150B; on Mary in Luke, cf. L. Alexander, 'Sisters in Adversity: Re-telling Martha's Story', in G.J. Brooke (ed.), *Women in the Biblical Tradition* (Lewiston, NY: Edwin Mellen Press, 1992), pp. 167-86; K.E. Corley, *Private Women, Public Meals: Social Conflict in the Synoptic Tradition* (Peabody, MA: Hendrickson, 1993); and W. Braun, *Feasting and Social Rhetoric in Luke 14* (SNTSMS, 85; Cambridge: Cambridge University Press, 1995).

82. Pliny the Younger, *Letters* 8.1.

83. Cicero, *De Senectute* 45–46; on meals shared outside the domestic setting, e.g., MacMullen, *Roman Social Relations*, p. 68. On meals and entertainment, see now the surveys in Corley, *Private Women, Public Meals*; and Braun, *Feasting*. On *thiasoi* see J.S. Kloppenborg and S.G. Wilson, *Voluntary Associations in the Graeco-Roman World* (New York: Routledge, 1996); and R.S. Ascough, *What Are They Saying About the Formation of the Pauline Churches?* (New York: Paulist Press, 1998).

the slaves who accompanied them around the city, and who were themselves by no means confined to the house. Pliny describes a young girl whose early death he laments, surrounded by 'nurses, attendants and teachers'.[84] Quintilian notes how impressionable young children are, and how powerful an impression a nurse or a *paidagogos* or slave playmate can make.[85] Much the same is noted in Ps.-Plutarch, *De Liberis Educandis*.[86] Slaves shared their beliefs, attitudes and stories with their young charges.

The aristocratic writers from around the first century, the ones I have been citing, and others like them, indicate at least elements of the popular oral urban culture of the day, the intertexture of people's discourse, the rich supply of threads with which people weave new patterns of words or reuse old ones. That is not to say that a *chreia* or a parable or a maxim from Seneca in Rome would necessarily have meant the same on the lips of a cobbler in Ephesus. But then it might have been used differently by Plutarch, and differently again by the man in the next cobbler's shop. Prima facie (and switching metaphors) these writings tell us something of what people had to chew on intellectually and aesthetically and morally (and religiously). They are part of the cultural *langue*. How they figured in various people's *parole* is obviously more difficult to discern.[87] That is always so (and is explored further in 'Words and Meanings', ch. 3, below). But knowing something more of the *langue* is an important first step. We proceed with caution—and confidence.

Oral communication, we have recalled in the foregoing, was dominant in the ancient Mediterranean world. A concentration on orality, on speech, can, however, lead to some false disjunctions between 'saying' and 'doing'. I discuss these fallacies in the next chapter.

---

84. Pliny the Younger, *Letters* 5.16.
85. Quintilian, *Institutes* 1.1.4-9; 1.2.4-5.
86. Ps.-Plutarch, *De liberis educandis*, *Moralia* 3E–5A.
87. The distinction stems from F. de Saussure, 1857–1913, and (if it needs explaining) contrasts the totality of language available to a linguistic community with what is used by individual speakers. The terms are usually kept in their original French.

Chapter 2

WORDS AS DEEDS AND DEEDS AS WORDS*

'Be doers of the word, and not just hearers' (Jas 1.22). 'People who say
fine things but don't do them, Diogenes said, were no different from a
harp—deaf and insensible.'[1] A contrast between words and deeds is
widespread in antiquity, and remains current today. In many contexts it
is useful. In some, as with other dichotomies, it can be harmful.[2] It will
be argued here that the disjunction of speech from other actions, and
then of action from the whole web of meaningful communication, can
be misleading, and in practice is particularly misleading when used as a
tool in interpreting narrative texts such as the Gospels and Acts.

Words, Deeds and Matters of 'Fact'

A sharp disjunction of this kind is used as an important hermeneutical
tool by E.P. Sanders in his *Jesus and Judaism*. 'Sayings' are clearly
distinguished from 'facts', and 'facts' are primarily actions, events
(well, accounts of actions and events).[3] The issue is somewhat complicated, because 'fact' is already a heavily value-laden term: a 'fact' is an
account of whose authenticity Sanders is convinced.[4] But the accounts
that convince him are narratives of events that he is able to distinguish

*   Reprinted from *BibInt* 3.1 (1995), pp. 129-53, by kind permission.

1.   Diogenes Laertius, *Lives of Eminent Philosophers* 6.4, in *Diogenes Laertius*
(trans. R.D. Hicks; LCL; London: Heinemann; Cambridge, MA: Harvard University Press, 1925).

2.   'Physical and spiritual', 'fact and value', 'science and art': J.L. Austin, *How
to do things with Words* (Oxford: Clarendon Press, 1962), observes in passing, 'the
familiar contrast of "normative and evaluative" as opposed to the factual, is in need,
like so many dichotomies, of elimination', p. 148.

3.   Sanders, *Jesus and Judaism*, pp. 13-18 and ch. 4; see further, below, on
'fact' see Downing, *The Church and Jesus*, pp. 132-48.

4.   Sanders, *Jesus and Judaism*, p. 11 n. 19, and p. 357.

sharply from 'sayings'. Accounts of events can provide 'facts' while accounts of sayings do not, for they may have suffered reinterpretation and re-casting in a way in which some at least of the accounts of 'events' will supposedly have escaped. Sayings can be used in historical reconstruction, but only to fill out, and that tentatively, the interpretation of the (supposedly) established 'facts'. So Sanders explains:

> The nature of the sayings material will not allow us to be certain about the precise nuance which Jesus wished to give such a large concept as 'the Kingdom of God'... We never have absolute certainty of authenticity, and probably have the original context of any given saying seldom, if ever. Facts allow us to be fairly sure that Jesus looked for a future kingdom. But to some degree conclusions about nuances and emphasis still rest on an analysis of sayings, and since this analysis will always be tentative, some things about Jesus' view of the kingdom can never be known with certainty.[5]

We are not concerned here with the issue of deciding the reliability of particular accounts, whether of sayings or of other actions, but only with the analytical tools whose validity is by Sanders here and by others elsewhere presupposed, not argued. Over against any reliance on an unexamined sayings–deeds dichotomy, there is a growing (if belated) agreement among a number of biblical critics that some variant of 'speech-act' analysis stemming from the work of J.L. Austin is not only true but importantly true.[6] Words are to be seen as having 'performative force', utterance is an action, we 'do things with words'. And we may accept a further refinement, between what we do 'in speaking'

---

5. Sanders, *Jesus and Judaism*, p. 156.

6. J.L. Austin, 'Performative Utterance', in J.O. Urmson and G.J. Warnock (eds.), *Philosophical Papers* (Oxford: Clarendon Press, 1961); and *idem, How to do things with Words*; and, for instance, the discussion and bibliography in H.C. White (ed.), *Speech-Act Theory and Biblical Criticism* (Semeia, 41; Atlanta: Scholars Press, 1988); J.G. Du Plessis, 'Speech-Act Theory and New Testament Interpretation with Special Reference to G.N. Leech's Pragmatic Principles', in P.J. Hartin and J.H. Petzer (eds.), *Text and Interpretation: New Approaches in the Criticism of the New Testament* (Leiden: E.J. Brill, 1991), pp. 129-42; and W. Houston, 'What Did the Prophets Think They Were Doing?', *BibInt* 1.2 (1993), pp. 167-88. Donald Evans attempted to introduce Austian analysis into biblical exegesis in his *The Logic of Self-Involvement* (London: SCM Press, 1963), but received little attention (and even less was accorded my own essay, 'Meanings', in M. Hooker and C.J. Hickling [eds.], *What about the New Testament? Essays in Honour of Christopher Evans* [London: SCM Press, 1975], pp. 127-42).

('illocution') and what we do 'by speaking' ('perlocution'). In saying 'I promise' (*ceteris paribus*) I make a promise; by dropping Austin's name in, I try to impress the reader, and so forth. An account of Jesus rebutting a challenge to his authority with the words, 'Was the baptism of John from heaven or from men?' (Mk 11.30) makes precisely the same prima facie claim to be an actual event, and authentic 'fact', as does the account of the (so-called) 'cleansing of the Temple' (Mk 11.15-19. 'In' both accounts of his actions, one verbal and the other (as narrated) initially non-verbal, Jesus is displayed as (among other things) asserting a rightful authority; 'by' both actions he is said to have disconcerted the authorities; and so on. 'In' each narrative Mark asserts (among other things) that each event took place; 'by' these assertions he intends his hearers' discipleship to be illuminated and enhanced; and so forth. (These are only some aspects of what is being done in and by these words.)[7]

But the inadequacy of any 'sayings–actions' dichotomy is perhaps still more clearly displayed if we start from the other side. When we talk of someone 'doing something', performing some action (such as Jesus' disruptive activities in the outer court of the Temple), we are normally taken to imply *intention*.[8] Some 'actions' are, of course, automatic ('she was breathing'), and some so habitual they demand no attention ('we can't help seeing'),[9] and some are accidental ('he tripped'). But if and when we take the trouble to narrate an action, and narrate it without any clear indication that it was 'unintentional' in kind or in this instance, then are we are assumed to be implying intention, purpose, meaning. It may well not be explicit, but clearly you see you are being told 'she meant to do it'. It was deliberate even if not deliberated. Jesus did not just trip over the tables (in Mark's narration). And even if this ascription of intention seemed not to be true of everyone's usage, it is certainly true of Sanders's usage.

---

7.   A great deal is implied without being stated. On 'implication' as an important term in such discussion ('implicature' is the favoured neologism), see H.P. Grice, 'Logic and Conversation', in P. Cole and J.L. Morgan (eds.), *Syntax and Semantics. III. Speech Acts* (New York: Academic Press, 1975), pp. 41-58.

8.   D. Davidson, *Essays on Actions and Events* (Oxford: Clarendon Press, 1980); J.R. Searle, *Intentionality* (Cambridge: Cambridge University Press, 1983). I sketched this part of my argument in my *Jesus and the Threat of Freedom*, pp. 151-52.

9.   For these qualifications, see C. Radford, 'The Power of Words', *Philosophy* 68.265 (1993), pp. 325-42.

Sanders is sure that Jesus performed some specific actions in this 'intentional' sense. He is certain that in the Temple Jesus overturned tables to indicate a destruction of that Temple that would precede its rebuilding. It was 'a demonstrative action', 'a gesture intended to make a point'.[10] In other words, it was (according to Sanders), intentional, it was a bearer of meaning; and, furthermore, its intention included communication. On both counts cited it is already as much a bearer of meaning as is anything from the sayings tradition. This story, and others on Sanders's list,[11] were always bearers of meaning, in Mark's (and the other evangelists') narratives, as well as earlier, in their likely rehearsal from memory in Christian communities. As bearers of meaning such accounts are always liable to be given a different context and a different nuance of meaning (as John does with this example), just as much as is any saying, and without any guarantee that some original 'intentional action' has been left discernible. The narratives of mute or largely mute action are in effect just as much 'sayings'—sayings of the early Christian communities—as are any others of their narratives of the teaching activity in which Jesus is said to have engaged; and no more and no less 'factual' for that.

Perhaps the crucifixion of Jesus might prove a clearer example of an event whose basic historical interpretation prior to any theological reflection among Jesus' followers is so obvious that it can readily count as a 'fact' with determinate meaning in Sanders's (and A.E. Harvey's) sense of 'fact'. Jesus was crucified under Pontius Pilate—as a royal (messianic) pretender.[12] That could well be the truth of it—but we still depend on the early (divergent) communities that have chosen to present this as the executing authority's *explicit* reason—rather than nonmessianic revolt, simple brigandage, involvement as a slave in the death of a master, or some other, unspecified; or any such combined with

10. Sanders, *Jesus and Judaism*, pp. 69-70.

11. Sanders, *Jesus and Judaism*, p. 11, lists eight 'almost indisputable facts': Jesus' baptism by John; Jesus was a Galilaean who preached and healed; called disciples, 'the twelve'; confined his activity to Israel; engaged in controversy about the Temple; was crucified outside Jerusalem by the Roman authorities; his followers continued as an identifiable movement; at least some Jews persecuted at least some parts of this movement.

12. Sanders, *Jesus and Judaism*, pp. 5-9; he cites A.E. Harvey, *Jesus and the Constraints of History* (London: Gerald Duckworth, 1982), who makes a similar point, ch. 2, pp. 11-25.

mistaken identity, or deliberate scapegoating. The only 'handle' Sanders has for his interpretation of Jesus' death by crucifixion in the time of Pilate, is a community tradition which insists that Jesus was an important, even a noble, criminal whose high status was thus acknowledged, if ironically and off-beam, by the authorities. At the very least it was, so to speak, high tragedy, not a squalid pointless mistake. Once we ask for meaning, 'meaningful facts', at this or any other point, we depend just as much on the community's (-ies') interpretation(s) as we do for any other account of what Jesus may have been involved in.

Sanders is not alone in this kind of programme aimed at isolating some bedrock 'facts', and cites Morton Smith as well as Antony Harvey as (albeit inadequate) predecessors.[13] It might be nice to have just such a firm basis on which to build one's own self-standing sandcastle of interpretation, decorated with such flags from the sayings tradition as would then fit one's chosen design. But there are—in fact—no such firm, unambiguous, self-interpreting 'facts' standing distinct from the shifting sands of the sayings tradition. There are only intentional narratives claiming to narrate intentional actions involving more or less or articulate speech. Hypothetical reconstructions of the Jesus tradition that eschew 'sayings', at least initially, in favour of supposedly 'factual' but still meaningful events are by that unsustainable distinction no sounder than any others; simply more confused and confusing.[14]

'Sayings Forms' and 'Narrative Forms'

The practice of working with a word–deed distinction goes back much further than Sanders and Smith, of course, as Sanders makes clear.[15] He is simply adopting an inherited distinction, but reversing the usual preference for the sayings strand of the Jesus tradition. The sayings–narrative dichotomy is in effect a major factor in 'classical' form criticism. For example, Rudolph Bultmann, in his *Die Geschichte der Synoptischen Tradition*, opens with this distinction, unexamined and taken for granted: 'Die Frage, ob die Überlieferung der Worte Jesu oder die der Geschichten von ihm früher zu festen Formen gelangt ist, scheint

---

13. A.E. Harvey, *Jesus*; M. Smith, *Jesus the Magician* (San Francisco: Harper & Row, 1978).

14. See, further, ch. 11 below: 'Shifting Sands'.

15. Harvey does not operate with this word–deed distinction.

mir kein debattierbares wissenschaftliches Problem zu sein.'[16] Thus the distinctiveness of the strands is simply assumed, so that successive sections of his work can be devoted to 'Die Überlieferung der Worte Jesu', and then to 'Die Überlieferung des Erzählungsstoffes'.[17] Contextless sayings are to be distinguished from those given a narrative setting ('apothegus'), and both these are to be distinguished from pure narratives (miracles, legends, myths). Even apothegms are included among sayings on sufferance, and only because 'manche Apothegmata durch die Erkenntnis vom secondären Charakter ihres Rahmens auf Herrenworte reduziert werden'.[18]

It has already been argued against this distinction both that to speak is to act, and that an ascribed action not otherwise qualified is, in normal usage, taken to be 'intentional'. But more than that, it is in the context of socially constituted meaning that (intentional) actions are perceived by those around, and by their performers; and certainly, if such actions are then narrated, they are only narrated in terms of socially constituted meaning.[19]

It is probably worth noting that this emphasis also counters any 'intentional fallacy' that supposes meaning resides in some inner process in the agent. The meaning—range of meaning—here at issue is socially constituted and shared—whether or not articulated in words

16. The question whether it was the tradition of Jesus' words or the tradition of the stories about him that first attained a fixed form does not seem to me a topic for serious scholarly debate.

17. 'The tradition of the words of Jesus'; 'The tradition of the narrative materials.' Bultmann, *Die Geschichte der synoptischen Tradition* (Göttingen: Vandenhoeck & Ruprecht, 1957), pp. 8 and 223.

18. 'Many apothegms can be reduced to pure sayings of the Lord when the secondary character of their structures is recognized.' Bultmann, *Die Geschichte der synoptischen Tradition*, p. 9.

19. Searle, *Intentionality*, ch. 5, 'The Background', pp. 141-59. In his *Speech Acts* (Cambridge: Cambridge University Press, 1969), pp. 50-53, Searle argued for 'institutional facts', where the formal or informal rules of human institutions provide the contexts within which we do things with words. It is a useful but restricted point; on which, see, e.g., G.N. Leech, *Principles of Pragmatics* (London: Longmans, 1983), pp. 106-107; 178-79, and the whole of his ch. 8: performative use is much less institutionally rule-bound, much more open and ad hoc. Perhaps see also my own earlier appraisal of this point of Searle's, in my 'Ways of Deriving "Ought" from "Is"', *PhilQ* 22.88 (1972), pp. 234-47.

spoken or written. It is a question of 'what it meant' rather than of what 'she/he [really] meant'.[20]

'Actions speak louder than words.' If they do not 'speak' in socially meaningful terms, they are unlikely to be noticed, and are very unlikely to be spoken of, narrated, written up. A healing, an exorcism can probably only be performed, and more certainly, can only be discerned and then told, in terms of the sorts of things it 'says', of how it is being understood. Even prior to narration it speaks, it communicates something (whether clearly, ambiguously or equivocally: just as with primarily 'verbal'—spoken or written—communications). Thus there is no sustainable dichotomy between the narration of a more or less or entirely mute act, and the narration of an utterance.

This theoretical conclusion can be substantiated in more detail for the New Testament material in particular with the help of an early study of Gerd Theissen's. Theissen explicitly allows for an overlap between *Lehre* and *Erzählung*, teaching and narrative.[21] But the diagram he deploys proposes a clearly bounded area of overlap, still distinguishing miracles and legends from narratives that teach; and he specifically insists, 'Mann kann die Wundergeschichten insgesamt durch ihr Motivinventar von allen anderen Gattungen abheben'.[22] In fact, his inventory (more elaborate than Bultmann's) seems on further examination to erase any such distinction, as the following table should show; for pretty much the same inventory of motifs is deployed for the narrating of sayings and of other events as is for miracle stories (although Theissen only notes four such: items 1, 6, 15 and 30, below). In addition, the major theme of 'boundary crossing'[23] which Theissen discerns

20. See, e.g., W. Charlton, *Aesthetics* (London: Hutchinson, 1970), pp. 109-11, referring to W.K. Wimsatt and M.C. Beardsley. That a performative analysis also makes it clear that those on the receiving end are presented with 'a range of meanings' is argued, effectively, for proverbs and wisdom sayings, and A.P. Winton in his *The Proverbs of Jesus* (JSNTSup, 35; Sheffield: JSOT Press, 1990), ch. 5, 'The Functions/Rhetoric of the Proverbial Sayings in the Synoptic Literature', pp. 129-40. 'Proverbs...give greater responsibility to the hearer in terms of interpretative choice' (p. 132). Such choice is almost certainly offered in some measure in every speech act (as well as all other acts).

21. Theissen, *Urchristliche Wundergeschichten* (Gütersloh: Gerd Mohn, 1974), p. 128.

22. 'We can clearly distinguish the miracle stories from any other form, by listing their motifs'. Theissen, *Wundergeschichten*, p. 92.

23. Theissen, *Wundergeschichten*, pp. 84-85.

in the miracles is well represented by similar clusters of motifs inviting the same interpretation, in the other narratives.

Only a selection of Theissen's motifs occur in any one miracle story, and some recur very infrequently. The same or very similar motifs (and similar clusters) are to be found among 'apothegms', sayings given an explicit narrative context. Theissen's headings are on the left in ordinary type; the same or similar motifs in other narratives are given in italics on the right.[24]

Miracles	**'*Apothegms*' as usually classified**

INTRODUCTORY

(1) Arrival of miracle worker first
Mk 1.21; 1.29, etc.

Appearance of actor (speaker) first
Mk 2.23; 11.27; 12.41 (though often it is opponent[s] first).

(2) Appearance of a crowd
Mk 3.1; 5.24; etc.

Appearance of a crowd
Mk 2.18; 3.20; 3.32; 4.1; 12.37
Lk. 3.7; 6.17; 7.25; 19.3.

(3) Appearance of distressed person
Mk 1.23; 1.40; 7.32, etc.

...of person with request/question
Mk 2.24; 3.22; 7.1; 8.27; 10.17; 11.27
Lk. 19.2-4.

(4) Arrival of companion with request
Mk 5.22-23; 9.17-24, etc.

...of representative with request
Mk 3.32; 10.13; 12.13.

(5) Secondary representative; delay
Mk 5.35; Lk. 7.6; etc.

Second verbal exchange; delay
Mk 3.33; 7.29; 11.31; 12.15b;
10.4-5; 10.20; Lk. 7.19.

(6) Appearance of opponent
(early) Mk 3.1; Lk. 14.1
(later) Mk 2.6; Lk. 13.14, etc.

Request is opposed
Mk 10.13; 11.33; 14.4-5;
Lk. 7.39; 19.7.

---

24. Theissen, *Wundergeschichten*, pp. 58-81. The headings here are given (with kind permission) from the ET, *The Miracle Stories of the Early Christian Traditio* (trans. F. McDonagh; Edinburgh: T. & T. Clark, 1983), pp. 48-72. I first sketched this part of the argument in an appendix to my 'The Woman from Syrophoenicia and her Doggedness', in G.J. Brooke (ed.), *Women in the Biblical Tradition* (Lewiston, NY: Edwin Mellen Press, 1992), pp. 129-49; but have omitted this part from the reprinted version of the article as it appears as ch. 5 of my *Making Sense in (and of) The First Christian Century* (JSNTSup, 197; Sheffield: Sheffield Academic Press, 2000).

EXPOSITION

(7) Reason for arrival of help-seeker   *Reason for coming*
    Mk 5.27; Lk. 7.3, etc.   Mk 7.2; 12.13; 12.28

(8) Exposition of distress (serious)   *Exposition of request (serious)*
    Mk 5.25-26; 9.21 Lk. 13.11; etc.   Mk 2.15-16, 18, 24; 7.3-4; 10.4, 13, 17;
                                         Lk. 7.37.

(9) Other difficulties   *Other problems*
    Mk 2.4; 5.24; 9.18   Mk 3.32a; 11.18; Lk. 19.3.

(10) Falling to knees   *Falling to knees*
     Mk 1.40; 5.6; 7.26, etc.   Mk 10.17 (only)

(11) Cry for help   *Cry for help*
     Mk 10.47; Lk. 17.13, etc.   Mk 10.17; (*mostly implicit*;
                                         e.g. Lk. 7.38; 19.3).

(12) Pleas, expressions of trust   *Pleas, expressions of trust*
     Mk 7.26-28; 9.22-24, etc.   Mk 10.17; 12.14.

(13) Misunderstanding   *Misunderstanding*
     Mk 5.39; 6.37; Acts 3.5, etc.   Mk 3.21; 10.18; 10.37.

(14) Scepticism, mockery   *Scepticism, mockery*
     Mk 5.40; 9.22   Mk 12.23.

(15) Criticism from opponents   *Criticism from opponents*
     Mk 2.6-7; 3.2; Lk. 14.1, etc.   Mk 2.16; 2.24; Lk. 7.39; 19.7

(16) Resistance, then submission of   *Resistance then submission*
     the demon: Mk 1.23; 5.7, 12   Mk 1.13, 17; Mt. 22.35, 46.

(17) Excitement, emotion (of healer)   *Excitement, emotion (of actor/speaker)*
     Mk 1.41; 6.34; 8.2, etc.   Mk 10.21; 14.34

(18) Assurance   *Assurance*
     Mk 2.5; 5.36; 6.50, etc.   Mk 12.34; 14.6; Lk. 19.5.

(19) Argument   *Argument*
     Mk 2.9; 3.4; Lk. 14.3, etc.   Mk 8.32; 10.13-14, 18; 10.41; 11.28-38;
                                         14.4-5; Lk. 7.39-43; 10.28.

(20) Thaumaturge reluctant, with-   *Reluctance, withdrawal, refusal*
     draws: Mk 4.38; 7.27, etc.   Mk 4.11-12; 11.33.

Miracles	**'*Apothegms*' as usually classified**

SCENE-SETTING

(21) Supplementary scene-setting
Mk 9.19; 10.49, etc.

Supplementary scene-setting
Mk 2.15, 18; 3.20b; 4.1b; 7.1b;
Lk. 7.36; 19.4.

(22) Touch
Mk 1.31; 1.41; 5.27; etc.

Wordless act of some kind, inc. touch
Mk 10.16; 11.2-7; 11.15-16; 14.3;
Lk. 7.38; 19.5.

(23) Healing matter
Mk 5.27-28; 7.34; 8.23, etc.

Significant matter
Mk 9.36; 11.2, 4; 12.15-16; 14.3;
14.22-24; Lk. 7.37-38.

(24) Miracle-working word
Mk 5.41; 7.34; 8.16, etc.

Clinching saying
Mk 2.17; 2.27-28; 3.34b-35; 7.15;
10.21; 10.42-45; 12.17; 12.27;
Lk. 7.47, 48; 9.58, 60, 62; 19.10, etc.

(25) Prayer
(Mk 7.34); Acts 9.40; 28.8

Prayer
(Mk 14.32-42)

(26) Recognition of miracle
Mk 1.42; 3.5; 6.51, etc.

Recognition of power of saying
Mk 7.19; 12.17; 12.32; 12.34.

CONCLUSION

(27) Miracle's effect demonstrated
Mk 1.31; 2.12; 10.52; etc.

*Decisive effect demonstrated: much as
above* (24), *but see also* Mk 10.22; Lk.
19.8.

(28) Dismissal
Mk 1.44; 5.19; 8.26, etc.

Dismissal
(Mk 10.21-22? 12.12?) Lk. 7.22; 11.37.

(29) Command to secrecy
Mk 1.44; 5.42; 7.36, etc.

Command to secrecy
Mk 8.30 (only).

(30) Wonder
Mk 2.12; 4.1; 7.37, etc.

Wonder
Mk 10.24; 11.18; 12.37.

(31) Acclamation
Mk 1.27; 2.12; 4.41, etc.

Acclamation
Mk 11.9-10; 11.18; 12.37.

(32) Rejection
Mk 3.6; 5.17, etc.

Rejection
Mk 10.22; 11.18; 12.12.

(33) Reputation spreads
Mk 1.28; 1.45; 5.15, etc.

Reputation spreads
(Mk 12.12?); 12.27.

Tales of powerful pronouncements and tales of powerful healings are tales of powerful activity, told with the aid of pretty well the same menu of motifs. The same vocabulary of narrative features is available and deployed whether the significant event is a healing, an exorcism, an assurance of forgiveness, an assurance of forgiveness accompanied by healing, a 'demo', a legal or ethical ruling, a theological pronouncement, a victory in a controversy or a demand. Neither form nor motifs encourage, let alone demand any dichotomy between narratives of verbal activity and narratives of mute or largely mute activity. All are meaningful, 'intentional' actions, to be narrated with the help of similar selections from a single menu. They share precisely the same continuous context of meaning, the same intertexture, in the Mediterranean world of late antiquity.

The Pragmatics of Useful Narrative: The Chreia

It should be clear, then, from the foregoing analysis of material in Mark, mostly, and Luke (with just a touch of Matthew), that the 'pragmatics' of these various narrations are very similar. The narrators seem to have a very similar range of aims in view in each instance, using very similar motifs to engage attention, hold it and transfer information to be noted, assimilated, responded to, stored; all the while expecting very similar kinds of perception and response from their hearers or readers.[25]

'Pragmatics' in this sense is concerned with still more of the aims and methods of persuading others to accept and maybe actively respond to information, than are dealt with in the classical discussions of rhetoric, the arts of persuasion. But it is perhaps worth noting that, at a much more sophisticated level than our evangelists, Cicero, and then Quintilian quoting him in agreement, are both sure that an orator's *narratio* will unquestionably include the narrating of things people have said.[26]

25. See especially, Leech, *Principles of Pragmatics*; but also S. Levinson, *Pragmatics* (Cambridge: Cambridge University Press, 1983). There is a helpful discussion of varying 'intentions' and 'motives' for texts (among which a motive to communicate is often one of a number) in M.G. Brett, 'Motives and Intentions in Genesis 1', *JTS* NS 42.1 (1991), pp. 1-16, especially in the concluding reflection that 'we could perhaps think of a continuum from the most explicit and conscious layer of communication down to the most hidden and sub-conscious layer of motives' (p. 16). (Whether restricting 'intention' and 'motive' respectively, to either end of the spectrum discerned will prove helpful time may tell.)

26. Quintilian, *Institutes* 4.2.107; himself quoting Cicero, *Partitiones* 9.31. So,

There is in fact a useful term from the classical discussions of com-munication, one which avoids the division which is here being rejected as artificial, unhelpful, misleading. Increasingly scholars have been resuming the use of the word *chreia* in preference to 'apothegm' (or 'paradigm', or 'pronouncement story').[27] And this category, of course, allows for '[mutely] acted *chreiai*' as well as for 'verbal' (the majority) and also for 'mixed' examples, along a spectrum; rather than encour-aging or imposing artificial distinctions.[28] Thus:

> Someone dropped a loaf of bread and was ashamed to pick it up; where-upon Diogenes, wishing to teach him a lesson, tied a rope to the neck of a wine-jar and proceeded to drag it across the Ceramicus.[29]

> Someone wanted to study philosophy under him. Diogenes gave him a tunny to carry, and told him to follow him. And when for shame the man threw it away and departed, and then sometime later Diogenes met him, he said with a laugh, 'The friendship between you and me was broken by a tunny'.[30]

> When someone said life was evil, he said, 'It's not living that's bad, but living badly'.[31]

A possible disadvantage of the term *chreia* is the stress in some ancient definitions on 'concision', brevity (as, indeed, in the examples above, and many more). Not many gospel *pericopai* might seem to fit within a category so defined.[32] It is clear, however, from the same clas-sical discussions, that students learned to expand these condensed nar-ratives.[33] It has also been argued cogently by J.F. Kindstrand that in

of course, Luke claims to have recorded what Jesus 'did and taught', Acts 1.1.

27. R.C. Tannehill (ed.), *Pronouncement Stories* (Semeia, 20; Atlanta: Scholars Press, 1981); D. Patte (ed.), *Kingdom and Children: Aphorism, Chreia, Structure* (Semeia, 29; Atlanta: Scholars Press, 1983); Berger, 'Hellenistischer Gattungen', pp. 1092-1110; and *idem*, *Formgeschichte*, pp. 80-93; Hock and O'Neil (trans. and eds.), *The Chreia*; B.L. Mack and V.K. Robbins, *Patterns of Persuasion in the Gos-pels* (Sonoma, CA: Polebridge Press, 1989).

28. Hock and O'Neil, *The Chreia*, p. 27, quoting Theon.

29. Diogenes Laertius, *Lives of Eminent Philosophers* 6.35 (LCL).

30. Diogenes Laertius, *Lives of Eminent Philosophers* 6.36 (LCL).

31. Diogenes Laertius, *Lives of Eminent Philosophers* 6.24 (LCL).

32. Cf. Hock and O'Neil, *The Chreia*, p. 26; only a few gospel *pericopai*, such as those in Lk. 9.57-62, are as brief as most of the examples in Diogenes Laertius; cf. Berger, *Formgeschichte*, p. 81.

33. On expansion, see Hock and O'Neil, *The Chreia*, p. 35; B.L. Mack, 'Elabo-

earlier usage the term applied to 'useful' pieces of much greater length, from which a number of the preserved abbreviated varieties very likely derive.[34] It is also clear that in collections such as those of Diogenes Laertius, ascribed sayings could be condensed still further into 'doxographic' summaries of views held, without even the repeated brief 'he said', or 'asked...he replied...'[35] Such briefly stated opinions in context are still not in general 'gnomes' or 'maxims': important elements both of their meaning and their force are still significantly constituted by their context, which is the narration of the characteristic actions (including effective utterances) of this particular person.[36]

Further support for the argument here being pursued may be afforded by considering the ease with which a chreia can be accorded an 'actantial' (story-line) analysis. For the first of those recounted above we may suggest:

[Sender] Diogenes	→	[object] 'a lesson'	→	[receiver] 'someone'
		↑		
[helper] Diogenes's wit	→	[subject] Diogenes	←	[opponent] the man and his shame

For the third:

[sender] 1st speaker	→	[object] an apt Cynic rejoinder	→	[receiver] 1st speaker and all hearers
		↑		
[helper] Diogenes's quick-witted word-play	→	[subject] Diogenes	←	[opponent] 1st speaker's shallow pessimism and ours'

rations of the Chreia in the Hellenistic Schools', ch. 2 of Mack and Robbins, *Patterns*, pp. 31-67.

34. J.F. Kindstrand, 'Diogenes Laertius and the Chreia Tradition', *Elenchos* 7 (1986), pp. 219-43; cf. the approving response from M.-O. Goulet-Cazé, 'Le Livre Six de Diogène Laërce', *ANRW* II.36.6 (1990), pp. 3978-981. There is a stimulating appraisal of the rhetorical pragmatics of Diogenes's *chreiai*, in R.B. Branham, 'Diogenes' Rhetoric and the Invention of Cynicism', in M.-O. Goulet-Cazé and R. Goulet (eds.), *Le cynisme ancien et ses prolongements* (Paris: Presses Universitaires de France, 1993), pp. 445-73.

35. E.g., Diogenes Laertius, *Lives of the Ancient Philosophers*, 6.27-29 and 70-73; on the latter see M.-O. Goulet-Cazé, *L'ascèse cynique* (Paris: Vrin, 1986).

36. See the discussion, in Hock and O'Neil, *The Chreia*, p. 26, again. (In the light of this it is particularly unfortumate that D. Dormeyer, *The New Testament among the Writings of Antiquity* (ET; Sheffield: Sheffield Academic Press, 1998 [1993]), not only fails to deal with 'action *chreiai*', but distinguishes *chreiai* too clearly from 'gnomes', pp. 174-78 and 86-89.

And we may do just as well for the following, from an amalgamated sequence: 'He would continually say that for the conduct of life we needed either reason or a rope (logon ē brochon).'[37] Thus:

[Sender] Diogenes	→	[object] an apt Cynic slogan	→	[receiver] supposed contemporaries and us
		↑		
[helper] Diogenes' mordant wit and sense for assonance.	→	[subject] Diogenes	←	[opponent] the stupidity of all civic societies

It should be obvious from this, if not already, that ascribed sayings, even lists of ascribed sayings (of which the above is a part) are always implicit narratives. On occasion elements of (supposed) context may be provided; but all narration of a character's views and opinions and utterances remain implicitly narratival, expecting the reader or hearer to fill in as much as is needed of what is unstated, to complete the story.[38]

In his *The New Testament and the People of God*, Tom Wright joins with others in forcefully arguing for 'story' as the dominant category for our proper understanding of early Christian communication.[39] Then the question of narratives and any sort of narrative structure in Q, currently much debated, becomes crucial. Wright speaks of 'the strange, unstoried world' of Q (and of the *Gospel of Thomas*), to be seen as quite alien to the pervasive narrative ethos of better-evidenced early Christianity. Only

> if Catchpole and others are right, and Q began with the story of John the Baptist, [and so] it may be the case that some sort of the total story of Jesus, rather than simply an abstracted collection of sayings, was present from the beginning[40]

can the Q hypothesis be thought of as at all plausible. When Wright and others are so busily pressing the category of 'story' it would be appropriate if they and more were to recognize how much more pervasive it really is.

---

37. Diogenes Laertius, *Lives of the Ancient Philosophers*, 6.24.

38. See n. 7, above, on 'implication'.

39. N.T. Wright, *Christian Origins and the Question of God*. I. *The New Testament and the People of God* (London: SPCK, 1992), ch. 3, pp. 47-80, and throughout Wright cites in support D. Patte, N.R. Petersen, R. Funk, A.C. Thiselton, and D. Rhoads and D. Mitchie in particular, p. 69.

40. Wright, *New Testament*, p. 435, 442.

Q as envisaged (the source of the non-Markan material that Matthew
and Luke in common include) already *narrates* a complex of the
teaching of Jesus, with plenty of clues to allow its early hearers to fill in
as much further narrative as they might need or wish to. It is a story of
Jesus teaching verbally (in the main) but also doing other things, in a
context amply signalled. In Q, for Jesus to have performed his teaching
and other actions in the setting indicated is all through to have *acted*
purposefully, meaningfully and effectively. And the 'plot' of the story
is patently summarized for us in the encounter with John's disciples
(Lk. 7.18-19, 21-28, etc.):

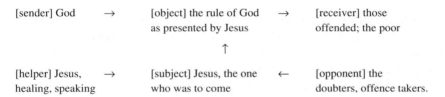

This 'plot' is very similar in content to the 'plots' Wright himself
discerns approvingly in various Jewish and Christian 'stories' in the
canon.[41] And even if we were to accept the conclusion advanced by
some that an earlier component of Q comprised solely sapiential sayings of Jesus (before being joined with matter including the pericope
just cited, matter comprising perhaps coaeval, perhaps later formed or
collected eschatological material), such wisdom sayings were (*ex hypothesi*) already being 'narrated' to an audience aware of and reminded of
the wider context, and as ever, expected to fill in any gaps needed for a
full appreciation—just as in the example from Diogenes above.[42]

Speaking, teaching, pronouncing, proclaiming, cursing, consoling are
actions, just as much as touching, healing, embracing, sharing food,
stoning. All such actions can be narrated as stories or parts of larger
stories, as in ancient Greek Lives of philosophers, or as in Q.[43] Any
given action may consist largely or partly of words spoken or written or
of conventional gestures or of any combination of these; or may be
entirely mute; and any may or may not be intended to communicate.

41. Wright, *New Testament*, pp. 221-23 and 378-90.
42. See especially, Kloppenborg, *Formation of Q*, pp. 238-45.
43. For an account of Q that tallies with the foregoing, see my 'Quite like Q',
Bib 69.2 (1988), pp. 196-225, reprinted with a response to criticisms, in my *Cynics
and Christian Origins*, ch. 5, pp. 115-42; and see also ch. 5 below.

Actions consisting largely of verbal utterances may be particularly ineffective, 'mere words'; but mute actions may also fail to achieve much if anything: 'empty gestures', 'pointless performances'. It is more helpful to consider the range of intent and effectiveness of verbal and other activity, than to note how readily words become mere words, and on that slender basis distinguish their utterances from other actions, their telling from other narrative.

The narration of the speaking, the writing, the gesturing, is part of the story. It could even be the whole story, if that were the action intended, effected and/or so perceived.

We have considered in some detail words as deeds and deeds as words. In the next chapter we ask how much clarity and precision we may justifiably expect in the use of words in our ancient sources—and whether some of the distinctions made in our interpretation of them may be unwarrantably imposed.

Chapter 3

WORDS AND MEANINGS

We have looked at some of the ways in which words are actions and some of the ways in which actions constitute communication. We need now to consider how much or how little verbal precision we may reasonably expect, in the light of what we find authors doing with words, and are found reflecting on what they and others do with them.

Questioning Common Assumptions

In studying literary remains from the ancient Mediterranean world (and further afield, of course) there is the underlying assumption that we can tell with a fair degree of plausibility quite precisely what words (or, better, words-in-sentences) mean or meant. Of course we depend on a long tradition of glossaries, commentaries, translations. For the Mediterranean world of late antiquity the cross-checks are so many and so complex that the likelihood of going systematically astray seems to most of us quite negligible.[1] The range of possibilities for a particular word can be determined, and the ways in which a particular set of words may modify and qualify each other in what we take to be a clause or a sentence can be discerned with some confidence. I shall argue, however, that it is less clear that we are justified in narrowing down the possibilities of 'meaning' in the ways we often do. We need to be much more sensitive than we seem in practice to be, to the ways in which speakers and writers themselves thought words worked and could be made to work.

Some of our decisions about the ways in which words have been

---

1. For the possibility of systematic mistranslation, see W.V.O. Quine, *From a Logical Point of View* (Cambridge, MA: Harvard University Press), 1953; *idem, Word and Object* (Cambridge, MA: MIT Press, 1960); and the discussion in F.G. Downing, *The Theologian's Craft* (Unsworth, Lancs: Downing, 1974), pp. 53-55.

deployed nonetheless seem quite secure. Words occurring only in a recent manuscript copy of a document, never in a range of older copies, are unlikely to be authentic; questions of their meaning and use have no bearing on the original. To take a different example, I have argued from instances we have of the ways in which ancient authors used others' acknowledged work, and from the practicalities of using documentary sources at the time, that we can decide fairly objectively that Matthew and Luke used Mark independently of each other, and also used another common source, 'Q', in very similar if not identical copies.[2] We do not need to decide what their sentences 'mean' to determine the fact of borrowing, and the order of it. And once that solution is accepted, then we can decide in some detail how Matthew and Luke respectively retained, rejected, reordered words and sets of words from Mark: still without needing to determine issues of meaning.

It is once we try to decide what each author used their words 'for', what they 'meant' by what they retained, by what they added or adapted or reordered ('redaction criticism'), that we need to ask not only about the range of uses for the words in question, but the largely overlooked question: Can we tell how these writers may have thought words in general worked, how they may have expected words in general to work? In particular do we need to know how precise and narrow or broad and flexible they expected the sense and reference of their words to be? Mark's Peter tells Jesus, 'You are the Christ'; Matthew's Peter expands this with '...the Son of the living God'. We might want to be able to determine whether Matthew is explaining what he took Mark to mean, or correcting Mark, or using a more sonorous and perhaps familiar phrase because he liked the sound of it (or just being careless). In fact we mostly assume without further question that ancient writers at large and our evangelists in particular intended precise meanings which we can then determine.

Some further examples are in order, and they will be drawn from discussions of and exercises in 'redaction criticism', the attempt not only to tell how our evangelists preserved, altered and expanded their (supposed) sources, but what all these findings may indicate for our interpretations of the end products.

In his very useful *Reading the New Testament* (1987) Christopher

---

2.   Downing, 'Towards the Rehabilitation of Q', pp. 169-81; *idem*, 'Compositional Conventions and the Synoptic Problem', ch. 8 below; and 'A Paradigm Perplex: Luke, Matthew and Mark', ch. 9 below.

Tuckett devotes a chapter to 'Redaction Criticism'. 'In the case of Matthew and Luke', he assures us, the method

> is relatively straightfoward, since we can make a direct comparison (via a synopsis) between the work of each evangelist and his Marcan source. In the case of the Q material in Matthew and Luke, the same may also be possible though the task is more complicated since we do not have Q directly available…

On the same page he adds,

> By the nature of the case, redaction-critical study of the earliest Gospel, Mark, is more problematical, since we do not have Mark's sources available to us… Redaction criticism has also been extended to try to analyse the sayings source Q. Problems are even greater here since, not only do we not have Q's sources directly available to us, we do not even have Q itself immediately before us.

He concludes, however, that as one tool in a literary-critical appraisal, redaction criticism can help us interpret a work as a whole.[3]

In practice, however, Tuckett (along with a number of others) is sufficiently confident actually to reverse the process, so sure that he knows what some sets of words in Q clearly mean as to be able to tell that they could not have been spoken or written originally by the same author as another part of the same sequence. I take my example from a discussion of the passage on 'cares', Lk. 12.22-31 and Mt. 6.25-34, giving the Lukan numbering for Q:

> It is widely acknowledged that Q 12:23 (the ψυχή is more than food, and the σῶμα more than clothing) does not fit well after the exhortation in v. 22 not to worry about food or clothing. The motives given in v. 23 on the one hand, and in vv. 22, 24, 26-28 on the other, for the general advice not to worry are different: in vv. 24, 26-28 there is no grading of concerns but simply an assurance that God will provide; v. 23, however introduces a contrast between the more important ψυχή–σῶμα and the less important food and clothing. It looks very much as if either v. 23 has been added secondarily to vv. 22, 24 and 26-28 or vice-versa… [This latter is judged less likely]… So, too, v. 25, interrupting the twin appeals to examples from nature (ravens/birds and lilies) and introducing a quite different kind of argument appealing to human inability to solve the problems of anxiety, is almost universally regarded as a secondary addition to the early tradition.[4]

---

3.   C.M. Tuckett, *Reading the New Testament* (London: SPCK, 1987), pp. 119, 123.

4.   C.M. Tuckett (the 'M' seems optional in his publications), *Q and the*

Tuckett does not think it necessary to tell us how he knows that the distinctions he and others find would have been so striking that a first-century east mediterranean speaker (Jesus or a follower) could not have combined them from the start; and this despite the fact that some supposed early redactor of the pericope (*ex hypothesi*) found them quite compatible and the sequence entirely coherent; as, obviously, also did both Matthew and Luke. In response to attempts to divide Q into two (or more) major strata with distinctive theologies, elsewhere, and by way of contrast, Tuckett himself demands to be told, 'If too much of a disjunction between layers is postulated...why the earlier tradition was ever used at all by the later editor?'[5]

Sequences enjoining the avoidance of cares about food, clothing and property appear in ancient Greek and Latin works ascribed to Cynics, and to Stoics with a Cynic cast to them. Among a score of passages I have assembled[6] two, three or four of the following strands occur in various combinations. Most often we find the example of adequately fed and clothed animals (8), plants less often (2). Their lack of property is noted four times. That it is 'God' who provides is made explicit in seven cases. A comparison of values occurs in six. Humans' limited powers are noted only three times, but are also implicit in the references to the divine care that obviates busy anxiety. It is quite clear that there is a cluster of themes available for any wanting to urge this case. Any smaller or larger selection of these themes can be brought in to make the overriding point: we should forgo anxious cares.

Quite apart from the question whether such Cynic material might have had a formative influence in the circles of Jesus and/or of Q (where Tuckett among others disagrees vigorously with my conclusions), at least these examples should have given him and those he quotes pause. If such themes could be combined at choice by some in the ancient east

---

History of Early Christianity: Studies on Q (Edinburgh: T. & T. Clark), 1996, pp. 149-50, citing D. Zeller, D. Catchpole, U. Luz, J.S. Kloppenborg, P. Hoffmann for v. 23, and R. Bultmann, J. Jeremias, D. Zeller, J.S. Kloppenborg, R.A. Piper and P. Hoffmann for v. 25. Possibly vv. 25-26 are intended. On this passage see also, more recently, A. Kirk, *The Composition of the Sayings Source: Genre, Synchrony and Wisdom Redaction in Q* (NovTSup, 91; Leiden: E.J. Brill, 1998), pp. 215-17.

5.   C.M. Tuckett, 'On the Stratification of Q: A Response', *Semeia* 55 (1992), pp. 213-22 (214).

6.   Downing, *Christ and the Cynics* §58, pp. 68-71; Lucian, *The Mistaken Critic* and *A Slip of the Tongue*; and see the quotation from Quintilian below and n. 14.

Mediterranean, how can one be so sure without argument that the author of the parts of the restricted sequence allowed by him as original could not have confidently uttered the whole passage as we have it? Or that the parts contrasted would have had such clear and distinctive meanings as to be unavailable for combining from the start in the sequence we find?

Perhaps most significant is Tuckett's phrase, 'introducing a quite different kind of argument'. It seems to be assumed that we know without asking that Q is (to use some classic terms) 'dialectic' rather than 'rhetoric', argument rather than persuasion. Yet in rhetorical persuasion cumulative force is regularly deployed, as we shall note in a little more detail below, and in particular do speakers rely on the cumulative force of motifs drawn from conventional clusters.

Further examples could have been drawn from many sources. I would note here only the related discussion stemming from work by John Kloppenborg, distinguishing (often rather more crudely than in Kloppenborg's own carefully qualified original) major 'strata' in Q on the basis of ideas judged to be distinctive: 'wisdom' over against 'prophetic/deuteronomic'. I discuss this particular issue further below, where I note that just such strands (and more) can be readily interwoven by Paul in Romans.[7] It is to be hoped that the foregoing will suffice to show that we do need to ask very carefully of our ancient sources, how their authors and hearers and readers thought words worked and could be make to work, what sorts of things they might seem to be doing with words in particular instances, how precisely or how flexibly; and that might then also allow us to address the question of what counted as coherence or incoherence in particular circumstances with particular aims in view. Certainly, before we continue to use 'incompatibility' as a criterion for slitting ancient documents into parts or strata, we need to check how far our sense of what is or is not compatible matches what we may discern of that of the author and the author's circle.

In Practice

As it happens, quite a lot of relevant work is available; its significance seems not to have been noted, its implications have not been brought to bear. We may recall the way children learned to use language in

7.   For references, see 'Word-processing in the Ancient World', ch. 4 below.

approved ways for speaking and for writing to be read aloud, very largely by imitation and repetition. You reproduced a story in your own words (but they had to be 'good Greek' or 'proper Latin' words),[8] expanded or condensed; you took a *chreia*, a significant act, verbal or wordless, ascribed to a known person, and expanded it or condensed it. Our best examples are drawn from the teachers' handbooks, the Greek *progymnasmata* that have been preserved for us,[9] but a summary in Quintilian from the late first century CE is worth quoting in part (Quintilian is taken as representative by commentators on Greek and Latin education in our period):

> I have now finished with two of the departments with which teachers of literature profess to deal, namely the art of speaking correctly and the interpretation of authors... There pupils should learn to paraphrase Aesop's fables...in simple and restrained language and subsequently to set down this paraphrase in writing with the same simplicity of style: they should begin by analysing each verse, then give its meaning in different language, and finally proceed to a freer paraphrase in which they will be permitted now to abridge and now to embellish the orginal, so far as this may be done without losing the poet's meaning [*mox mutatis verbis interpretari, tum paraphrasi audacius vertere, qua ex breviare quaedam exornare salvo modo poetae sensu permittitur*].[10]

Our New Testament documents are, of course, in Greek, the product of a Greek-language upbringing, stemming from communities that were articulate in Greek, inscribed by people literate in Greek. That Jesus and his first followers conversed mostly if not entirely in Aramaic still seems most likely, but there also seems every reason to believe that education at that time in Judaea and Galilee conformed to much the same style.[11]

---

8.   Diogenes Laertius, *Lives of Eminent Philosophers* 7.59.

9.   Hock and O'Neil, *The Chreia*; Marrou, *A History of Education in Antiquity*, pp. 142-75, but especially pp. 172-75; S.F. Bonner, *Education in Ancient Rome from the Elder Cato to the Younger Pliny* (London: Methuen, 1977), pp. 165-276, but especially pp. 229-36 and 250-58.

10.   Quintilian, *Institutes* 13.2 (LCL).

11.   M. Hengel, *Judaism and Hellenism* (ET; 2 vols.; London: SCM Press, 1974); and *The 'Hellenization' of Judaea in the First Century after Christ* (ET; London: SCM Press, 1989); G.J. Brooke, *Exegesis at Qumran* (JSOTSup, 29; Sheffield: JSOT Press, 1985), pp. 6-8. On awareness of the *chreia*, one of the staples of the Greek teachers' *progymnasmata*, see A.J. Avery-Peck, 'Rhetorical Argumentation in Early Rabbinic Pronouncement Stories', *Semeia* 64 (1993/94), pp. 49-72; H.A.

The importance of this aspect of ancient education for our appreciation of 'apothegms' and other elements in the gospel tradition has been noted by quite a few scholars.[12] What is to be emphasized here is the extent to which it was presupposed that you could 'say the same thing', tell 'the same story' in other words, more briefly or more elaborately. You chose different phrasing—but you were doing 'the same thing', conveying 'the same' idea, urging 'the same' response.

The lessons learned were used in adult life. Hock and O'Neil cite Dio Chrysostom *Oration* 32.44, relating at length a *chreia* involving Anacharsis that is found in a brief version in Diogenes Laertius' *Lives of Eminent Philosophers* 1.104;[13] but there are many more examples, especially in Dio's Cynic *Orations* (telling Alexander to stop blocking his sunlight [4.14-15]; offering therapy [8.5]; managing without a slave [10.1-16]); and again, many more in the *Cynic Epistles*.

An adult public speaker, insists Quintilian, should practice translation from Greek into Latin, as Messala, Crassus and Cicero did:

> The purpose of this form of exercise is obvious. For Greek authors are conspicuous for the variety of their matter, and there is much art in all their eloquence, while, when we translate them, we are at liberty to use the best words available, since all that we use are our very own. As regards figures, too, which are the chief ornament of oratory, it is necessary to think out a great number and variety for ourselves, since in this respect the Roman idiom differs largely from the Greek. But paraphrase from the Latin will also be of much assistance, while I think we shall all agree that this is especially valuable with regard to poetry...for the lofty inspiration of verse serves to elevate the orator's style and the bold licence of poetic language does not preclude our attempting to render the same things in the appropriate [sc. prose] language (*et verba poetica libertate audaciora non praesumunt eadem proprie dicendi facultatem*).[14]

So long as they are licit Latin or good Greek a wide choice of words, phrases and figures are expected to be available for selection to convey

Fischel, *Rabbinic Literature and Greco-Roman Philosophy* (Leiden: E.J. Brill, 1973); M. Luz, 'Oenomaus and Talmudic Anecdote', *JSJ* 23.1 (1991), pp. 42-80; P.S. Alexander, 'Rabbinic Biography and the Bisography of Jesus: A Survey of the Evidence', in Tuckett (ed.), *Synoptic Studies*, pp. 19-50.

12. Hock and O'Neil, *The Chreia*, pp. 1-47; Mack and Robbins, *Patterns*. On compression of a longer original rather than expansion of the brief *chreia*, see Kindstrand, 'Diogenes Laertius', pp. 219-43.

13. Hock and O'Neil, *The Chreia*, p. 40.

14. Quintilian, *Institutes* 10.5.3-4, LCL amended (cf. translator's note).

the intended sense and/or reference, only more or less elegantly, persuasively. This is the import of much of Quintilian's discussion of rhetoric (itself, of course, explicitly similar to that of many Greek and Roman predecessors). Particularly significant for the opening example in this present chapter is the discussion of 'amplification', and there especially of 'augmentation', piling up a number of complementary or supplementary details to emphasize 'the meaning' intended, elaborating a general principle with as many relevant commonplaces as possible;[15] a procedure quite distinct from the 'digression' from the main point that Tuckett and others discerned in the passage from Q. (Be it said, 'digression' is also a permitted rhetorical ploy.)[16]

It is probably time to 'come clean' with the reader. There are powerful modern arguments against any such trust that words can be made to work like this. Words, many would persuasively argue, do not (phrases and sentences do not) 'clothe', 'contain', 'meaning' as though 'the meaning' were some discrete contents within a package. I am not aware of ancient writers making any such claim explicitly[17] but this would seem to have been the common tacit assumption. As words such as *translatio* ('translation') and μεταφορά ('carrying across') suggest, you could expect to dress an idea, or a meaning in all sorts of clothes, all sorts of packaging, and still convey 'it' safely to the hearer or listener. Although it seems clear to many nowadays that you can not,[18] yet that is what ancient practice and technical advice presupposes.

---

15. Cicero, *Orator* 125-26; *Partitiones* 52-53; Quintilian, *Institutes* 8.4, and especially 8.4.26-27; cf. Aristotle, *Rhetoric* 1.9.38-41; 2.19.26; Ps.-Cicero, *Ad Herrenium* 2.20.47-49; 3.7.15; 4.28.38.

16. On digression, Cicero, *De Oratore* 3.203-204; Quintilian, *Institutes* 4.2.19; 4.3.14-17; 9.1.28; 10.1.33.

17. But cf. 'the cloak of many colours which Demetrius of Phalerum was said to wear', as a metaphor for an elaborate digression, Quintilian, *Institutes* 10.1.33 again.

18. L. Wittgenstein, *Philosophical Investigations* (Oxford: Basil Blackwell, 1953); *idem*, *On Certainty* (Oxford: Basil Blackwell, 1969); and Downing, 'Meanings', pp. 127-42; see further below. A 'transportable contents' sense of 'translation' was still being deployed by G. Ebeling in *An Introduction to a Theological Theory of Language* (ET; London: Collins, 1973). For a recent discussion, J.T. Reed, 'Modern Linguistics and the New Testament: A Basic Guide to Theory, Terminology and Literature', in S.E. Porter and D. Tombs (eds.), *Approaches to New Testament Study* (JSNTSup, 120; Sheffield: Sheffield Academic Press, 1995), pp. 222-65; noting p. 232, 'Principle: Words as physical objects do not "possess" meaning, they are "attributed" meaning by speakers and listeners in a context'; and

So Flavius Josephus takes a Greek original, the *Letter of Aristeas*, already in quite good Greek, and produces a version of his own. It was studied some 40 years ago by A. Pelletier. I quote from a previous summary of my own:

> Pelletier makes it clear that Josephus' prime intention is to paraphrase, 'to change whatever he can', if only by inversion. Apart from inventories, and one or two set formulae, Pelletier finds just one (broken) sequence of twelve words, and another of ten, that are [near-] identical in both. Other than these there are only short phrases or individual words. Even with the individual words Josephus will sometimes for (a) substitute synonym (b), only later, on finding (b) in his source, render it by (a).[19]

Josephus follows standard practice. It is important to use your own words (that makes it your own work); but your own words are assumed to be entirely capable of conveying 'the meaning', 'the same meaning'.

So Josephus is to be taken at his word (!) when he insists early in his *Antiquities* that his version of the Jewish traditions drawn mainly from sacred Scripture will neither add nor omit anything.[20] As he explains at another point,

> While the relation and recording of events that are unknown to most people because of their antiquity require charm of exposition, such as is imparted by the choice of words and their proper arrangement and by whatever else contributes elegance to the narrative, in order that readers may receive such information with a certain degree of gratification and pleasure, nevertheless what historians should make their chief aim is to be accurate and hold everything else of less importance than speaking the truth to those who must rely on them in matters of which they themselves have no knowledge.[21]

Of course Josephus does leave out much that might be embarrassing, such as the golden calf incident; and includes non-scriptural matter (and not only the *Letter of Aristeas*), as well as speeches he himself composed. One can only assume that he supposed that to include the golden calf episode would be to risk a misunderstanding of the tradition as a

P.M.S. Hacker, 'Davidson on Intentionality', *Philosophy* 73.286 (1998), pp. 539-52.

19. A. Pelletier, *Flavius Josèphe, adaptateur de la lettre d'Aristée* (Paris: Cerf, 1962), referring in particular to p. 29; Downing, 'Redaction Criticism', I, pp. 46-55, referring in particular to p. 48.

20. Josephus, *Ant.* 1.17; cf. 20.261.

21. Josephus *Ant.* 14.1-3 (LCL).

whole, that it could only mislead. Still, however we judge Josephus'
integrity as an apologist to and for his people, his working assumption
is that a wide choice of words and phrases are equally available for conveying 'the meaning' of the original. His work is accurate in just the
same sense as the Septuagint translators' was (*Ant.* 12.104). I have
shown in an earlier discussion that other near contemporary writers
making similar claims to an accurate reproduction of sources work on
the whole even more 'freely' than critics conclude that Josephus does.[22]

When it comes to the text of sacred Scripture itself, of course, different rules apply: then the text must be to the syllable maintained with
total accuracy (*Apion* 1.37-42; even if, again, we know that contemporary texts in fact varied, and often widely). Once a translation
(the Septuagint) has become sacred Scripture, the same applies; witness
Josephus' insistence at *Ant.* 12.109, although he does not include
Philo's conviction that each of the translators independently produced
exactly the same words for the entire text,[23] which simply presses the
expected consistency of the copies back to source. Translation in this
instance ought to have something like formal geometric or dialectical
precision, argues Philo, the right words for the right words (*kuria
kuriois*).[24] With this insistence we may compare Mt. 5.18 (and Lk.
16.17, *mian kerian*), but also, for instance, Dio of Prusa's aside on the
sacrosanctity of officially inscribed laws, where, too, *mian kerian* must
not be removed.[25] As we shall note shortly, the underlying presupposition in fact remains the same, but with the reverse implication in practice. The outer form is sacred, precisely because it can clothe, contain,
convey a wide range of meanings, and you need in Greek words that
will do this as well as the Hebrew did. In fact Philo makes the point
about words and meanings here being urged in this very context:

> Who does not know that every language, and Greek especially, abounds
> in terms (*onomata*) and that the same thought (*tauton enthumēma hoion*)
> can be put in many shapes (*schēmatisai pollakōs*) by changing single

22. See 'Compositional Conventions and the Synoptic Problem', ch. 8 below.
23. Philo, *Vit. Mos.* 2.37-38.
24. On which see the discussion in D. Runia, 'Naming And Knowing: Themes
in Philonic Theology, with special reference to the *De mutatione nominum*', in
R. van den Broek *et al.* (eds.), *Knowledge of God in the Graeco-Roman World*
(EPRO, 112; Leiden: E.J. Brill, 1988), pp. 48-75; repr. D. Runia, *Exegesis and
Philosophy: Studies on Philo of Alexandria* (Aldershot: Variorum, 1990).
25. Dio Chrysostom, *Discourse* 31.86.

words (*metaphrazonta*) or whole phrases (*paraphrazonta*) and suiting the expression to the occasion?[26]

When it comes to a sacred text (legal codes included) 'Lawyers,' notes Quintilian, 'frequently raise the question of the letter and the intention of the law (*scripti et voluntatis quaestio*); in fact a large proportion of legal disputes turn on these points.'[27] The fact is, once the words have been 'canonized', many different contents may be found 'in' the one container, just as the same dress may clothe a succession of characters in turn. (Clement of Alexandria later distinguished four sets of possibilities, *Stromata* 1.28 *et passim*, followed by mediaeval Christendom.) Philo is quite sure that most recorded events happened as recounted,[28] and that one sense of the ritual prescriptions certainly is an enjoinder to overt performance: 'There is the temple made with hands.'[29] However, the account of Eve being made from Adam's side, for instance, is 'mythic', only; while much of what is said elsewhere contains at least two meanings.

> It is true that the seventh day is meant to teach the power of the Unoriginate and the ineffectiveness of created beings; but let us not for this reason abrogate the laws laid down for its observance, and light fire or till the ground or carry loads...[30]

And of the patriarchs Philo writes, 'These words do indeed seem to refer to men of holy life, but they are reminders of an order of things which is less obvious but far superior to things of sense'.[31] More than two senses may be available: Moses, the 'fine child' (*asteios*) of LXX Exod. 2.2, is 'goodly' in the strongest usage of the word, but also [world-]citizen, in the word's original use.[32] (*Conf. Ling.* 106–109). The 'pruning' of Lev. 19.23 is interpreted horticulturally at *Virt.* 155–160, where it also betokens the breadth of God's generous creative care; but it means ridding ourselves of self-conceit at *Leg. All.* 1.52. At *Plant.* 104–116 the pruning initially means doing away with pretence,

---

26. Philo, *Vit. Mos.* 2.38 (LCL).

27. Quintilian, *Institutes* 7.6.1, cf. 5.5-6; and Ps.-Cicero, *Ad Herrenium* 1.11.19-23; Cicero, *De Inventione* 2.116-17 (with some very sensible comments on resolving ambiguity).

28. Philo, e.g., *Vit. Mos.* 1.1-2;

29. Philo, *Spec. Leg.* 1.67.

30. Philo, *Migr. Abr.* 91 (LCL).

31. Philo, *Abr.* 52 (LCL).

32. Philo, *Conf. Ling.* 106-109.

especially in our approach to God; but then Philo notices various possible punctuations of what follows, and interprets the two that most appeal to him—purifying teaching (114) or self-evident eternal truth (116). But to be fair, a spot check suggests that Philo is mostly consistent in the deeper meaning he finds in any given passage.[33]

Stoic and other commentators had long been quarrying in Homer's and Hesiod's myths of the gods for expressions of truths about how things are. The methods of Stoic *allegorēsis* (allegory) are different from Philo's, but he shares the underlying conviction about how words work.[34] The deeper meanings Philo discerns are general truths about God and human life, and later rabbis had similar aims for their researches (midrash) into the inexhaustible treasure house of the Scriptures. 'A deeper meaning in Scripture preserves the more profound meaning of the everyday world of Israel even now', is how Jacob Neusner summarizes the approach, while commenting in modern literalist fashion, 'the exegete reads Scripture in terms other than those in which the scriptural writer speaks'. Neusner distinguishes this still less sympathetically from 'midrash as paraphrase...imposing fresh meanings by the word choices or even adding additional phrases or sentences and so revising the meaning of the received text'.[35] In between these two he places 'midrash as prophecy', to which we now turn; but his comments afford us a further reminder of how hard it is for us today to allow for a different understanding of how words and meanings may relate.

Our most plentiful examples of 'midrash as prophecy' are provided by some of the Dead Sea Scrolls, with their *pesher* reading of ancient texts, concluding that they are 'to be interpreted' as referring to recent or current events as they affect the author's (or authors') community.

---

33. For the systematic care with which Philo discerns the deeper meaning, see Brooke, *Exegesis at Qumran*, pp. 17-25.

34. Cf. A.A. Long 'Allegory in Philo and Etymology in Stoicism', *StudPhilAnn* 9 (1997), pp. 198-210; but also Cicero, *De Natura Deorum* 1.36-41; 2.59-72; Plutarch, *De Iside et Osiride, Moralia*, e.g 363D, 367C; Athenagoras, *Legatio* 20-24; stressing the classical precedent for Philo; E. Ferguson, *Backgrounds of Early Christianity* (Grand Rapids: Eerdmans, 1987), pp. 98, 282, 284, citing first-century CE Heraclitus of Alexandria, *Homeric Questions*; and for Stoics, cf. also Diogenes Laertius, *Lives of Eminent Philosophers*, 7.147, 187.

35. J. Neusner, *What is Midrash?* (Philadelphia: Fortress Press, 1987), pp. 7-8; cf. also P.S. Alexander, 'Midrash and the Gospels', in Tuckett (ed.), *Synoptic Studies*, pp. 1-18.

Some while ago George Brooke (following William Brownlee) argued persuasively that a similar range of careful exegetical techniques were being deployed in discerning these meanings as were used by Philo in Alexandria and by later rabbis, occasional diverse meanings again not excluded.[36] Brooke was arguing against those who supposed that such 'meanings' could only have been received through dream revelations, which latter suggestion again shows how hard it is for our contemporaries to accept that ancient exegetes could suppose in the cold light of day that some deeper meaning was actually 'there', awaiting discernment. We have noted the companion reluctance to allow that authors could suppose themselves to be 'clothing' in more than one way 'the idea' they were intending to convey (where their rhetorical variations may make us today suspect different hands at work).

The Theory that Reflects the Practice

Ancient Graeco-Roman writers consistently take 'naming' as the basic model for understanding language. In today's terms we might somewhat unreflectively expect names to 'label', to refer hearers succesfully to things or persons named, while also readily allowing that 'the Cynic', 'the Sinopean' as well as 'Diogenes' may all refer us to the same person (or 'the Evening Star' and 'the Morning Star' to the same planet). Then words might be expected to name and so refer us to (the same) ideas, thoughts, impressions, in much the same way.[37]

There was some controversy over origins: was our use a matter purely of convention? Or was the basic vocabulary 'natural', formed perhaps by assonance, by onomatapoeia in particular, so that 'etymology' might allow one to clarify 'the truth' (*to etumon*) of the matter in hand? In *Kratylos* Plato offers an account of the working compromise accepted by most.[38] In the first century CE we may also compare Philo, *Op.*

36. Brooke, *Exegesis at Qumran*, pp. 36-44, and the study as a whole; on diverse meanings in one passage, pp. 354-56. Cf. P. Borgen, 'Philo of Alexandria: Reviewing and Rewriting Biblical Material', *StudPhilAnn* 9 (1997), pp. 37-53.

37. See the contributions in S. Evason (ed.), *Companions to Ancient Thought. III. Language* (Cambridge: Cambridge University Press, 1994). My thanks to Dr Gillian Clark for bibliographical leads; for what follows see also her *Augustine: The Confessions* (Cambridge: Cambridge University Press, 1992).

38. J. Pinborg, 'Classical Antiquity: Greece', in T.A. Sekeok (ed.), *Current Trends in Linguistics* 13: *Historiography of Linguistics* (The Hague: Mouton, 1975), pp. 69-126, here referring to pp. 69-70; cf. also A.A. Long, *Hellenistic*

Mund. 149-50, where the names Adam chooses express perfectly the natures of the animals presented to him.

There were also differing attempts to understand just how this 'naming reference' worked, and how verbs, as a distinct group, worked (and modern authors seem to differ in their explanations of the explanations).

However, Jan Pinborg summarizes Aristotle on language thus:

> The semantic conception involved in his [Aristotle's] definitions and their context is rather primitive. The written symbols are arbitrary signs of the spoken symbols which are arbitrary signs of the mental concepts which in turn are 'likenesses' of the things themselves. The conception presupposes a theory of natural 'forms' according to which the forms embodied in the things themselves and giving them their nature are grasped directly by the intellect.[39]

To quote Aristotle himself:

> Words spoken are symbols or signs (*sumbola*) of affections or impressions (*pathēmatōn*) in the soul; written words are the signs of words spoken. As writing, so also is speech not the same for all peoples. But the mental affections themselves, of which these words are primarily signs, are the same for all, as are also the objects of which those affections are representations or likenesses, images, copies (= *homoiōmata*).[40]

More influential still, one gathers, were the Stoics. Following Pinborg again:

> They distinguish three components in the analysis of meaning: 1. the sign or the expression signifying; 2. what is signified; and 3. the object referred to. The expression and the object are corporeal entities while what is signified is incorporeal and cannot act upon anything... 'In Stoic

Philosophy (London: Gerald Duckworth, 1974), p. 132; B. Williams, 'Cratylus' Theory of Names and its Refutation', in Evason (ed.), *Language*, pp. 23-36; and Evason, 'Epicurus on mind and language', in *idem* (ed.), *Language*, pp. 91-99 ('Linguistic naturalism and the origin of language').

39. Pinborg, 'Classical Antiquity', p. 76, referring to Aristotle, *Peri Hermeneias*, which, he adds, 'depends rather heavily on Plato... The semantics of the mature Aristotle as expressed especially in the *Metaphysics* are much more sophisticated. They were not, however, to play any important role in the development of grammar...'

40. Aristotle, *Peri Hermeneias* 1.4-8, in *Aristotle: Categories, On Interpretation, Prior Analytics* (trans. H.P. Cooke and H. Tredennick [LCL; London: Heinemann; Cambridge, MA: Harvard University Press, 1905]), slightly amended.

theory acts of thought are private physical modifications of the *hēge-monikon* (soul) but the sense of words in which they (i.e., the concepts) are expressed is immaterial, objective and something which others can grasp'.[41]

Implications

It was realized that in some contexts words could be misleadingly ambiguous, creating a problem that needed to be dealt with. Stoics wanted their philosophical definitions to be precise, to be able to be clearly true or obviously false, and so argued (sensibly) that contexts can remove ambiguities. Galen, as another example, understandably, wanted precise clinical terms for physicians. In other schools and in other fields there is little sign of such concerns.[42]

For most purposes, then, it was enough to agree, some words are smarter, more fashionable than others (better Greek, better Latin), and some if only by convention more suitable than others as vehicles for one's intended meaning. But words by and large are thought to work by containing meanings that the words simply clothe, and that have to be grasped with the help of the words but are themselves prior to and other than the words. And then, of course, any given set of words may 'contain' a number of meanings, including varied meanings, quite different meanings; and the obverse also holds: any given specific meaning or set of meanings can remain 'the same' when clothed in fresh words, even quite different words. This creates a very varied and pliable intertexture for common discourse, even if it does not suit tidy modern minds.

Important corollaries, already indicated, would seem to follow. Any given author may intend to say 'the same thing' two, three or more times in different ways, even quite different ways in the same sequence; but we cannot be certain. There may, on the other hand, be new thoughts. Perhaps the shorter and simpler the (apparent) 'expansion'

41. Pinborg, 'Classical Antiquity', p. 79, slightly amended; he refers to Sextus Empiricus, *Adversus Mathematicos* 7.11-12 (but cf. also Diogenes Laertius, *Lives of Eminent Philosophers*, 7.44-63), and in the final lines is quoting A.A. Long, 'Language and Thought in Stoicism', in A.A. Long (ed.), *Problems in Stoicism* (London: Athlone Press, 1971), pp. 83-84; cf. *idem*, *Hellenistic Philosophy*, pp. 118-41.

42. C. Atherton, *The Stoics on Ambiguity* (Cambridge: Cambridge University Press, 1993); R.J. Hankinson, 'Usage and Abusage: Galen on Language', in Evason (ed.), *Language*, pp. 166-87.

the more likely is it to betoken reaffirmation rather than a fresh idea; but there is no knowing for sure. And if we cannot be sure that it is 'a different thought', *even less can we tell that it indicates a different author*, a redactor.

Of course, a given word, phrase or sentence in a sequence could also stem from a different author, even if for us it seemed to be clarifying or reinforcing precisely the same message in characteristic style as the rest of the text, because menus for amplification were widely shared. But the upshot is that without textual evidence in support we should not pretend to be able to discriminate objectively where ancient ways of using words and ancient reflections on the ways words work render our discriminations so unsure. (In practice, of course, our inability to persuade one another might lead to the same effective conclusion: witness the recent careful collations of discrepant conclusions on the detailed extent of Q.)[43]

Twentieth-Century Postscript

> When they, my elders, named some object, and accordingly moved towards something, I saw this and grasped that the thing was called by the sound they uttered when they meant to point it out… Thus, as I heard words repeatedly used in their proper places in various sentences, I gradually learned to understand what objects they signified; and after training my mouth to form these signs, I used them to express my own desires.[44]

So Ludwig Wittgenstein begins his *Philosophical Investigations*, with Augustine's version of the common classical view of how words work and their use is acquired. Wittgenstein continues,

---

43. E.g., J.S. Kloppenborg, *Q Parallels: Synopsis, Critical Notes & Concordance* (Sonoma, CA: Polebridge Press, 1988); and the painstaking series edited by S. Carruth and A. Garsky, *Documenta Q* (Leuven: Peeters, 1996-). (For some similar discussion of ancient uses of words, cf. A.F. Person, 'The Ancient Israelite Scribe as Performer', *JBL* 117.4 [1998], pp. 601-609.)

44. Augustine, *Confessions* 1.8, quoted in L. Wittgenstein, *Philosophical Investigations*, 2e: 'Cum ipsi (maiores homines) appellabant rem aliquam, et cum secundum eam vocem corpus aliquid movebant, videbam, et tenebam hoc ab eis vocari rem illam, quod sonabant, cum eam vellent ostendere… Ita verba in variis sententiis locis suis posita, et crebro audita, quarum rerum signa essent, paulatim colligebam, measque iam voluntates, edomito in eis signis ore, per haec enuntiabam.'

Augustine does not speak of there being any difference between kinds of words. If you describe the learning of language in this way, you are, I believe, thinking primarily of nouns like 'table', 'chair', 'bread' and of people's names, and only secondarily of the names of certain actions and properties; and of the remaining kinds of words as something that will take care of itself.

Wittgenstein then argues at length that this is a misleading account of language as we use it,

> for giving orders and obeying them—describing the appearance of an object, or giving its measurements—constructing an object from a description (a drawing)—reporting an event—speculating about an event—forming and testing an hypothesis—presenting the results of an experiment in tables and diagrams—making up a story; and reading it— play-acting—singing catches—guessing riddles—making a joke; telling it—solving a problem in practical arithmetic—translating from one language into another—asking, thanking, cursing, greeting, praying.—It is interesting to compare the multiplicity of the tools in language and of the ways they are used, the multiplicity of kinds of words and sentence, with what logicians have said about the structure of language. (Including the author of the *Tractatus Logico-Philosophicus*.)[45]

The author referred to is Wittgenstein himself, of course, who in that earlier work had elaborated what was in effect a sophisticated form of the Stoic 'picturing' view of language noted above. Here he tries to persuade us out of seeing words as 'names for objects' (27e). Not everyone is persuaded by Wittgenstein, admittedly. But if we are, there is still less reason for supposing we can make fine discriminations of 'meaning' and then of authorship in the works of people who used words in fact as freely as we know we do, but were even less worried

---

45. L. Wittgenstein, *Philosophical Investigations* 11e–12e. On the foregoing, again, see Downing, 'Meanings'; O. Hanfling, *Wittgenstein's Later Philosophy* (Basingstoke: Macmillan, 1989); F. Kerr, *Theology after Wittgenstein* (London: SPCK, 2nd edn, 1997). M.F. Burnyeat, 'Wittgenstein and Augustine *De Magistro*', *AristSocSup* 61 (1987), pp. 1-24, defends Augustine's account of how we learn; but Wittgenstein's concern is with words as names rather than with our acquisition of language; cf. C. Kirwan, 'Augustine on the Nature of Speech', in Evason (ed.), *Language*, pp. 188-211: 'Augustine was tempted to assume that whatever corresponds to a sentence, in the mind or in the world, must be formed of parts—be they "inner words" or ideas—which correspond to the parts—words—forming the sentence. This beguiling error is the picture theory of language…it was to impede the philosophy of language for many centuries after Augustine' (p. 211). See also B. Stock, *Augustine the Reader* (Cambridge, MA: Belknap, 1966), pp. 246-47.

than we are that their intended 'meaning' might suffer from paraphrase and amplification, or their words not be flexible enough for all the meanings that should be discerned.

Ancient authors did not have to 'get it right' on their own under threat of the finality of print. They expected far more 'feedback' during the composition of their works than we today usually accept. They would have lots of reassurance that their ideas were in fact being adequately conveyed before they 'authorized' and circulated copies of their shared efforts. It is to ancient ways of shared composition that we now move.

Chapter 4

WORD-PROCESSING IN THE ANCIENT WORLD:
THE SOCIAL PRODUCTION AND PERFORMANCE OF Q*

Discussions of the synoptic Gospels, their sources, interrelationships and composition, still tend to ignore the pragmatics of compositional methods prevalent in the first-century Mediterranean world. Even when questions of contemporary narrative genres are addressed, the implicit model of 'the author' seems to be drawn from the experience of the present-day scholar alone in his or her book-lined study.[1] A previous generation imagined 'scissors and paste'; our own knows even easier methods of 'word-processing'. It is worth reflecting on such evidence as we have for the specific, *oral*, ways in which words actually do seem to have been 'processed' in the first century.

The implications of the evidence assembled will then be illustrated with reference to some recent studies of 'Q'. We are asked by a number of scholars to imagine an author or authors for Q, embedded in a pleb-eian community, at work from time to time revising, even drastically revising, that community's practical handbook(s) for it, in ways that leave discordances clear enough for us to discern. We have to ask how realistic this is, in the light of the evidence we have; or, alternatively, are the contents of Q really so discrepant as to entail quite unconventional authorial procedures, otherwise unevidenced?

Oral Social Performance

The culture of the ancient Mediterranean world was primarily oral. There was writing, and there were visual and plastic arts. But the spoken

*   Reprinted from *JSNT* 64 (1996), pp. 29-48, with kind permission.
1.   In his account of Mark at work, Burton Mack pictures 'a desk in a scholar's study lined with texts...', Mack, *A Myth of Innocence*, pp. 322-23. It is a long tradition: John O'Neill notes Schleiermacher raising a similar objection against his

and heard word was paramount. The conclusion is commonplace,[2] but its implications for literary composition are perhaps not yet fully understood. Even among the highly educated, both in theory and in practice, writing was secondary. For the theory, Loveday Alexander has recently reminded us of the very widespread preference for 'the living voice', adducing evidence from Plato through to Galen and beyond, as well as among early Christians.[3] For the practice one may note the judgment of Kenneth Quinn, 'the written text played very much the role which the printed score of a musical composition plays today...you acquired a copy with the intention of having it performed for you...'[4]

That set speeches of all kinds were prepared for oral performance is obvious, and Quintilian, for instance, shows how elaborate their enactment was meant to be. But however carefully the script had been written, the rhetor was expected to pretend to be speaking spontaneously, responding to his audience. The listeners had to be in mind when the

contemporaries; J.C. O'Neill, 'The Lost Written Records', *JTS* NS 42 (1991), pp. 483-504 (501).

2.   See Downing, '*A bas les aristos*', ch. 1 above, and especially references there both to primary and to secondary sources.

3.   L. Alexander, 'The Living Voice: Scepticism towards the Written Word in Early Christian and in Graeco-Roman Texts', in D.J.A. Clines, S.E. Fowl and S.E. Porter (eds.), *The Bible in Three Dimensions* (Sheffield: JSOT Press, 1990), pp. 221-47; cf. P.J. Achtemeier, '*Omne verbum sonat*: The New Testament and the Oral Environment of Late Western Antiquity', *JBL* 109.1 (1990), pp. 3-27; P.J.J. Botha, 'Greco-Roman Literacy as Setting for New Testament Writings', *Neot* 26.1 (1992), pp. 195-215; *idem*, 'The Verbal Art of the Pauline Letters', in S.E. Porter and T.H. Olbricht (eds.), *Rhetoric and the New Testament* (JSNTSup, 90; Sheffield: JSOT Press, 1993), pp. 409-59; J. Dewey (ed.), *Orality and Textuality* (Semeia, 65; Atlanta: Scholars Press, 1995).

4.   Quinn, 'The Poet and his Audience', p. 90, and insisting that 'score' (for performance) affords a better analogy than 'play-script' (though that term will also be used in what follows). Quinn (pp. 75-150) is writing about poetry in particular, but his model is more widely apposite, as the passages to be quoted should show; and see also G. Anderson, 'Sophists and their Outlook in the Early Empire', *ANRW* II.33.1 (1989), pp. 79-208. P.J.J. Botha appositely cites Pliny the Younger's dependence on a reader to demonstrate how his words will sound as he composes ('The Verbal Art', p. 414, citing Pliny the Younger, *Letters* 8.1). Although silent reading may not have been quite as rare in the ancient world as is sometimes supposed, F.D. Gilliard, making this point, accepts that the predominance of orality in the ancient world is beyond question—see his 'More Silent Reading in Antiquity: *non omne verbum sonabat*', *JBL* 112.4 (1993), pp. 689-96.

ideas were being worked up, but had also to be played to and improvised for (even if the orator also had a prompter).[5] Quintilian tells us something of what this meant when pleading in the courts:

> we must often express our views before an ignorant audience (*apud imperitos*), and quite ordinary people in particular (*populumque praecipue*), of whom most are uneducated (*indocti*)... Not every judge is learned (*eruditus*)—you may find a simple soldier or a countryman.

As we saw in Chapter 1, you have to understand and respond to your total audience if you are to win its sympathy, and a case can be swayed by the applause drawn from the crowd.[6] Pliny, a pupil of Quintilian's, claimed a similar concern to move a mixed audience, popular and patrician, for as much as seven hours—without having to pay for his applause.[7]

In other contexts the public speaker could be still more in the hands of his hearers:

> Dio attributes the Alexandrians with cries of 'When will he finish?', 'Bring on the juggler!' and 'Nonsense!' And he complains of hubbub, laughter, anger, cat-calls and jokes, by which the Alexandrians were able to terrify and prevail over laymen and princes alike.[8]

'When the would-be orator mounts the platform—like a slave in the market,' notes Philo, 'he becomes a bond-servant instead of a free man.'[9] And it was not only deliverers of more or less spontaneous speeches who performed in such circumstances. Dio imagines, in addition to 'crowds of wretched sophists around Poseidon's temple, and their disciples, as they are called, fighting with one another, [also] many writers reading aloud their stupid works, many poets reciting poems while others applauded them'. This is pictured at the Isthmian Games in the late fourth century, but it is very similar to what he recounts of Tarsus or Alexandria in the late first century.[10]

5. Anderson, 'Sophists', pp. 89-101; Ps.-Cicero, *Ad Herennium* 1.6.10; for 'prompter', Quinn, 'The Poet and his Audience', p. 85.

6. Quintilian, *Institutes* 3.8.2, 7, 11; 5.7.31; 8.3.3; 11.1.45, 3.131; 12.5.6, 9.4; (LCL); cf. Chapter 1 , '*A bas les aristos*' for these references.

7. Pliny the Younger, *Letters* 4.16, 19; cf. 2.14; cf. Philo, *Abr.* 20; Dio, *Discourse* 31.68, passages we also considered in Chapter 1.

8. Anderson, 'Sophists', p. 96, citing Dio, *Discourse* 32.7, 22.

9. Philo, *Jos.* 35 (LCL); cf. 67; and Seneca, *Epistulae Morales* 29.10-12; and 52; Diogenes Laertius, *Lives of Eminent Philosophers* 6.41.

10. Dio, *Discourse* 8.9 (LCL) but cf. also Dio, *Discourses* 11.6, 27.5-6, 32.9-

More select gatherings may have been less rowdy: a paying audience in a lecture hall, pupils in school being taught by a professional rhetorician or listening to one another's efforts.[11] Or it might be friends gathered for a relaxed symposium, though Dio suggests that the satirists' accounts of such occasions may have some truth in them: 'Some attend for the sake of drinking...the naturally loquacious, feeling they've got their table companions for an audience, recite stupid and tedious speeches, while others are singing in tune and out of it...'[12] Pliny would have expected more decorous behaviour, when he chides a guest for letting him down: 'You would have heard a comic play, a reader, or a singer—or all three if I had felt generous...a feast of fun, laughter and learning.'[13] But it is clear that most if not all of what is written is a script for oral performance—and the audience is part of the performance.[14]

This all means (as the complaints show) that the audience had considerable control over the contents of what was being performed.[15] Even when you were attempting to move your audience in some fresh direction, most of what you said had to be familiar, commonplace, echoing the present ideas and opinions of those listening.[16] And that this betokens more than a simple awareness of the need to use understandable language is shown by the frequent warnings of the ease of a descent into flattery, of being the captive of your audience.[17] The audience's anticipated and expressed expectations would seem to have

12, 33.1-7, 42.4-5, 57.10-12, for the audience's impact.

11. Marrou, *A History of Education in Antiquity*, pp. 160-75, 194-205; Bonner, *Education in Ancient Rome*; D.L. Clark, *Rhetoric in Greco-Roman Education* (New York: Columbia University Press, 1957).

12. Dio, *Discourse* 27.2-3.

13. Pliny the Younger, *Letters* 1.15 as quoted above, Chapter 1; cf. *Letter* 9.17.3.

14. Quinn, 'The Poet and his Audience', argues that specifically in Latin poetry there was a move towards producing texts that would be read by others in private; yet even so, thinks 'it is clear that the Romans even as late as the first century AD still felt that performance was the real thing' (p. 90); cf. Seneca, *Epistulae Morales* 64.2; and Plutarch, *De Recta Ratione Audiendi, Moralia* 37B–48D.

15. Cf. Quintilian, *Institutes* 3.8.35-48.

16. Cf. Aristotle, *Rhetoric* 1.5.1-6 and all of 2, on the importance of what is genuinely 'commonplace'; so too, Cicero, *De Oratore* 14.47; Ps.-Cicero, *Ad Herennium* 2.9-13; 4.3-4.

17. Cf. Philo, *Migr.* 111, and the references in n. 9 above.

a powerful effect in social composition, and the effect would for the most part have been 'conservative' in the sense of largely conserving their preconceptions and prejudices.

Oral Social Composition

Further, it is not simply the case that the future performance and audience are 'in mind' in the process of initial production. A select part of the intended audience, an early smaller audience, may very well have been part of the production from the very start. Discussing Josephus's writing, Tessa Rajak noted some while ago that the help he acknowledges from others matches closely the procedures Cicero earlier alluded to when corresponding with Atticus and L. Cossinius, and 'the final product would have evolved out of many journeys by many messengers and much mutual assistance'. Rajak then adds,

> Or, again, we think of the younger Pliny telling us it was customary for authors to give readings from their productions before invited audiences in order to gather useful criticisms and be able to insert corrections before the final version was issued.

Pliny was unusual only in adopting this procedure with speeches, too (where others would have expected the final 'published' version to have emerged only from the open public—and itself 'creative'—performance).[18] It is just so that the pseudo-Socratic Letter 22 imagines Xenophon writing,

> I do not yet have anything of the sort that I would have the confidence to show to others without being there myself, as when I readily chatted with you (Simmias and Cebes) in the house where Eucleides was lying ill. And you must know, friends, that it is impossible to take back a writing once it has reached the hands of the public.[19]

We must of course, take into account the possibility that in some instances at least, a secretary may also have been encouraged or

---

18. T. Rajak, *Josephus* (London: Gerald Duckworth, 1983), p. 63, citing Cicero, *Atticus* 2.1.1-2 and also Pliny the Younger, *Letters* 7.17.

19. In S.K. Stowers (trans.), 'The Epistles of Socrates and the Socratics', in A.J. Malherbe (ed.), *The Cynic Epistles* (SBLSBS, 12; Missoula, MT: Scholars Press, 1977), p. 273. Malherbe dates the letter early in the second century (p. 28). Quintilian, *Institutes*, *Dedication* and *Preface*, indicates other social factors in the publication of lectures as such—the urging of impressed friends and the mistaken initiative of devoted students.

enjoined to share in a given composition, and note specifically the oral and critical role of Pliny's reader Encolpius.[20]

It seems, then, that oral performance will in many if not all instances have been part of the production of any piece—its production, not just its goal. And a smaller or larger audience will always (or most often) have been part of the still exploratory and creative performance. Word-processing in the ancient world was a social activity. There is, for sure, still an 'author', a main focus for the production, a band-leader as it were. It is not a spontaneous group activity over a shorter or longer period.[21] But it is certainly 'a complex communal event'.[22]

By contrast, it would seem that most historians of Christian origins and early Christian writings operate with a nineteenth-century image of the author as individual working in romantic isolation until presenting a finished work for the public to take or reject as issued. If an audience enters the picture ('the Markan, Q, Johannine community'), it seems to be an audience as imagined by the author, the audience as passively mirrored in the work, rather than in any way as active collaborator in its production—and performance.[23] A useful recent survey bears out this generalization. Barry W. Henaut's *Oral Tradition and the Gospels* discusses various attempts to discern oral tradition on the basis of forms that might be clearly distinguished from the written material in which it might be supposed to have been embedded.[24] Henaut argues effectively (against the form critics, and against Riesenfeld, Gerhardsson and Kel-

20. Pliny the Younger, *Letters* 8.1 (as noted by Botha, 'The Verbal Art', p. 414); and see, for instance, the discussion in Betz, *Galatians*, pp. 312-13. J.L. White notes that the messenger sent with a letter might well be expected both to read and amplify it, then leave it as a record, *Light from Ancient Letters*, pp. 216-17; M.L. Stirewalt, *Studies in Ancient Greek Epistolography* (Atlanta: Scholars Press, 1993), p. 5; cf. Jer. 36.

21. As suggested very vividly by K.E. Bailey, 'Middle Eastern Oral Tradition and the Gospels', *ExpTim* 106.12 (1995), pp. 363-67, but rightly rejected by C. Bryan, *A Preface to Mark: Notes on the Gospel in its Literary and Cultural Settings* (New York: Oxford University Press, 1993), pp. 153-54.

22. Botha, 'The Verbal Art', p. 417.

23. I was feeling towards the view advanced here in my 'Ears to Hear', in relation to content, but not the pragmatics of composition as such ('Ears to Hear', pp. 97-99).

24. B.W. Henaut, *Oral Tradition and the Gospels: The Problem of Mark 4* (JSNTSup, 82; JSOT Press, 1993), cf. Achtemeier, '*Omne verbum sonat*', p. 15 n. 87, against Kelber.

ber in particular)[25] that this cannot be done, for the supposed oral forms can clearly be seen to have remained available to such *writers* as Mark, Luke and Matthew. But Henaut himself is still not free from the over-clear division between 'oral' and 'written'. He concludes,

> The problems encountered—working back from the textual medium to the oral phase itself—may be summarised as follows. First there is the problem of writing itself, which may be termed the existential moment. Words must be chosen and the author becomes bound to one particular expression for the ideas to be conveyed to the audience. Innovation is highly prized, and hence it need not surprise us that over 40 versions of the Golden Rule can easily be found... Only in textuality can thoughts be distilled from their particular expression and recast in an endless variety of possibilities.[26]

This just does not seem to be true for the ancient Mediterranean world. Oral performance without a script or with one is much freer. For sure, once a particular script has been copied onto papyrus, it is difficult to alter that copy.[27] But prior to that inscribing matter written on tablets or on parchment can be changed, and any script can still be performed afresh, with that performance providing the basis for the next use of the text, or for the next transcription, or both. That must surely be so when the author is the performer; but it must needs also be so even with any other reader (slave included) expert enough to be entrusted with a performance for others.[28] As Kenneth Quinn concludes,

> Books were for professionals—for the professional writer to record the work he had written, or to interpret his work by reading it to others; for the professional reader to interpret the work privately to his master or employer, or for a larger audience. The ancient book was for those who had acquired fluency in reading at sight from a text which was not easy to read from, and some proficiency in the harder skill of interpreting the text which was read, so that it made sense and came alive.[29]

25. The form critic chosen is R. Bultmann, *History of the Synoptic Tradition* (ET; New York: Harper & Row, 1963); H. Riesenfeld, *The Gospel Tradition* (ET; Philadelphia: Fortress Press, 1970); B. Gerhardsson, *Memory and Manuscript* (ET; Lund: C.W.K. Gleerup, 1961); W.H. Kelber, *The Oral and the Written Gospel* (Philadelphia: Fortress Press, 1983).

26. Henaut, *Oral Tradition*, pp. 295-96.

27. Cf. Ps.-Socratic Letter 22, quoted above.

28. Cf. Dio, *Discourse* 42.4-5.

29. Quinn, 'The Poet and his Audience', p. 82; he has earlier (p. 81) cited on

It is, of course, important not to misconstrue the word 'interpret' in this context. Interpretative performance is above all a matter of stress and pitch and timing. But it is also a matter of discerning words and phrasing; and in attempting this, what is expected, and what sounds best according to accepted rules are likely to have their effect for any reader responding to his or her audience—but especially for the author so engaged, as Quinn illustrates, citing for instance Suetonius's story of Virgil completing some lines of *Aeneid* 6 'in the heat of performance'.[30]

As Quinn notes, even from among aristocratic circles there is no fully detailed description of this creative performance, only the hints that show this is what was taken for granted as common practice. It must be stressed, however, that there is no direct evidence whatsoever for any other procedure, anything more akin to what our contemporaries seem unreflectively to presuppose, the romantic solitary doing her or his own thing.

The illustrations so far have been from the highly educated and highly articulate, save only the pseudo-Socratic letter cited. But there is nothing to suggest that 'middle-' and 'low-brow' composition followed any different procedures; indeed, social oral composition leading into social oral performance and would seem likely to have been still more the norm. Writing materials were scarce and costly. We would expect notes at an early stage to be on readily reusable surfaces—waxed tablets, or at most, parchment which could be sponged.[31] A text would in all likelihood only very slowly reach a form in which the 'trial' audience might start to urge the author to release it for others to perform; and even then he might well revise it in the light of his own subsequent readings and his hearers' responses.[32]

As I have argued above, citing others in support, ideas and practices in the oral culture of the ancient world had a great many avenues by which they could disperse 'downwards' and outwards from the educated aristocracy—through public performance itself in courts and

---

this point Marrou, *A History of Education in Antiquity*, the relevant passages are pp. 379 and 434.

30. Quinn, 'The Poet and his Audience', p. 85, citing Suetonius, *Vita Vergilii* 132-39 R; cf. all of Quinn, 'The Poet and his Audience', pp. 83-88; Achtemeier, *'Omne verbum sonat'*, pp. 17-18.

31. Quinn, 'The Poet and his Audience', pp. 169-70; cf. E.G. Turner, *Greek Manuscripts of the Ancient World* (Oxford: Clarendon Press, 1971).

32. Cf. Quintilian, *Institutes* 1.Pr.1-8.

theatres, and through educated slaves and freedmen and women.[33] Quite clearly, too, the only formal education in the use of language had this as its ultimate goal (even if not many were likely to reach the heights attained by a stonemason's son such as Lucian of Samosata). As we saw in Chapter 3, children were taught to declaim from texts by teachers who declaimed; children were taught to produce texts for declamation, and were taught how to produce variations, and choose what their peers and their elders applauded.[34] Nor is there any indication that Jewish practice, for instance, differed at all markedly.[35] Word-processing in the ancient Mediterranean world will have been consistently oral *and collaborative*.

The Oral Performance and Social Composition of Q and other Early Christian Writings

There is no indication that early Christians escaped this pervasive approach to communication, rather is there clear evidence that here as elsewhere they shared fully in the culture of their time and place. Our main example is Q; but first we consider briefly Paul and Mark as they appear in some recent scholarship.

The Corinthian Christians allow that Paul's letters 'performed' well (2 Cor. 10.10), when given to one of their competent readers; but Paul himself was very unimpressive and unpersuasive as a speaker. Paul of course insists frequently that this is his own deliberate choice (1 Cor. 1.17–2.5, etc.) Whatever we may make of this demurrer (cf. 2 Cor. 11.6), there is every indication in his writing as it comes down to us that he was well aware of how words should be put together to influence a contemporary audience. There is, for instance, the wealth of material collected by Margaret M. Mitchell to illuminate Paul's rhetoric in 1 Corinthians, as well as plentiful illustrative matter gathered by

---

33. Downing, '*A bas les aristos*', ch. 1 above.

34. Marrou, *A History of Education in Antiquity*, pp. 154 and 165-66; Quinn, 'The Poet and his Audience', pp. 167-69, citing Horace, *Epistles* 1.18.12-14 and Quintilian, *Institutes* 2.5.4; cf. M.L. Clarke, *Higher Education in the Ancient World*, ch. 6, 'The Elementary Exercises'; and see Chapter 3, above, pp. 61-63.

35. Cf. L. Alexander, 'The Living Voice', pp. 222-23: 'the rabbinic schools form part of a cultural continuum covering the whole of the eastern Mediterranean'. Cf. M. Goodman, *State and Society in Roman Galilee AD 132–212* (Totowa, NJ: Rowman & Allanhead, 1983), p. 80, 'not dissimilar in method'.

others with similar interests.[36] The importance of rhetoric in Paul's world has been forcefully argued recently by Duane Litfin, even if one is not convinced that 'the complaints against Paul had to do essentially with the form of his preaching, not its content'.[37] Paul's refusal to deploy the arts of persuasion (1 Thess. 2.4; Gal. 1.10) is itself a *topos* from the world of rhetoric, evincing a common awareness of the dangers involved in being too adaptable to one's audience.[38] Ronald F. Hock has made a cogent case for seeing Paul's public communication in the setting of shop-front conversations (rather than the set-piece speech to a larger audience suggested in Acts).[39] This context would have allowed a still greater interaction with his partners in conversation, and it is this that will have allowed Paul to dispense with superficial 'pleasing' and drive for a verifiable understanding and conviction. Paul's other context is that of the gathered congregation where he composes in company with such as Aquila and Prisca and their house church (1 Cor. 16.19-20; Rom. 16.21-23; cf. 2 Cor. 1.1, etc.) or, at the very least, in company with the intended messenger who will most likely also be the interpretative performer.[40] It is only in these social settings that Paul the erstwhile Pharisee could have set about processing his words so that he could be satisfied that they said much at least of what he wanted to say and also might well convince Gentile Greek converts in letters that would read well when well read.[41] That he succeeded at all must show

36. Mitchell, *Paul and the Rhetoric of Reconciliation* and, e.g., Betz, *Galatians*; F.W. Hughes, *Early Christian Rhetoric and 2 Thessalonians* (Sheffield: JSOT Press, 1989); J.-N. Aletti, *Comment Dieu est-il juste? Clefs pour interpréter l'épître aux Romains* (Paris: Seuil, 1991).

37. D. Litfin, *St Paul's Theology of Proclamation* (SNTSMS, 79; Cambridge: Cambridge University Press, 1994), quoting from p. 199.

38. Cf. Betz, *Galatians*, p. 54; Dio, *Discourses* 4.10, 15, 124; 32.10-12.

39. Hock, *The Social Context of Paul's Ministry*.

40. Botha, 'The Verbal Art', pp. 415-19.

41. This is the necessary context for the 'considerable care' with which it has been 'shown Paul composed his letters and framed his arguments...to inform, instruct, explain, and persuade. One finds him defining and seeking to clarify issues, reasoning things out, anticipating objections, and developing counter-argument... lifting the truth claims of the gospel to the level of explicit understanding. Apart from this achievement...there could have been no effective missionary proclamation, least of all among the Gentiles', V.P. Furnish, 'On Putting Paul in his Place', *JBL* 113.1 (1994), pp. 3-17, 15-16, SBL Presidential Address 1993. Cf. also J.D.G. Dunn, 'Prolegomena to a Theology of Paul', *NTS* 40 (1994), pp. 407-32, emphasizing the 'character as dialogue' of Paul's letters (p. 414). Careful communicative

that he made good use of the conventions of social composition.

Mary Ann Beavis's study, *Mark's Audience: The Literary and Social Setting of Mark 4.11-12* clearly and cogently sets Mark in the context of oral performance: 'The Gospel was not written for private study, but *in order to be read aloud* (or recited from memory) to an audience, probably by the evangelist himself, with all the rhetorical flourishes at his command.'[42] Nonetheless, Beavis makes no reference to the social pragmatics of composition as such.

Those who write about Q these days seem for the most part at least convinced that it was written for a 'community' of 'Q Christians', by an author or authors acting as more than compiler(s). But how this composition may be thought to have operated within or for this community is (in the works here cited) never explained in any detail. Richard A. Edwards decided that 'the search is for a community which preserved Q and not the individual responsible for its final form...this community would be a group of like-minded individuals who used Q in their activities'. The method remains unspecified, although it seems to be 'literary'.[43] Dieter Lührmann had earlier distinguished '"collecting" of materials by catchword and common topic' from redaction as 'deliberate composition with a particular theological point of view', but still without indicating how this might have been done.[44] Dieter Zeller accepted the distinction, assigning early collection and redaction to itin-

---

aim is discerned by both writers, but not the social composition that would have been the normal procedure, the process by which the aim would be achieved.

42. M.A. Beavis, *Mark's Audience: The Literary and Social Setting of Mark 4.11-12* (JSNTSup, 33; Sheffield: JSOT Press, 1989), pp. 30-31, original emphasis; cf., again, my own 'Ears to Hear', pp. 97-99; but also, now, Bryan, *A Preface to Mark*; cf. L. Hurtado, 'Greco-Roman Textuality and the Gospel of Mark: A Critical Assessment of Werner Kelber's *The Oral and the Written Gospel*', *BibRes* 7 (1997), pp. 91-106.

43. R.A. Edwards, *A Theology of Q* (Philadelphia: Fortress Press, 1976), pp. 21, 73. In fact H.E. Tödt, *The Son of Man in the Synoptic Tradition* (ET; London: SCM Press, 1965), pp. 246-69, talks simply of 'the community which collected'. For resistance to talk of a 'Q community', while accepting Q as such, M. Hengel, 'Aufgaben der neutestamentlichen Wissenschaft', *NTS* 40.3 (1994), pp. 311-57, 336.

44. D. Lührmann, 'Q in the History of Early Christianity', in J.S. Kloppenborg (ed.), *The Shape of Q* (Minneapolis: Fortress Press, 1994), pp. 59-73 (59) (first pub. as 'Q in der Geschichte des Urchristentums', in D. Lührmann, *Die Redaktion der Logienquelle* [WMANT, 33; Neukirchen–Vluyn: Neukirchener Verlag, 1969], pp. 88-104).

erant preachers in the communities they founded, with the final work done by 'early Christian teachers', with again no suggestion as to the practicalities.[45]

A slightly clearer indication of what he envisaged has been offered by John S. Kloppenborg: 'the *actual* audience of these Q speeches is the community itself, i.e., those already sympathetic to the preaching of the kingdom...' and the speeches will have been delivered by 'Q preachers'—and such speeches and units will have been 'interpolated' into a prior collection of 'wisdom speeches' that by now are '*already in written form*', and this major redaction is now 'literary'—'otherwise one would expect a greater degree of homogeneity and fewer abrupt transitions'.[46] However, a clear distinction between oral and literary composition is here again assumed without further argument, although the assumption is clearly important in the case being made (as Kloppenborg has earlier announced, in methodological agreement with Arland D. Jacobson and Dieter Lührmann). Whereas the presence of 'grammatical shifts, breaks in the train of thought, shifts in audience, shifts in tradition or theology', generally speaking 'aporiae',[47] might seem to most of us entirely to be expected (see the previous chapter), and signs that we most likely had a transcription of more-or-less

45. D. Zeller, 'Redactional Process and Changing Settings', in Kloppenborg (ed.), *The Shape of Q*, pp. 128-29 (first pub. as 'Redaktionsprozesse und wechselnder "Sitz im Leben" beim Q-Material', in J. Delobel [ed.], *Les paroles de Jésus* [BETL, 59; Leuven: Peeters, 1982], pp. 395-409). It will be obvious to any informed reader that I have not gone back through all of even the main discussions of Q over the past three decades, but only checked with others' surveys and the works here cited that my memory is not misserving me; a further such survey is F. Neirynck, 'The Sayings of Jesus', in F. van Segbroeck (ed.), *Evangelica II: 1982–1991 Collected Essays by Franz Neirynck* (BETL, 99; Leuven: Peeters, 1991), pp. 409-568.

46. Kloppenborg, *Formation of Q*, pp. 167, 244; cf. *idem*, 'Jesus and the Parables of Jesus', in R.A. Piper (ed.), *The Gospel behind the Gospels: Current Studies on Q* (NovTSup, 75; Leiden: E.J. Brill, 1995), pp. 275-319 (275) and *passim*; and also B.H. McLean, 'On the Gospel of Thomas and Q', in Piper, *The Gospel*, pp. 321-45 (324): 'fundamentally two different ways, orally and scribally'. None of the contributors to Piper's volume discuss our evidences for contemporary compositional procedures, apparently assuming that their implicit model is unproblematic.

47. Kloppenborg, *Formation of Q*, pp. 97-98, quoting A.D. Jacobson, 'Wisdom Christology in Q' (PhD dissertation, Claremont, 1978), p. 9; see now A.J. Jacobson, *The First Gospel* (Sonoma, CA: Polebridge Press, 1992), p. 252.

spontaneous speech, it is taken by Kloppenborg as a conclusive sign of purely literary editing. And the practical relationship between the agent of such major and perhaps final redaction, and any audience, is still left unstated. More recently Kloppenborg (in association with Leif E. Vaage) has again insisted that

> The reality that Q was a written text…is the first datum to be reckoned with… At the very least, the reading of any text ought now to begin with a serious consideration of its character as text before imagining the seemingly infinite variety of pre-textual (oral) performances to which the text may bear witness.[48]

The dichotomy between 'oral' and 'textual' remains central—and remains unsubstantiated. Even Heinz O. Guenther, arguing vigorously that 'the Christian content [of Q] is embedded in typically Hellenistic conventions' pays no attention to such conventions of social composition as are evidenced for us.[49]

There are tantalizing hints from Burton L. Mack that he might have picked out a detailed and realistic contemporary model of composition—speakers responding to a chance public audience, house groups in conversation—but we still only have vague references to 'the authors of Q', 'the people of Q', 'mythmaking in the Jesus movement' and suchlike.[50] Migaku Sato usefully suggests that notebooks formed from parchment sheets tied loosely together might have been used,[51] but makes no attempt to picture the social setting for their employment.

It is hard from all the hints in the authors mentioned to piece together any clear, let alone evidenced, picture of the procedure that is being implicitly presupposed. The discussion is conducted primarily in terms of content consistency and style as these appear to well-educated, twentieth-century Western scholars. The process of composition seems

---

48. J.S. Kloppenborg and L.E. Vaage, 'Early Christianity, Q and Jesus: The Sayings Gospel and Method in the Study of Christian Origins', *Semeia* 55 (1992), pp. 1-14 (9).

49. H.O. Guenther, 'The Sayings Gospel Q and the Quest for Aramaic Sources: Rethinking Christian Origins', *Semeia* 55 (1992), pp. 41-76 (73).

50. B.L. Mack, *The Lost Gospel: The Book of Q and Christian Origins* (Rockport, MA, and Shaftesbury, Dorset: Element, 1993), pp. 130, 146-47, 149.

51. M. Sato, *Q und Prophetie: Studien zur Gattungs- und Traditionsgeschichtliche der Quelle Q* (WUNT, 2.29; Tübingen: J.C.B. Mohr, 1988), pp. 62-65, 390-93; cf. Marrou, *A History of Education in Ancient Rome*, pp. 154-55; Bonner, *Education in Antiquity*, pp. 126-30.

then to be tacitly constructed on the basis of the way some of us would conjecture *we* might have produced some such results: and the impression that comes to mind is sometimes of an individual, sometimes a series of individuals drafting and amending a report that is then to be published for (and perhaps delivered to) some late-twentieth-century Western voluntary association. It is supposed to 'mirror' the concerns of that association,[52] but does so at any given point only through the mind or minds of the editor(s). It is, we must conclude, a picture drawn from modern authorial practice, quite without reference to the way words seem to have been processed in the first century, involving the frequent social interaction indicated in the sources quoted above.

It could be, of course, that Q was initially produced by and performed only among a very restricted circle of friends; but that seems somewhat unlikely. The authority Matthew and Luke appear to accord its contents, coinciding so much more extensively in their reproduction of it than in their use of Mark, certainly suggests otherwise. And an isolated and unrepresentative origin is certainly not the hypothesis of the scholars here cited, and others besides, who emphasize the importance of the 'Q community'.

The conclusion being argued is similar to but stronger than those of Christopher M. Tuckett and Harold W. Attridge responding to some of the essays already here referred to, and questioning some or much of the 'stratification', the discerning of supposedly distinct and discrepant 'layers' in Q.[53] We need not only to ask (with Tuckett), 'If too much of a disjunction between layers is postulated…why the earlier tradition was ever used at all by the later editor…within the same social group' (pp. 214-15), but also, how and why could our editor(s) ever have got away with it, in testing this drastically revised version out with a few friends, or in responding to the reactions of the majority when this strange new version was performed? There is room in the model of

---

52. Kloppenborg accepts from A.J. Malherbe the caution that 'it would be naive to suppose that every document associated with primitive Christianity in fact mirrored the viewpoints of that community'—but is sure this holds for Q; 'Literary Convention, Self-Evidence and the Social History of the Q People', *Semeia* 55 (1992), pp. 77-102 (78).

53. Tuckett, 'On the Stratification of Q', and H.W. Attridge, 'Reflection on Research into Q', *Semeia* 55 (1992), pp. 223-34, respectively; and cf. Tuckett's *Q and the History of Early Christianity*, pp. 69-74, and the whole of his ch. 2, 'Redaction Criticism'.

composition here proposed for all manner of subtle changes from one performance to another (room, not necessity), and so for minor inconsistencies to appear (or disappear).[54] There seems to be no room for large or drastic changes—ever. If the argument of the first part of this essay holds, then whatever was added to any current form of Q, *on its first appearance* the expanded version must have appeared largely consistent to the members of the community, if the basic matter had hitherto been (as the hypothesis supposes) the foundation charter and manual for life of that community.

Are the Contents so Discrepant as to Presuppose a Distinctive Compositional Procedure?

Those who argue for strata in Q are sure that the contents are so patently disparate that diverse sources, times and contexts must have been involved, leaving behind blocks of matter that we must today accept as distinct. Are recent arguments about 'strata', arguments conducted in terms of contents currently judged to be consistent or more or less inconsistent, sufficient to outweigh the indications here assembled of the likely 'conservative' effects of conventional social compositional procedures? Further, are they also enough to outweigh the arguments of the previous chapter against inventing discrepancies in ancient Graeco-Roman texts?

The sharpest contrast between 'layers' in Q is drawn by such as John D. Crossan[55] and Burton Mack, distinguishing 'wisdom' from 'apocalyptic': 'the contrast in mood is overwhelming'.[56] Yet not only do we find that (*ex hypothesi*) the Q community is by no means 'overwhelmed' by the combination of these strands as distinguished by just some moderns, there are other contemporary scholars who allow no such contrast: Paul D. Hanson, Michael Stone and Jonathan Z. Smith, for instance, have all insisted on the positive intermingling from much earlier times of what are here designated separate strands and even distinctive genres.[57] To (try to) understand divine reality in itself and in

54. See for instance Mack and Robbins, *Patterns*.

55. J.D. Crossan, *The Historical Jesus: The Life of a Mediterranean Jewish Peasant* (San Francisco: Harper, 1991), pp. 227-28.

56. Mack, *The Lost Gospel*, p. 131, and, e.g., pp. 29-39.

57. P.D. Hanson (ed.), *Visionaries and their Apocalypses* (London: SPCK, 1983), pp. 9-10; J.Z. Smith, 'Wisdom and Apocalyptic', in Hanson (ed.), *Vision-*

its effects both now and in the near and more distant future is a constituent function of the wise.

In the analyses of Lührmann, Kloppenborg and Jacobson the preferred distinction is stated more in terms of 'wisdom' over against a 'prophetic' or 'deuteronomic' 'threat of judgment'.[58] It is worth noting that Kloppenborg carefully explains, 'to say that the wisdom components are formative for Q and that the prophetic judgment oracles and apothegms...are secondary is *not* to imply anything about the ultimate tradition-historical provenance of any of the sayings' (p. 244). Nonetheless, the sapiential and prophetic/deuteronomic strands are supposedly distinctive enough to entail the hypothesis of separate stages in the composition of Q. And again it is difficult to imagine the first performance of the combined strands. Either the two sets of material have been performed as distinct units in the life of the community—in which case it is hard to tell why they should have been combined, what was being gained by interweaving them, 'spoiling' their thematic unity, or the prophetic/deuteronomic is new, a large import of fresh ideas. In that case the community is being asked to accept not just some new ideas, but a radical re-casting of the sapiential tradition of Jesus' teaching which has been the ideological core of its common life. And this is then to ignore the pressure on authors and/or performers to keep their communities with them in any given performance.

It is also the case that the 'interweaving' of the two strata imagined is far more detailed and painstaking than any for which we have evidence: compare the discussion of 'Compositional Conventions', Chapter 8 below. A strong cultural argument for Q having existed is the implausibility—in the light of contemporary practice—of whichever evangelist worked last having 'unwoven' and 're-woven' his predecessors. So a major argument for the Q hypothesis is at the same time a strong

---

aries, pp. 101-20 (repr. from B.A. Pearson [ed.], *Religious Syncretism in Antiquity* [Missoula, MT: Scholars Press, 1975]); and M.E. Stone, 'New Light on the Third Century', in Hanson (ed.), *Visionaries*, pp. 85-91; *idem*, 'Enoch and Apocalyptic Origins', in Hanson (ed.), *Visionaries*, pp. 92-100 (repr. from M.E. Stone, *Scriptures, Sects and Visions* [Philadelphia: Fortress Press, 1980]).

58. D. Lührmann, *Die Redaktion der Logienquelle* (WMANT, 33; Neukirchen–Vluyn: Neukirchener Verlag, 1969), based in part on O.H. Steck, *Israel und der gewaltsame Geschick der Propheten* (WMANT, 23; Neukirchen–Vluyn: Neukirchener Verlag, 1967); Kloppenborg, *Formation of Q*, esp. ch. 4, 'The Announcement of Judgment in Q', pp. 102-70; and Jacobson, *The First Gospel*, pp. 48-51 and *passim*.

argument against it having been produced by the interweaving of previously distinct 'strata'.

But just as the wisdom versus apocalyptic contrast is suspect, so too is any hard line between wisdom and prophecy (deuteronomic or other). The example of Paul's letter to the church in Rome affords a useful comparison from around the same period among Christian groups not totally isolated from one another. Clearly it is possible to find contrasts, contradictions, aporiae within this one text (and not only between this and other writings widely ascribed to the one writer, Paul, in modern scholarship). There is, for instance, as pointed out among others by Heikki Räisänen, at the very least an apparent contradiction between the suggestion that Gentiles may well do what the law requires (Rom. 2.14) and the insistence very shortly after that 'all have sinned' (Rom. 3.23).[59] There are also problems outlined by David Seeley with what Paul has to say about law and grace, so that 'Romans 1–2 reflects a different message from Romans 6–8'.[60] Not many, however, have followed John C. O'Neill (and C.H. Weisse and A. Loisy before him) in deciding that 'the words of the epistle handed down to us were not written by one man, were not written at one time, were not written to one audience',[61] not even Räisänen, who quotes O'Neill's assessment of the conflict with approval. Yet these apparent (and maybe very real) contradictions in Romans are surely greater than any supposed contrast in Q between wisdom and prophecy or apocalyptic; or, for example, between Lk. 16.17-18 (Q 56) on the law in general and divorce in particular on the one hand, and the apparently much less 'observant' material elsewhere in Q.[62]

We see in fact in Romans a mid-century Christian author-with-friends (Rom. 16.21-23) producing with them a script to be performed entire for an audience elsewhere (quite likely tried out in advance in Corinth [?] where it was written) that includes most if not all the variety—and disparate variety—of kinds of material that appear in our reconstructions of Q. We have apocalyptic eschatology (Rom. 1.18;

---

59. See, e.g., H. Räisänen, *Paul and the Law* (ET; Philadelphia: Fortress Press, 1986), pp. 97-109.

60. D. Seeley, *Deconstructing the New Testament* (Leiden: E.J. Brill, 1994), p. 154.

61. J.C. O'Neill, *Paul's Letter to the Romans* (Harmondsworth: Penguin Books, 1975), p. 11.

62. E.g., Mack, *The Lost Gospel*, p. 176, a 'truly surprising novelty'.

8.18-25, 37-39; 11.25-36; 13.11-14); interspersed with this we find a 'deuteronomic' account of Israel's past, in chs. 9–11, quoting Deuteronomy itself and cognate passages noting the people's constant refusal of God's messengers; and this latter leads straight into a sapiential sequence, chs. 12–13, ending, as just noted, in apocalyptic eschatology (just as ch. 1 combined both strands: 1.18-20). Paul could draw on all these strands and more,[63] to create a rich intertexture that was his own but that many could share.

If Paul with friends could write all this, most likely try it out in one community on one occasion, and then send it with some confidence to another, why should not Q with its rather more limited mix of materials (but some of similar kinds) have been put together over a shorter or longer period by one author-with-friends in one community, more or less as we reconstruct the 'final' version today? Or, rather, what is there in contemporary Jewish or Christian literature preserved for us and in our knowledge of the pragmatics of composition in the Mediterranean world of the first century that in any way demands or warrants a 'stratified' account of Q along the lines proposed by Kloppenborg, Jacobson, Mack and others?

Even if (with Mack and—rather differently—with the present writer) weight is given to possible Cynic analogies, there is still no basis for distinguishing 'sapiential' from 'judgmental' from 'apocalyptic' material: all these can be found in sources widely recognized as Cynic.[64]

Both Jacobson and Kloppenborg argue initially for the literary unity of Q.[65] It seems entirely reasonable to suppose that prior to its performance in some such coherent form as is currently reconstructed the community had been used to hearing recited individual sayings and maybe clusters, from the full range of matter that was then included (and, very likely, more of the same that was not brought in). The material was already in Greek (even if it had once been in Aramaic).[66] A collection

---

63. See Downing, *Cynics, Paul and the Pauline Churches.*

64. Mack, *The Lost Gospel*, pp. 105-130; Downing, *Cynics and Christian Origins*, pp. 115-68. Diogenes and Heraclitus and Socrates can all be presented as judges in a future celestial world, Ps.-Diogenes 30, Ps.-Heraclitus 5 and 9; *Socratic Letter* 25 (A.J. Malherbe [ed.], *The Cynic Epistles*, p. 279); cf. Epictetus, *Encheiridion* 15. Vituperative rebukes are pervasive.

65. Jacobson, 'The Literary Unity of Q', pp. 365-89; Kloppenborg in his *Formation of Q*, pp. 89-95.

66. Kloppenborg, *Formation of Q*, pp. 51-64.

of the sayings of a teacher was a commonplace form in the Hellenistic world, it formed his *bios*, Life.[67] It would have been almost inevitable that some in the community would consider at some stage performing a fairly comprehensive presentation of the teaching of the school.[68] An individual in a small community, or a group of friends with perhaps a leader would draft the piece on tablets. In the latter case particularly the scribe can readily respond to suggestions: 'I think we could have a bit more about Jesus and John now we've included some of the special things Jesus taught.' 'But if we're putting in that story of John sending from prison we must have a healing story first.' 'Right, then, the one about the centurion, he understood about orders and obedience, and that links nicely with that bit about saying "Lord" and doing his Father's will which we've just finished up with. So, how does it go now?' The details are not recoverable. But some such *simple and imprecise* procedure is the only one likely.

Any such Life would most likely begin by linking the leading figure with some known predecessor. After that there is little overall organization; rather is material ordered by theme and catchword, in the main. It might end with an account of the philosopher's death, but need not. Unlike other 'wisdom' collections, here the sayings are ascribed, and the central figure predominates in references in the nominative, a subject of verbs, and as the utterer of verbs of speech.[69] The actual content of a Cynic Life flows between exposition of elements of the preferred life-style, critique of aspects of convention, admiration for some, trenchant criticism of others. I have tried to show elsewhere in some detail the extent to which the *entire* content of Q (not just the bits that appeal to such as Burton Mack) can be matched, often very closely, with Cynic traditions—and much more extensively than they can be paralleled in Jewish prophetic or Jewish or other wisdom documents

67. See F.G. Downing, 'Quite Like Q: A Genre for Q: The "Lives" of Cynic Philosophers', *Bib* 69.2 (1988), pp. 196-225, repr. in *idem, Cynics and Christian Origins*, ch. 5, pp. 115-52; and 'A Genre for Q and a Socio-cultural Context for Q', ch. 5 below, in discussion with R.A. Burridge, *What are the Gospels?*

68. For early Christians and their teachings as a 'school' with its traditions, see for instance, L. Alexander, 'Acts and Ancient Intellectual Biography', in B.W. Winter and A.D. Clarke (eds.), *The Book of Acts in its First Century Setting*. I. *The Book of Acts in its Ancient Literary Setting* (Grand Rapids: Eerdmans, 1993; Exeter: Paternoster Press, 1994), and other work likely to be forthcoming.

69. Burridge, *What are the Gospels?*, pp. 134-38.

(bedded though Q obviously also is in Jewish Scripture and tradition).[70] It would not be appropriate to attempt to go back over all that material. But what we may discern of the social practicalities of composition in and for performance would lead us to expect Q to have been composed from the start very much as we find it. Given that the supposedly distinctive strands in Q do not appear discrepant to others in the first century, there seems to be no good reason to imagine some otherwise unevidenced pragmatics of composition, in which individuals, of their own initiative, produce in their studies and publish fresh versions of the community handbook for its members to accept or reject *en bloc*.

It would nonetheless be interesting to have an attempt to defend a 'stratigraphic' account of Q's formation that began, not simply with distinctions in thought that appeal to late-twentieth-century Western academics, but with the evidenced pragmatics of first-century Graeco-Roman (including Jewish) social compositional performance *and* then only with distinctions in thought for whose acceptance *as importantly discrepant* there is good evidence in contemporary sources.[71]

Yet can Q indeed be seen as a Life, as an instance of the Life of a philosopher, a teacher? and how clear-cut, anyway, are such questions of genre? We pursue these issues in the next chapter.

70. See n. 66 above.

71. In response to the foregoing the question has been very properly raised as to how the 'social composition' for which I argue could be thought to have produced Matthew and Luke as we have them. In brief I would respond: Mark and Q already have themes in common, discourse material which is (on my hypothesis) not at all discrepant (wisdom, prophecy, apocalyptic), and both are Lives. They would invite union (unlike the supposed layers of the stratigraphic models, which should have repelled any merger). There are plenty of examples of expanded Lives, including ones where one source at least had mostly narrated discourse. For the procedure one might imagine for Luke, see F.G. Downing, 'Theophilus' First Reading of Luke–Acts', in Tuckett (ed.), *Luke's Literary Achievement*, pp. 91-109, repr. as ch. 10 below. For Matthew the proposal would marry well with previous suggestions of a 'school' setting. In his *The Composition of the Sayings Source: Genre, Synchrony and Wisdom Redaction in Q* (NovTSup, 91; Leiden: E.J. Brill, 1998), Alan Kirk argues a quite different case for Q as the product of a single redaction, one complexly and deliberately structured in detail and overall to a supposedly known genre by a skilled scribal author. There is, however, no evidence for any explicit recognition among contemporaries of either the major or the minor generic categories Kirk finds in other ancient sapiential work. No one analyses in such detail, nor expects to be guided in such detail.

Chapter 5

A GENRE FOR Q AND A SOCIO-CULTURAL CONTEXT FOR Q:
COMPARING SETS OF SIMILARITIES WITH SETS OF DIFFERENCES*

Studies of rhetoric in the New Testament, Jean-Noel Aletti has suggested, readily allow themselves to be divided into two kinds: one school imposes an early identification of the genre on the basis of a few, often superficial similarities, and then reads the whole in that light. The other (his own preferred) looks first to content and arguments, and only then attempts to discern the rhetorical structure of the whole.[1]

Aletti is discussing rhetorical models as they may appear in Paul's and others' letter writing; but a similar division may be argued among discussions of narrative genres. In his *What are the Gospels?* Richard Burridge outlines just such a critique of a number of previous suggestions as to 'a genre for the gospels', among them those of C.H. Talbert and P.L. Shuler, where, he argues, a supposed sub-genre (e.g., 'encomiastic biography') is deduced from a small and arbitrarily chosen range of facets, to the neglect of many others. Burridge himself proposes a much more extensive set of similar features, large sub-sets of which are to be found in works clearly discerned as Lives, *bioi*, *vitae*, in late east Mediterranean antiquity.[2] It is also worth noting some of the related theoretical reflections offered in studies by Margaret M. Mitchell and by George E. Sterling: a careful discussion in detail of the contents of a

---

*   Reprinted from *JSNT* 55 (1994), pp. 3-26, with kind permission.

1.   J.-N. Aletti, 'La présence d'un modèle rhétorique en Romains: Son rôle et son importance', *Bib* 71.1 (1990), pp. 1-14 (8); cf. his 'La *Dispositio* rhétorique dans les épîtres pauliniens: Proposition de méthode', *NTS* 38.4 (1992), pp. 385-401; Tuckett urged a similar conclusion in his *Reading the New Testament*, p. 70: 'in general terms, we can only determine the genre of a text as a whole by looking at its individual parts'.

2.   Burridge, *What are the Gospels?*; discussing, among others, Talbert, *What is a Gospel?* and Shuler, *A Genre for the Gospels*.

text must precede any conclusions as to genre and any interpretative deductions based on supposed genre.[3]

For all their occasional differences in critical detail and emphasis, these writers clearly agree in accepting that the issue of genre nonetheless remains significant in our appreciation of a writing. An awareness of the genres in use, or in use and under discussion in the Graeco-Roman world around the time of the production of the New Testament documents helps to give them a context (rather than leave them floating 'sui generis'), and affords some real if limited help to us in our attempts to discern and understand what was being said and written in the succeeding individual parts.

But we must also realize how flexible was the use made of genre models, actual or theoretical, and (I would add) the extent therefore to which genres overlapped in practice. There are no hard-and-fast rules (as theoreticians such as Quintilian himself insist); and still less are there clearly defined and normative sub-genres of, say, 'encomiastic biography'.[4] We do best to attempt to recognize 'family resemblances', various common features, similarities, that cluster to suggest a genre, but which may be variously shared with others.[5] So, when Burridge picks out and analyses the items of his extensive 'menu' (my term) of features to be found in 'Lives', from the centuries either side of the first, none of these features is necessary, and none constitutes on its own a sufficient sign of a *bios*. But a cluster of them would suggest that the author intended and the hearers or readers would have discerned that, 'here is a *bios*', a 'character sketch'. And first-century readers would most likely have discerned just such significant family resemblances, similarities, of a *bios* kind in all four of our canonical Gospels.

---

3.   Mitchell, *Paul and the Rhetoric of Reconciliation* and G.E. Sterling, *Historiography and Self-definition: Josephos, Luke–Acts, and Apologetic Historiography* (NovTSup, 64; Leiden: E.J. Brill, 1992); cf. also S.E. Porter and T.H. Olbricht, The Rhetorical Analysis of Scripture (JSNTSup, 146; Sheffield: Sheffield Academic Press, 1997). (I reviewed Burridge and Sterling together in *JTS* NS 44.1 [1993], pp. 238-40.)

4.   As proposed by Shuler, *A Genre for the Gospels*, pp. 24-57.

5.   The Wittgensteinian model is proposed explicitly by Burridge, *What are the Gospels?*, p. 39 and *passim*, though I shall argue that he does not maintain consistently this important insight; cf. Wittgenstein, *Philosophical Investigations*, §67, p. 32e.

Features of Lives

In what follows I want to make a critical use of Burridge's menu (à la carte, that is) for a *bios*, but to deal with a text which he cursorily dismisses from consideration: Q. 'Fascinating though...speculations [concerning Q] are, they concern texts which, if they existed at all, have not survived; therefore we cannot be certain about their genre.'[6] However, neither do we have original or first-century texts of Mark, Matthew, Luke or John: only text critics' and others' reconstructions; it is with these that we concern ourselves (Mark with or without 16.9-20, John with or without ch. 21, and so on). There are a number of different reconstructions of 'final' Q, of Luke's Q and Matthew's Q.[7] But we have every right to attempt a genre analysis of our favoured or even of various reconstructions of Q.

I shall illustrate my critical proposals with references in the main to Burridge's treatment of one of his chief examples, Lucian of Samosata's *Demonax*, clearly seen as a *bios* by others. But I shall also consider similar Lives from Diogenes Laertius, Suetonius and Philostratus. I shall follow Burridge's system of headings and sub-headings.

Introductory

Lucian was born in Syria, around 120 CE. Initially apprenticed to his uncle as a monumental mason or sculptor, he soon switched to train in rhetoric, to be a sophist, a learned but (he hoped) popular entertainer. He was much influenced by the Gadarene Cynic writer Menippus, as well as, later, by his urbane Cynic teacher, Demonax. It is therefore worth noting Menahem Luz's recent detailed argument for a 'general Gadarene Cynicism' evidenced in ongoing rabbinic tradition, a tradition thus influential in the general area of southern Syria where Q is usually thought to have originated a century earlier.[8]

Opening Features

Titles. Lucian's work is entitled *dēmōnaktos bios* in the manuscripts. The words *bios* or *vita* often occur in individual titles, or in the titles of

---

6. Burridge, *What are the Gospels?*, p. 248.
7. Cf. Kloppenborg, *Formation of Q*; *idem*, *Q Parallels*. More recently, now, also Jacobson, *The First Gospel*; and Mack, *The Lost Gospel* and n. 12 below.
8. Luz, 'Oenomaus', pp. 46, 50, 80.

collections of similar pieces, but by no means always.[9] We have no title, nor any clear allusion to any title for Q as commonly reconstructed.

Opening Formula/Prologue/Preface. We have no obvious incipit or prologue for Q, which we do have for *Demonax*. However, if we include for comparison other works that are classed as *bioi*, and are otherwise similar in containing lots of sayings of teachers, the beginnings vary even more than Burridge notes.[10] If the first section of Q is taken to have focused on a predecessor (John), we may note that Dio's character sketch of Diogenes (*Discourse* 8) also gets under way with indications of a (somewhat precarious) relationship between Diogenes and his predecessor, Antisthenes. Lucian's prologue to his *Demonax* also begins with reference to another Cynic figure, Sostratus, one who lived out in the open, slept rough, slew robbers, made roads in untravelled country, and built bridges where passage was difficult.[11] Even if the main resonances here are with Mark (and are surely coincidental), yet it shows clearly that one could readily begin a Life centred on one man with recollections of another, including implicit similarities and contrasts: Demonax the urbane figure in every way, Sostratus the wilder wilderness figure. (If the start of Q is taken as including the baptism of Jesus,[12] so too does Mark, and Mark is clearly a *bios*, by Burridge's criteria. A 'call' story of some kind will often feature in the Life of a philosopher-teacher, and can be used to introduce it.)[13]

Subject

Analysis of Verb Subject. In my judgment this is the most cogent and most important part of Burridge's argument, not least if one's reaction is 'of course'. Burridge notes that only in a Life (as distinct even from a history) will a single named person predominate among references in the nominative, as the subject of verbs, and as the utterer of verbs in

---

9. Burridge, *What are the Gospels?*, pp. 160-61.

10. Compilers of collected Lives (e.g. Diogenes Laertius) seem to begin with the subject's name. A single character sketch such as Dio's *Discourse* 8, or Lucian's *Demonax* can have a more individual commencement.

11. Lucian, *Demonax* 1.

12. As argued recently, for instance, by D.R. Catchpole, 'The Beginning of Q: A Proposal', *NTS* NS 38.2 (1992), pp. 205-21; repr. in *idem*, *The Quest for Q* (Edinburgh: T. & T. Clark, 1993).

13. E.g. Diogenes Laertius, *Lives of Eminent Philosophers* 6.1-2, 20-21, 82, 87.

speech.[14] Even leading figures in 'histories' do not figure nearly so prominently. So,

> Much of the *Demonax* consists of witty conversations between Demonax and someone else, leading up to a witty saying or clever pronouncement of the sage himself. This is reflected in a manual analysis of the verbs: Demonax is the subject of a third of them (33.6%) and speaks a further fifth (19.7%), whereas all those with whom he converses only make up another fifth when taken all together (20.9%).[15]

There are longer continuous stretches of discourse in Q than in *Demonax*. We are told around 33 times that Jesus 'said' or 'did' something, 26 times that some other(s) did (of these the Devil comes next with 7 or 8 references. The figures depend, of course, on the extent of Q in various reconstructions). Jesus is the utterer of between 630 and 700 verbs; others of only around 60. '*Bios* literature is characterized by a strong concentration and focus on one person, and this is reflected even in the verbal syntax.'[16]

There is, however, a further significant point of syntax which Burridge has overlooked. A large number of units of discourse in Greek Lives of teachers, for instance both in *Demonax* and in Diogenes Laertius's *Diogenes*, are introduced in the first person, 'I tell you…' We find this also in Q (between 16 and 25).

So, whereas Q is clearly seen by some as a wisdom collection,[17] it is, at least by these criteria, rather different from most such collections usually included for comparison. Although the first person is sometimes used in wisdom collections in an appeal to the sage's authority and/or experience (e.g. Prov. 4), the sayings themselves seem always to be 'gnomic', 'impersonal'. The compiler subscribes to the teaching, but it stands on its own feet. He does not appear in the nominative as author of the utterances, he is rarely if at all the subject of verbs. In the canon Ecclesiastes might figure as a partial exception; but that is only to note that here we have a much more 'autobiographical' experience (again), and one opposed to the common thrust of the 'sayings of the wise'.[18]

---

14. Burridge, *What are the Gospels?*, pp. 134-35, etc.; and his Appendices, pp. 261-74.

15. Burridge, *What are the Gospels?*, p. 163.

16. Burridge, *What are the Gospels?*, p. 163.

17. J.M. Robinson and H. Koester, *Trajectories through Early Christianity* (Philadelphia: Fortress Press, 1971); Kloppenborg, *Formation of Q*, pp. 263-306.

18. My generalization seems to hold for the canonical and deutero-canonical

The *Gospel of Thomas* is also often included in the 'trajectory' of Sayings of the Wise. Burridge notes that *Thomas* lacks some important features among those he argues are in some combination constitutive for the *bios* genre: for example, narrative, chronological and geographical settings.[19] However, *Thomas* does include frequent references to Jesus in the nominative, and he is the subject of a great many of the verbs (admittedly, repetitiously, 'Jesus said'). If we do not arbitrarily refuse to allow that genres can overlap each other, in this area, which seems fairly distinctive of a Life, *Thomas* overlaps, and Q at the very least overlaps quite significantly with the genre of *bios*.

Even these syntactical features, however, ought not to be taken as necessary features of a *bios*; yet a piece that includes them would have to lack a great many other features often appearing in a *bios* (similarities), and also contain a great many not normally found in a *bios* (differences) for us to be justified in subsuming it under some other heading.

Others again (e.g. Migaku Sato) choose to see Q as a prophetic collection.[20] Some of the prophetic books do include occasionally a few of the features that Burridge notes, though only Jeremiah does so at all extensively. Most of the features of a *bios* that Burridge prompts us to discern in Q (ones discussed so far, and more to follow) figure little if at all in the prophets as a set. And there are a great many contrasts, not least that the prophets quite specifically do not announce their teaching in their own name: they proclaim, 'So says Yahweh' rather than, 'I tell you'.[21]

Allocation of Space. In *Demonax* Burridge finds a brief note of the philosopher's birth and education and character; most space is given to 'many stories and anecdotes, each leading up to a pronouncement or saying of the sage'.[22] In fact, as I have noted, the Life begins with a

wisdom literature, but also for *Ahiqar*, and for such later compilations as *m. Ab.*, the *Sentences of Sextus*, and the traces of earlier Pythagorean collections that seem to have provided some of the matter for the latter; also for the main examples in Kirk, *Composition: Ps. Phocylides, Testaments of the Twelve Patriarchs*, Sirach and Wisdom of Solomon (despite Kirk's chs. 7–9).

19. On the 'trajectory', cf. Robinson and Koester, *Trajectories*; on *Thomas*, Burridge, *What are the Gospels?*, p. 250.

20. Sato, *Q und Prophetie*.

21. See my article/review of Sato, *Bib* 72.1 (1991), pp. 127-32, but also the discussion in my *Cynics and Christian Origins*, pp. 122-46; and further below.

22. Burridge, *What are the Gospels?*, pp. 166-67, with table.

summary of a companion sketch of another linked but contrasting character, Sostratus. Likewise in Q we begin, on most reconstructions, with the appearance of John as a teacher; according to fewer critics, that includes a sort of 'call' story in the baptism of Jesus. Then follows a character-revealing test encounter with dialogue ('the Temptation'), followed for the most part by spontaneous pronouncements from Jesus but including a few further encounters involving dialogues and near dialogues (featuring the centurion, disciples of John, the crowds and would-be disciples), all in *chreia* form ('asked...he said...' or such like).[23] The sayings may sometimes echo those of 'the wise', but they are not presented as such. What Jesus pronounces (mostly spontaneously, occasionally prompted) constitutes almost the entire text. As Burridge says of *Demonax*, 'Of course, since the focus of interest in a philosopher is in his teaching, this is to be expected'.[24] Laertius's *Life of Diogenes* is very similar, as are other briefer Lives of teachers in Laertius's collection, but also in other collections ascribed to Suetonius and to Philostratus.

Discussing this and others of his examples, here and elsewhere, Burridge also places considerable stress on references to the family and on accounts of the death of the main character. Neither, of course, appear in Q. It is therefore important to point out here as well as later that many of the Lives just mentioned (in Diogenes Laertius, Suetonius and Philostratus) also lack one or both of birth and death. In the first book of Philostratus's *Lives of the Sophists* such items are more often lacking than present, even though these are all figures long dead; but accounts of birth and/or death are not universal in the second volume either, even for the more recently departed. The same may be said of many of the briefer Cynic Lives in Diogenes Laertius, *Lives of the Eminent Philosophers* 6. What is important in an ancient character sketch is attitudes to questions of family and to death (and other common but personally crucial circumstances) that display the *ethos* of the subject of a Life; external events as such are much less important than attitudes to them (as, for instance, Quintilian insists).[25]

23. See n. 32 below.
24. Burridge, *What are the Gospels?*, p. 166.
25. Quintilian, *Institutes* 3.7. On death narratives, see further below, under 'Topics', and n. 40.

External Features

I would suggest that the traditional pair 'form and content' would serve better for this and the next main sections; but for ease of reference I continue to cite Burridge's headings as given.

Mode of Representation. Burridge's term for the (very common) 'mode' adopted for *Demonax*, 'prose narrative', fits Q quite happily. Burridge then adds, 'the bulk [of *Demonax*] is not continuous, but, rather, a string of unconnected anecdotes and stories'.[26] Just below, I shall raise a query against this 'unconnected' (for *Demonax* as for other similar compositions).

Size. I find this item in Burridge's discussion the least satisfactory— in fact, quite unacceptable. He takes it that a Life will be of 'medium length' among ancient tomes, that is, 10–25,000 words, though he himself notes that some of his own chosen examples are shorter or longer. *Demonax* is shorter, at around 3000; and Philostratus's *Life of Apollonius of Tyana* is much longer (82,000). But it must be noted that Philostratus's *Lives of the Sophists* range from shorter to very much shorter than Burridge's arbitrarily chosen norm, as do those of teachers ascribed to Suetonius, and many of the Lives in Diogenes Laertius's collection (although their *bios* character based on still earlier *bios* sources—so generically very significant—is undisputable).[27] Q (at around 3500) is much the same length as *Demonax* and Diogenes Laertius's *Diogenes* (of Sinope): if this is significant for genre at all.

Structure. Citing H. Cancik, Burridge characterizes *Demonax* as a 'loosely connected sequence of stories and sayings...with less integration of teaching and activity than even Mark's Gospel', though allowing in conclusion that there is some topical arrangement in collections like *Demonax*.[28] Scholars have found connections by catchword and topic in Q, as well as structures of inclusio and chiasm (though not always the same ones!). Certainly there are also catchword and thematic

---

26. Burridge, *What are the Gospels?*, p. 168.

27. See the discussion in Kindstrand, 'Diogenes Laertius', pp. 217-43; and Goulet-Cazé, 'Le Livre Six', pp. 3933-37.

28. Burridge, *What are the Gospels?*, p. 170; H. Cancik, 'Logos. Formengeschichtliche Untersuchungen zu Lukians "Leben des Demonax" ', in *idem* (ed.), *Markus-philologie: Historische, literargeschichtliche und stilistische Untersuchungen zum zweiten Evangelium* (WUNT, 33; Tübingen: J.C.B. Mohr, 1984), pp. 115-30 (128).

links in *Demonax* and in Diogenes Laertius's *Diogenes*.[29] If it is agreed that Q is somewhat more carefully ordered by theme, this would align it that much closer with one common way of ordering a character sketch, a *bios* (chronology is the other main option).[30]

Burridge again stresses the structural importance of bracketing a Life between birth and death; it must therefore be re-emphasized that many acknowledged Lives lack one or both of these elements.

Scale. Perhaps 'scope' would have been more appropriate. The scope 'is limited to the subject's life, deeds and character', with at most passing reference to the wider world, to great contemporary events, or to time before or after. 'Each story is about Demonax himself.'[31] As we have seen that is not quite accurate: Lucian began with Sostratus, just as Dio can begin a portrait of Diogenes by sketching in his relationship with Antisthenes. However, even giving full weight to John's appearances in the text, Q is very clearly focused on Jesus' teaching, together with occasional references to his actions.

Literary Units. Q, as we have recalled, is made up of brief units. Some of them may have been transmitted in clusters prior to the final assembly of Q. Some of these units take a typical condensed *chreia* form.[32] Other short sequences are almost 'doxographic'.[33] So Burridge concludes,

> [A]ll our examples [of *bios*] are formed from a similar range of literary units of stories and anecdotes, sayings and speeches, with some being

29. See my 'Quite like Q', pp. 196-225; see also C.M. Tuckett in his 'A Cynic Q?', *Bib* 70.3 (1989), pp. 344-76 (362). Tuckett's article subjected mine, along with some other scholars' suggestions of Cynic resonances in Q, to a detailed critique. I have attempted to respond to the several cogent and to the rather more numerous ill-founded points he made, in my *Cynics and Christian Origins*; but now further in this chapter.

30. Burridge, *What are the Gospels?*, pp. 139-41, 169-71.

31. Burridge, *What are the Gospels?*, pp. 141, 172.

32. On the *chreia* form ('asked...he said...', etc.), see the discussion in my 'Quite like Q', pp. 199-200, and Tuckett, 'A Cynic Q?', p. 361, and references there. My resistance to any tight definition of a *chreia*, already supported by Hock and O'Neil, *The Chreia*, and by Mack and Robbins, *Patterns*, is further strengthened by Kindstrand's 'Diogenes Laertius'.

33. 'Doxographies', lists of the leading views of important teachers, appear frequently in Diogenes Laertius, *Lives of Eminent Philsophers* (e.g. 6.70-71, 103-105), but also in Cicero and others, as well as in the early Christian Fathers. Luke 6.20-49 could well be taken to function as an introductory summary of Jesus' ethical views.

rather carefully composed while others [including *Demonax*] are more of a loose connections of units.[34]

'Connections' I discussed just above. The standard building blocks for the kind of character sketch that the term *bios* indicates are also the basic units of which Q is made up. The closest analogies remain with the Lives of teachers such as Demonax and Diogenes of Sinope.

Use of Sources. Most of our Lives of teachers rely on written and oral tradition. Lucian bases his *bios* on his own memories as a disciple of Demonax, though he has shaped his reminiscences very much as popular *chreiai* of the developed terse kind also found in Diogenes Laertius and others. Q seems to be almost as close to the live recollections of original disciples, also cast or recast in similar memorable oral forms.

One minor but significant source for Q is the Jewish 'canonical' Scripture, with half-a-dozen explicit quotations and about the same number of further clear allusions. Our undisputed Cynic sources contain scattered quotations from and allusions to Homer, Hesiod, Plato and others. Though we have no similar quotations in these documents from 'barbarian' writings, positive allusions to and citations of barbarian wisdom, albeit expressed in poor Greek, would be entirely in character. Barbarians were seen as being likely to be closer to 'nature' and how life should be, than those corrupted by Greek culture and convention.[35]

Methods of Characterization. Lucian offers a brief abstract analysis of Demonax's character, and such analyses occur in a few of Burridge's other chosen examples. But, as he emphasizes, mostly character is portrayed in words and deeds without further comment. Particularly in Plutarch there may be overt illustrative comparisons between characters; I have noted the implicit comparison with Sostratus in *Demonax*, and there are more in Demonax's encounters with other philosophers. Just such a comparison between Jesus and John seems to many readers to be a significant strand in Q.[36] Taking this facet a stage further than Burridge does, we may also note that Jesus in Q deals with many of the

---

34. Burridge, *What are the Gospels?*, p. 173.

35. Cf. Ps.-Anacharsis; Onesicritus in Strabo, *Geog.* 15.1.63-65; C. Muckensturm, 'Les Gymnosophistes étaient-ils des Cyniques modèles?', in Goulet-Cazé and Goulet (eds.), *Le cynicisme ancien*, pp. 225-40, and C.P. Jones, 'Cynisme et "sagesse barbare": Le cas de Pérégrinus Proteus', in Goulet-Cazé and Goulet (eds.), *Le cynisme ancien*, pp. 305-18.

36. Cf. J.S. Kloppenborg, 'City and Wasteland: Narrative World and the Beginning of the Sayings Gospel Q', *Semeia* 52 (1991), pp. 145-60.

topics that contemporary convention holds indicate a person's character.[37]

Internal Features

Setting. The focus in a *bios* in not place but person. However, it probably is significant that Demonax is implicitly in Athens for all the anecdotes related: he is another Socrates,[38] but an 'urbane' figure compared with Sostratus in the wilderness. Kloppenborg argues that the references to John in the wilderness and the one reference to Jerusalem are significant in Q.[39] Though the wilderness on Kloppenborg's view has a somewhat different significance from that in *Demonax*, Jesus does seem to stand in relation to Jerusalem's characteristic hatred for prophets as Demonax does to the Athenians' 'characteristic' response to Socratic figures. Similar motifs in their respective narratives help us to interpret the characters portrayed.

Topics. Burridge includes a formal list—ancestry, birth, boyhood, great deeds, virtues, death and its consequences[40]—and, to be sure, these can be very telling in a character sketch. Burridge admits that

37. E.g. power, glory, hunger and thirst, comfort and hardship, poverty and wealth, reliance on the 'natural' world around, ostentation and generosity, unpopularity and physical suffering, and the foes who inflict them: these and many more issues in Q are very much more characteristic of Graeco-Roman popular philosophy than of canonical Jewish literatue; and attitudes on these issues evinced in Q are very much more those of the Cynics and the more Cynic-like Stoics: see my 'Quite like Q', but also my *Christ and the Cynics*; and my *Cynics and Christian Origins*; cf. also my *Cynics, Paul and the Pauline Churches*, pp. 141-73, discussing 'tribulation lists', and esp. p. 169, for the contrast with Jewish lists.

38. Lucian, *Demonax* 11 and 58.

39. Kloppenborg, 'City and Wasteland'.

40. Burridge, *What are the Gospels?*, pp. 178-80. On Lk. 14.27 as expressing a typically Cynic or Cynic-Stoic attitude to the teacher's death, see D. Seeley, 'Jesus' Death in Q', *NTS* 38.2 (1992), pp. 222-34. And once we accept that a death narrative is not obligatory it is even less surprising to find no resurrection narrative. However, Lk. 12.8-9 expresses a conviction of post-mortem living effectiveness that can, of course, be paralleled in Cynic sources—mockingly in Lucian's *Peregrinus*, quite seriously in Ps.-Diogenes 39, Ps.-Heraclitus 5, 9; Epictetus, *Encheiridion* 15; *Ps.-Socratic Letter* 25.1; Lucian, *Downward Journey* 23. Stories of life after death or life with the gods are firmly part of the Menippaean Cynic tradition: cf. R. Bauckham, 'The Rich Man and Lazarus: The Parable and the Parallels', *NTS* 37.2 (1991), pp. 225-46. I would not wish to argue that the silence of Q on the resurrection traditions betrayed a deliberate Cynic scepticism! Yet what is in Q on death and effectiveness after death does fit well with some Cynics' approaches.

some Lives lack one or more of them. In fact, some lack all of them, but include others that Burridge has himself noted elsewhere such as public appearance; and of course one should also include among these 'great deeds' the enunciation of great thoughts, the most significant content for the life of a philosophical teacher, who will be expected to pronounce on or otherwise respond to issues of power, glory, comfort, voluntary and enforced hardship, poverty, wealth, generosity, friendship, enmity and so on as Jesus does in Q.[41]

Style. Demonax is written at a popular level, with a simple and clear style. As Burridge says of the Gospels, their *koine* style should not be seen as peculiar; it would by no means have set them apart from writers such as Lucian. The same would be true of Q. (Lucian can even affect a dialect style, as in his *De Dea Syriae*.)

Atmosphere. Burridge considers 'tone, mood, attitude and values'. The tone of a Life is usually serious, the mood positive, the attitude to the subject respectful, and the hearer or reader is encouraged to emulate the attitudes evinced in the actions and sayings narrated. Burridge finds Demonax light-hearted, but he himself does not seem to have had occasion to reflect on the Cynic *spoudaiogeloion*—serious fun. Lucian explicitly hopes that his audience will see his *Demonax* as a pattern to copy, not just as a wit to admire from a distance.[42] In his attitudes to wealth, power, glory (and much more) Jesus in Q has been presented as a pattern to be admired and imitated. His values are God's values. In my *Cynics and Christian Origins* I hope to have shown that the ensuing Christian centuries, while Cynicism remained a living movement as well as an important intellectual and ethical stimulus, clearly and in many cases explicitly acknowledged that many of the standard ethical themes of popular Graeco-Roman philosophy were here at issue, and that largely Cynic-like attitudes are on Jesus' lips in the parts of the Gospel tradition we here take to have constituted Q. These are largely

41. See n. 37 above. Burridge criticizes my earlier 'Contemporary Analogies', for placing too much emphasis on 'topics' and 'motifs', to the disadvantage of other generically significant items. I shall return to this issue towards the end of the present chapter. A distinction is made by some between narrative motifs, and teaching, as though the latter were somehow different in kind, so as to render a Life such as Q 'strangely unstoried' and quite other than the more obviously narrative Gospels (see, e.g., Wright, *New Testament*, p. 435). I have attempted to undo this false disjunction in my 'Words and Deeds and Deeds and Words', ch. 2 above.

42. Burridge, *What are the Gospels?*, p. 182, Lucian, *Demonax* 2 (as noted elsewhere by Burridge, on authorial intent).

the values a Greek audience would have expected to find promoted in the Life of a Cynic philosopher.

Quality of Characterization. Q, as we have seen, lacks anything like the 'stereotypical' generalizations that Burridge notes at *Demonax* 6–11; but, as he comments, 'the picture that emerges from the actual anecdotes has a more "real" and individual feel about it', as Lucian himself intends.[43] The actions narrated and the many more attitudes evinced on the very full range of expected topics covered in Q would have allowed the character, the *ethos* of Jesus to emerge with at least as much vividness.

Social Setting and Occasion. Lucian's *Demonax* seems set for a popular audience (its author an intellectual entertainer, a sophist), even though the philosopher is said to have been cultured and from a 'good family'. Demonax is presented, we have observed, as a model to be copied, not just as a wit. The occasion for Q to be heard would seem likely to have been somewhat different: within a community already largely committed, rather than to an ad hoc popular gathering. But the social level aimed at, among competent 'plebeian' Greek speakers, would seem to overlap. There are some very similar criticisms of the wealthy and powerful, some very similar affirmations of poverty and simplicity.[44]

Authorial Intent and Purpose. Burridge divides intent and purpose under a number of somewhat overlapping sub-headings, noting that the genre was 'extremely flexible'.[45] Lucian certainly intends to praise Demonax ('the best of all philosophers') as Q does Jesus ('greater than Solomon', 'greater than Jonah', Lk. 11.29-32); though in neither case does this make the work into 'an encomium'. 'Example' we have already touched on for both. 'Inform' is a very general category; but the preservation of people's memory of his subject is an aim announced by Lucian (*Demonax* 2), and is often suggested as a reason for the move to written records of Jesus and his teaching among early Christians. 'Entertainment' in the witty manner of Lucian is not there in Q, although I have noted Lucian's underlying seriousness (*spoudaiogeloion*). 'Engaging', intent to gain and hold the hearers, would be true of both

---

43. Burridge, *What are the Gospels?*, p. 183.

44. Lucian, *Demonax* 5, 7, 9, 34, 41, 50-52, 59, 66; for many other parallels, see my 'Quite like Q', *Christ and the Cynics* and *Cynics and Christian Origins*.

45. Burridge, *What are the Gospels?*, p. 188, quoting C.R.B. Pelling, 'Plutarch's Adaptation of his Source Material', *JHS* 100 (1980), pp. 127-40 (139).

(as of other more obviously serious Lives). Both Q and *Demonax* obviously (and as has been already much repeated) display their subjects' teaching on a range of topics seen as important. Both are often polemical; unlike some Lives, neither seems particularly defensive, 'apologetic'.

One may fairly conclude that, if Burridge is on the right tracks, Q would have sounded to contemporary Greek audiences more like a *bios* of a teacher—and, I would add, of a Cynic teacher—than anything else (even if some or all were aware of its long traditional Jewish sources, and of other possible Hebrew and Aramaic as well as Greek Jewish models besides). Q displays a rich intertexture, but the largest single set of threads is Cynic.

Other Motifs and Other Genres

In conclusion Burridge reaffirms his Wittgensteinian model of 'family resemblances'. We obtain a clear picture of the family that constitutes and exemplifies the *bios* genre, diverse and flexible, yet recognizable, from collocations of the features he outlines, and which have been briefly and mostly approvingly surveyed here, particularly 'the major determining feature...the subject; all these works concentrate on one individual'. In contrary vein Burridge then insists, 'However, it should not be assumed that there are no boundaries',[46] and he also places Acts out of bounds in this discussion (for no other stated reason than that it never appears paired with Luke's Gospel in the manuscripts).[47] By way of contrast Gregory E. Sterling, in his *Historiography and Self-definition* considers the pair Luke–Acts in the light of a tradition which he discerns, one that has clear enough generic features to influence Josephus, generic features that appear clearly in the Gospel and Acts when read together. But can Burridge and Sterling both be right—or do their arguments to diverse genre models (and there are others mooted, of course) suggest that the quest is futile?

It seems much more significant than Burridge allows that we can find long 'biographical' sequences in the historians. Romulus, Numa, Publicola and Camillus are treated very similarly by Plutarch in his *Parallel Lives* to the ways they are presented in Dionysius of Halicarnassus's *Roman Antiquities*; as are Joseph and Moses in Philo's Lives of them

---

46. Burridge, *What are the Gospels?*, p. 189.
47. Burridge, *What are the Gospels?*, p. 248.

and in Josephus's *Antiquities* respectively. It is particularly significant that Josephus refers us to his *Jewish War* for his own *Life*'s continuation (413). If we want, we can read much of the former not so much as a history, but as part two of a *bios*. Thus one could read Luke's Gospel on its own as a Life of Jesus, or a part of an apologetic history of the Christian people, with Acts as part two. Just so, of course, Plutarch reads Livy's *History* and Dionysius's *Antiquities* with *bioi* in mind— and could paraphrase much of the material pretty well as it stood.[48]

The family resemblance model in Wittgenstein specifically excludes firm boundaries.[49] Because there are so many topics or motifs in common, especially between history and *bios* (but also with the romances),[50] it is very easy to 'read' them for different purposes. The point can be illustrated from other generic sets: Dio of Prusa tells us explicitly that he expected to declaim his speeches to very different audiences—what would be deliberative in one town might be epideictic in another. Pliny the Younger's *Letter* 10.96 to Trajan was initially deliberative, forensic in outcome, but epideictic—for display—all along in intention.

Approaching the issue from a slightly different and more theoretical angle, when we are discussing genres we are obviously, as already noted, discussing similarities: and the discussion of similarities clearly entails, at least implicitly, differences—or else we would be talking of type identity. The suggestion is being made that there are extensive and significant similarities outweighing—at least for the purposes in hand— any differences. But the similarities tend to be 'similarities under some particular description'. And there's the rub. Those of us who claim to have discerned and wish to propose similarities will frame our descriptions accordingly. Thus, in his study of the Q temptation narrative, Kloppenborg concludes,

> The testing stories mentioned here are similar enough in structure and function to invite comparisons with the Q temptation account. In both the Abraham stories and the Q temptation the testing occurs away from society. Job's testing does not occur in a desert, but it happens after the elements which tie him to society...have been removed.[51]

48. Cf. my 'Compositional Conventions and the Synoptic Problem', ch. 8 below.

49. Wittgenstein, *Philosophical Investigations* §67 onwards, especially §71, pp. 34-47.

50. For the romances and some interesting comparisons, see chs. 6, 7 and 10, below.

51. Kloppenborg, *Formation of Q*, p. 260; compare the headings in the generic

What might appear to some on closer examination to be very disparate elements of very different importance in each story are here being subsumed under the category 'away from society': that is now a supposedly important similarity. (I am not alone in thinking that similarities with some accounts of Herakles on trial are much more significant.)[52]

How can we assess such competing claims to have found the most or even the only significant 'similarities'? It is worth looking again at, say, Shuler's conviction that he had found a genre of 'encomiastic' biography, over against Burridge's insistence that Shuler had managed to demonstrate neither the existence of this genre nor that the Gospels belonged to it. It is also worth looking at Kennedy's and others' conviction that a full theoretical *dispositio*, 'table d'hôte' menu for a rhetorical speech, is to be found in many of the New Testament letters, over against Aletti's insistence that this is simply being imposed by force.[53] Burridge usefully cites Alastair Fowler on 'mode'. A writing may be dramatic, maybe more specifically tragic in 'mode', without being a drama, let alone a tragedy of a classical kind.[54] A letter may contain exhortations without authorizing us to split it up into the parts a deliberative speech 'ought' to display. A Life may praise its subject, may be encomiastic, without 'being' an encomium. A 'mode' is best indicated adjectivally rather than by a noun. A single feature, even a strong 'modal' feature, does not suffice for the identification of a genre.

Elements of tragedy, of praise, of exhortation may constitute similarities between various literary works, at a very general level of description, without constituting sufficient similarity for them to have been seen or for them to be seen by us as comprising instances of a genre. Only a detailed comparison warrants a firm genre classification.

In his introductory manual, *Reading the New Testament*, Christopher Tuckett properly asserts,

structure A. Kirk finds or imposes, in his *Composition*, e.g., pp. 130-32 and 294-95. A similar point is made against me (with some justification; but see below) by Tuckett, 'A Cynic Q?', e.g. pp. 569-70.

52. Cf. A.J. Malherbe, 'Herakles', *RAC* 14 (1988), pp. 569-70.

53. Burridge, *What are the Gospels?*, p. 89; Aletti, 'La *Dispositio*', especially p. 390; G.A. Kennedy, *New Testament Interpretation through Rhetorical Criticism* (Chapel Hill: University of North Carolina Press, 1984); and comments on A. Kirk, *Composition*, p. 92 n. 71, above.

54. Burridge, *What are the Gospels?*, pp. 41-42, citing A. Fowler, 'The Life and Death of Literary Forms', in R. Cohen (ed.), *New Directions in Literary History* (London: Routledge & Kegan Paul, 1974), pp. 77-94 (56-57).

circularity in determining the genre of a text is to a certain extent inevitable... Our understanding of [it] should be constantly influenced, rein-
forced, or perhaps modified by our understanding of the individual parts,
and conversely, our developing understanding of the genre will continually influence our understanding of the individual parts of the text.[55]

The contribution of still quite diverse scholars such as Burridge, Sterling and Mitchell has been to insist on taking their descriptions much
further down the line, going into much greater detail than do many
others, with much richer comparisons, both of parts and whole. In particular, Burridge's elaborate 'menu' (while open to some criticism, as
outlined above) encourages us to look in considerable detail at each text
under discussion, under a great many quite precise descriptions, and
even in side-by-side comparison. At least as much as this is necessary
before Q is subsumed under any generic heading, and before any
generic classification is used to aid our understanding of the parts and
the whole.

For a fuller understanding of Q in its possible wider socio-cultural
contexts, a comparison *in detail* of the individual parts between a standard reconstructed Q and as full as possible a range of data from around
its time and area of origin is indisputably essential. What are the
respective similarities, what are the respective differences, and what are
we to make of them?

I have offered in various studies already noted here just such detailed
comparisons of the contents of Q with the contents of other prima facie
plausible partners. I have argued that compared with evidence adduced
from elsewhere, Q (in its parts) has much more in common with Cynic
sources, and often with Cynic character sketches, *bioi*, than with any
other proposed set of near contemporary or currently influential writings, far more than with the canonical prophetic literature (though there
are a few very similar passages there), and far more than with any
gnomic collection of Sayings of the Wise (even though there are also a
few wisdom sayings in Q).[56]

It seems at least plausible that a comprehensive comparison at this
level of contents, item by item, is far more significant still for our
understanding of the text itself, than is any discerning of genre. As
Burridge remarks, once one has accepted that a genre, in this instance
that of *bios*, is to be seen as flexible and therefore widely inclusive, the

55. Tuckett, *Reading the New Testament*, p. 70; cf. n. 1 above.
56. See nn. 21 and 29 above.

less helpful for our understanding is any conclusion as to genre that we reach.[57] People may note initial pointers to a genre when they start to listen or to read, and their genre-based expectations may help (or hinder) them as their reading progresses, in the circular procedure described by Tuckett. But it is the contents, part by part, that are read, not the generic structure (unless one is a specialist in this fashion of analysis!) Nonetheless, it must be significant that Burridge's selection of generically significant features seems capable of pointing to the same conclusion as to the genre of Q as my own earlier comparisons of content (and just a few generic features) did.

Similarities and Differences

The first step, then, towards the reading of a text in its socio-cultural context is the interpretative comparison or series of interpretative comparisons in detail between a given text (say, a reconstructed Q) and other literature from its apparent environment that affords at least some prima facie plausible comparability. The contents are to be compared item by item, whether the items seem generically significant or not.

The next step is to recall, again, that this is a matter of similarities, not (save in close copying) identity. Q (our present example), as I have recalled, occasionally cites canonical Jewish Scriptures in recognizable form, or includes a handful of other clear allusions. They are close enough to be worth printing alongside their sources. The similarities are then so clear that they sometimes can be left to speak for themselves, with little or no commentary. So, too, I have printed passages of Q along with Cynic texts.[58] Some of these are so obviously similar at first sight that, again, the similarities need no pointing out. Other similarities are less obvious and need to be indicated for readers to assess. It is very rare for texts to be so closely and so extensively similar that no more than this is ever needed. Even the synoptic Gospels elicit reams of commentary, as scholars attempt to discern how close or distant from one another apparently 'parallel' passages are.

57. Burridge, *What are the Gospels?*, pp. 255-56. There is an interesting discussion of genre issues by C.J. Classen, 'Paulus und die antike Rhetorik', *ZNW* 82 (1991), pp. 1-33, pointing out how little later scholars versed in classical rhetoric use it in their exegesis: this reinforces Burridge's admission, though hardly shows that Paul and others were not still influenced by structural models.

58. In my collection, *Christ and the Cynics*.

So, scholars may well discern less obvious analogies, where (they suggest) quite similar ideas or attitudes are being expressed, yet in rather different words and images. These cannot be ignored: if the likeness is genuine, then it may well be significant for placing and understanding the text that is the focus of attention. And one may well need to assess whether such apparently very similar passages and ideas noted are set in broadly similar or very different contexts in the respective documents being compared. Thus Kloppenborg's very general common theme of testing in Q and in some ancient Jewish sources taking place 'away from society' might have appeared as an important underlying similarity in ethos, if it has been accompanied by other still closer parallels in theme, wording or imagery.

Broad statements of similarity have their place; I doubt if any scholar engaged in this kind of endeavour avoids them. It would seem possible for it to be the case that very significant, readily acknowledged similarities might obtain between two documents, but similarities that could only be stated in general terms, without there being any passages from them worth printing in parallel at all. On the other hand, it is possible to conclude that readily paralleled passages are being used very differently in different texts (compare Chapter 3, above).

The mere generality of statements of similarity indicates no necessary weakness in the case being proposed, tempting though the dismissive charge of 'generality' may be. For example, in his criticism of attempts by Kloppenborg, Vaage and myself to point up analogies between Q and broadly Cynic sources, Tuckett focuses much attention on the 'generality' of some of the similarities adduced.[59] Yet their generality as such is no drawback, if these similarities are real, and numerous, and are adduced in support of other still closer similarities; and if competing sets of material suggested for comparison from around the time and area appear to afford fewer and slighter parallels.

We all generalize; Tuckett himself is no exception. Countering the suggestion that Christians obeying the Q mission charge would have looked like Cynics, Tuckett himself (in company with others) advances the broad generalization that all Cynics were dressed and equipped alike in a way that would have left the Q Christians looking quite distinctive, even deliberately so: a general similarity suggested between some Cynics and some Christians is, Tuckett avers, therefore not so

59. Tuckett, 'A Cynic Q?', pp. 366, 367-68.

very close after all. If the evidence supported Tuckett's conclusion, it would be a weighty counter to the analogy claimed. In fact, that all Cynics dressed the same way, and none in the way enjoined on the Q emissaries, itself constitutes an unfounded generalization about Cynics.[60] A generalization about 'dissimilarities' is as much weakened by lack of valid evidence as any about similarities will be.

In attempting to counter claims to similarity it is almost inevitable that Tuckett should produce sweeping generalizations like this of his own. The most significant such generalization for him seems to be à propos 'the eschatology which underlies so much of Q'.[61] This underlying eschatology, the expectation of an imminent judgment, is proposed as the key by which much in Q is to be interpreted, especially any and every ascetic injunction (which is where the Cynic parallels are often at their closest). This eschatology constitutes a quite distinctive ethos, which shows that even passages that on the surface may look very like some from Cynic sources, are 'really' quite distinct, quite different.[62]

It is clear that Tuckett has persuaded himself that all commands in Q to ascetic practice share this underlying similarity, they are all coloured by an imminent expectation of judgment; and to be sure there are other scholars who would agree. But it is not obvious from the text of Q, nor to every scholar (quite apart from those of us who espouse alternative 'Cynic' readings).[63] In Q there is actually nothing that says, 'the time is short, do this or that'. 'This generation' may well be under threat, and that may well imply a fairly swift end (though it need not). But the

---

60. Tuckett, 'A Cynic Q?', p. 374; answered in detail in my *Cynics and Christian Origins*, pp. 10-12, 32-33.

61. Tuckett, 'A Cynic Q?', p. 375.

62. Tuckett argues for this 'pan-eschatologist' interpretation of Q in his 'Q, Prayer, and the Kingdom'. I have attempted elsewhere to raise serious questions against a use of eschatological motifs as though they were distinctive of only some strands of first-century east Mediterranean thought: 'Cosmic Eschatology in the First Century: Pagan, Jewish and Christian', *AC* 64 (1995), pp. 99-109; and 'Common Strands in Pagan, Jewish and Christian Eschatologies in the First Century', *TZ* 53.1 (1995), pp. 196-211, repr. in F.G. Downing, *Making Sense*, ch. 9.

63. D.R. Catchpole in reply finds no good reason to allow eschatology so dominant a role: see his 'Q, Prayer and the Kingdom: A Rejoinder', *JTS* NS 40.2 (1989), pp. 377-88, repr. in *idem, The Quest for Q* (Edinburgh: T. & T. Clark, 1993), pp. 201-28.

shortness of the time is never adduced in Q (unlike Paul)[64] as a motive for adopting any aspect of the life-style enjoined. The lilies and the ravens have not changed their way of life under threat of the end, to provide the Q community with an urgent new example of appropriate behaviour. There is no evidence for Tuckett's hermeneutical key to Q's asceticism, other than Tuckett's own generalization: the ethos of Q's asceticism 'must' be coherently and distinctively coloured by the judgment passages he has chosen as the universal key to most or all of the rest.

Now, admittedly, Tuckett may have guessed right. This might have constituted a genuine similarity in ethos underlying all the ascetic commands, even all else that Q enjoins. But this interpretation is only an embracing hypothesis. It is not a given 'factual' difference in Q against which a Cynic interpretation, for instance, must founder as mere hypothesis. It is simply a different general hypothesis, parading as fact.

Yet, how about differences? Differences are even harder to quantify or to compare than are sets of similarities: harder, or maybe impossible. Apart from explicit contradictions, how does one compare what is by definition 'dissimilar'? Where do the more significant differences lie: between Q and the canonical prophetic literature, Q and the 'Sayings of the Wise', or Q and Cynic tradition?

As I have allowed, where similarity, not type-identity, is asserted, differences there must be. But it would seem that only the comparative similarities are 'visible' or readily statable and available for comparison. We decide that we have discovered an extensive range of clear and precise similarities, perhaps supported by some less clear ones, perhaps accompanied by some only demonstrable in general statements, between Q and the prophetic books in the canon. We can perhaps set this list alongside another (wisdom writing, the Cynics, both, or yet more), and decide which impresses us most. (Or that none impress us very much; in each comparison on its own we decide that the differences outweigh the similarities: the sui generis position.) Just such detailed sets of comparisons I have tried to produce for Q (and for other New Testament material).

Yes, we could perhaps list sets of 'differences', vague though such a programme must be. But how can we possibly compare them? How could we compare the respective silences of prophets, wisdom collections and Cynics (over against Q) on exorcism? on anything amounting

---

64. 1 Cor. 7.29; Rom. 13.11.

to a 'Christology'? or on the absence from wisdom and the prophets of any kind of 'mission charge' whatsoever, against the absence from Q of any overt mention of Cynicism?

Because differences there must be when similarity, not type-identity, is being asserted, differences are all too easy to assert. But in a comparison of competing sets of supposed similarities, a reference to differences simply distracts attention from the only possible critical task, that of assessing the respective extents and weights of the sets of similarities that are said to be discernible. What remains when all the similarities have been noted are the differences, but they are irrelevant once we have decided that they are not so extensive as to render fruit-less a comparison of the extent and weight of the sets of similarities.

We still have not found any clear way to decide between these (and other) competing hypotheses as to what is most similar to or more different from whatever we have chosen for comparison among evidences roughly contemporary and roughly from the same geographical and social areas. We have to accept that there is never likely to be a conclusive decider.

However, in this instance, I have adduced a large amount of evidence (in my *Cynics and Christian Origins*) to show that Christians in the early centuries, and others too, for whom Cynicism was a live tradition and an important literary influence, discerned, often explicitly, the Cynic resonances of what was by our definition the Q tradition of the teaching of Jesus. I could well have added that, had Q survived, it would most likely have gone on being read alongside the other Gospels as a fifth and impressive *bios* of Jesus the teacher. Its general features would have pointed the way (Downing, here, after Burridge). Its contents certainly continued to do so (Downing).

As I have argued (in my *Cynics and Christian Origins* and else-where), if those using Q had wanted to avoid such a reading in favour, say, of the pervasive eschatology Tuckett proposes, they would have had to make that very much clearer. Instead they left the ascetic teach-ing in particular wide open to be read as Cynic, even after it had been absorbed into Matthew and Luke. I have argued that this latter reading looked so obvious to later readers that it must surely have been obvious from the start, and the compiler(s) of Q must have been content that it should have appeared so. If they intended something different (of the sort Tuckett and others with him prefer) they left it for the latter to guess.

The similarities I adduce, from precise to general, are similarities seen by people much closer to the culture of the time than I or Tuckett and others are who offer his or alternative non-Cynic interpretations. The differences that he and others find so significant between Q and Cynicism go by and large unnoticed by people of the culture in which Cynicism was naturalized. The similarities that he, following Sato, sees with canonical prophets—apart from the handful of direct quotations and allusions—do not appear significant or even noteworthy to the early Christians, immersed though they are in the prophets as forerunners of Christ.[65] With an implicit choice of interpretative key between scriptural prophets or scriptural wisdom, and much else, the key most clearly selected for interpreting the tradition of Jesus' ascetic ethic was that provided by Cynic tradition.

Burridge, as here noted, makes a good case for taking Mark as a Life. But that (as we have argued for Q) is not the only model that warrants consideration. There are features of Mark that do not often appear in surviving Lives but that nonetheless demand attention, which is accorded in the next two chapters.

65. Tuckett ended his critique of various suggestions as to 'a Cynic Q' by proposing instead the parallels adduced with the canonical prophets by M. Sato. I have pointed out elsewhere (n. 21, above) that Sato only claims parallels with one quarter of the text of Q, and have then argued that only half of those parallels are at all close. Sato himself notes the absence from Q of a number of very significant features, particularly 'thus says the Lord' and similar formulae. Some of the parallels for the one eighth (or even one quarter) of Q are assuredly important. The Jewish canon certainly provides the only discernible *literary* sources behind Q. But the Cynic parallels—as close as or closer than all but a handful of direct quotations from the canon—are far more extensive.

Chapter 6

MARKAN INTERCALATION IN CULTURAL CONTEXT*

1. *Intercalation*

There have been a number of monographs and articles discussing 'inter-calation' in Mark's writing. He repeatedly 'sandwiches' one narrative that would seem able to stand on its own within another that would seem entirely coherent without it, 'cutting' sharply from the one to the other and back again: a1-b-a2 Yet, independent as they seem, each narrative, inner and outer, would seem to illuminate the other. Attention has tended to focus on examples where the inner story (b) includes a character or characters who do not appear in the 'framing' episode (a); but other instances are suggested, for instance, where the 'inner' (b) is a monologue, discourse material. The history of research, from Ernst von Dobschütz onwards is summarized by others (and I have not pursued it myself). I am largely persuaded by Tom Shepherd, 'The Narrative Function of Markan Intercalation', but accept some critical comments from Geest van Oyen.[1]

Where earlier commentators have discerned simply (but still significantly) a device to engage and maintain interest, more recent ones find it used to emphasize important theological themes: for instance, faith, witness, judgment, apostasy.[2]

* Also to appear in G.J. Brooke (ed.), *Narrativity and the Bible* (Leuven: Peeters); included here by kind permission; papers from the 1996 Manchester–Lausanne Colloquium.

1. T. Shepherd, 'The Narrative Function of Markan Intercalation', *NTS* 41.4 (1995) pp. 522-40; G. van Oyen, 'Intercalation and Irony in the Gospel of Mark', in F. van Segbroeck *et al.* (eds.), *The Four Gospels 1992: Festschrift Frans Neirynck* (3 vols.; BETL, 100; Leuven: Peeters, 1992), II, pp. 949-74.

2. J.R. Edwards, 'Markan Sandwiches: The Significance of Interpolations in Markan Narratives', *NovT* 31.3 (1989), pp. 193-216 (216); as noted with apparent agreement by van Oyen, 'Intercalation', p. 962; cf. Shepherd, 'Narrative Function',

Most of the authors I have read seem content to restrict their discussion of the narrative function and force of this phenomenon to its appearance in Mark. James R. Edwards does call attention to instances of 'flashback' in Homer that 'interrupt' a narrative; but only Mk 6.14-29, the death of the Baptist, seems at all analogous. In 2 Maccabees, vv. 8.30-33 seem to disrupt the main sequence of the battle with Nicanor, 8.23-36; but Edwards cannot discern there any of the kinds of interconnection that most now perceive in the Markan examples. He has more confidence in proposing the discourse material of Hosea 2 within the narrative of chs. 1 and 3; or Nathan's dialogue with David, within 2 Sam. 11.1–12.25. However, he then points out that here, too, there is an important difference, the inner matter is in each case an intentional comment on the flanking narrative, whereas in Mark this is true only of 4.1-20 (which others, of course, often exclude from their lists); and himself concludes, 'We are thus left to examine Mark's material on its own'.[3] My main concern in what follows is to see whether analogies to this procedure of Mark's may be found elsewhere in the available literature of Mediterranean late antiquity.

Of course, it is not impossible that Mark may have been very innovative; but at least it would seem obvious that we should look further for possible precedents. If recent commentators are right, that this is a frequent and significant device in Mark's construction of his narrative, but one for which there is no indication that his lector is expected to provide any explanation (there is no 'let the reader understand' inserted at these points), then it would seem likely that Mark expected the hearers to be equiped to appreciate the device.

Other studies over the past 15 years or so, often picking up much older ones, would at least tend to encourage such a search. Strong arguments have been advanced against concluding that Mark (and the other Gospels) were in any strong sense *sui generis*; we may note in particular Richard Burridge's *What are the Gospels?*[4] Vernon Robbins has argued cogently that Mark will have learned his 'three-step progres-

---

p. 540, 'secrecy and revelation, life and death, cleansing and cursing, poverty and riches, suffering and resurrection'.

3. Edwards, 'Markan Sandwiches', p. 203; as noted with apparent agreement by van Oyen, 'Intercalation', p. 961 n. 58.

4. Burridge, *What are the Gospels?*, building on while criticizing Talbert, *What is a Gospel?*; Shuler, *A Genre for the Gospels*; cf. the discussion in Chapter 5, above.

sions' 'where he learned to compose in Greek'; and suggests various analogies from Graeco-Roman literature for Mark's portrayal of Jesus with disciples.[5] In his study of the abrupt ending of Mark, J.L. Magness has adduced relevant comparisons from Homer, Virgil, Xenophon and Philostratus.[6] Mark's composition is significantly formed by the Jewish Scriptures, for sure, but by other influences and expectations besides, it would seem.

We need now to define a little more clearly that for which we are seeking analogies. Although a main character or characters (in this case, mostly, Jesus) may act in both stories, there are always characters who (or items that—the fig-tree in ch. 11) appear only in the middle; 14.53-72 (with Peter's Denial) has no protagonists common to both narratives;[7] nor has 6.7-32 (with the death of the Baptist). Although mostly the inner tale fits within the time of the outer one (and both makes and fills a gap there), the two may well in one instance be contemporaneous (14.53-72, again).[8] The two events are located in different even if nearby places. Similar or else very clearly contrasting actions are performed (including ideas enunciated) by contrasting or similar protagonists in each, so that each tale seems to interpret the other, with the resonances drawing our attention to the themes at issue as well as engaging our interest, as indeed the interruption does itself. There is then a dramatic irony evoked, for the author and the hearer obviously understand more than the protagonists can, unable as the latter are to

5.   V.K. Robbins, 'Summons and Outline in Mark: The Three-Step Progression', *NovT* 23.2 (1981), pp. 97-114; *idem, Jesus the Teacher: A Socio-Historical Interpretation of Mark* (Philadelphia: Fortress Press, 1984); cf. his careful consideration of the abusive mockery of a prisoner in the wider Mediterranean world, 'The Reversed Contextualisation of Psalm 22 in the Markan Crucifixion', in van Segbroeck *et al.* (eds.), *The Four Gospels*, pp. 1161-1182; cf. also, F. Neirynck, *Duality in Mark: Contributions to the Study of the Markan Redaction* (BETL, 31; Leuven: Peeters, 1972).

6.   J.L. Magness, *Sense and Absence: Structure and Suspension in the End of Mark's Gospel* (Atlanta: Scholars Press, 1986).

7.   Agreeing with van Oyen, 'Intercalation', p. 967, against Shepherd in his earlier dissertation, *The Definition and Function of Markan Intercalation as Illustrated in a Narrative Analysis of Six Passages* (PhD dissertation, Andrews University 1991), pp. 327-28; but see Shepherd's response, 'Narrative Function', pp. 527-28.

8.   Again agreeing with van Oyen, 'Intercalation', as in n. 7 above.

share in comparing and contrasting the stories that both link and separate them.

We need then to list and label those common features that are widely discerned in the Markan intercalations.

1. Some distinct or entirely distinct character(s) [item(s)] in the middle sequence (b).
2. A distinct even if neighbouring locality for the middle sequence (b).
3. An a1-b-a2 time sequence (even a1-b1-a2-b2, as at Mk 11.25) *or* contemporaneity (but not 'a' complete before 'b' starts).
4. There are similarities and contrasts in characters and actions.
5. We may well discern a dramatic irony—as hearers we know more than do the actors.

Nonetheless, even should we find that some or all of these motifs so described and labelled occur together in other narratives, we might well want to make yet more detailed comparisons, and might still find Mark distinctive, even if perhaps not quite as unprecedented in his intercalations as recent studies of the device may lead us to conclude.

Lives and Histories

We are, however, presented with a somewhat unpromising start. However effective some of today's readers find this aspect of Mark's storytelling, it is well known that Matthew and Luke seem to have been much less impressed. In only one instance from the most frequent list of six do both find Mark's sandwich worth preserving, at Mk 5.21-23 (Jairus's daughter and the woman with a haemorrhage).[9] In two cases neither follows Mark (Mk 3.20-35, Jesus' family and 'Beelzebul'; and Mk 11.11-25, the fig-tree and the Temple). Luke takes one more that Matthew refuses (from Mk 6.7-30), and Matthew two more that Luke refuses. Perhaps their sense for narrative logic and hearers' expectations indicate that Mark was indeed innovating—and not all that acceptably?

We might certainly draw just such a negative conclusion from surveying Josephus' retelling of the Jewish Scriptures. We have seen from

9. Assuming Matthew and Luke both used Mark (a common conclusion for which I have myself offered supporting arguments). Any who suppose Mark used the other two can rephrase, perhaps to read, 'Matthew and Luke only once (or twice) join in offering Mark a ready-made intercalation, and in all use the device only half as often'.

James Edwards that there are not in the Scriptures many intercalations of the sort analysed above for Josephus to deal with; but, as I have myself illustrated elsewhere, Josephus is in fact noticeably concerned to 'improve' the flow of his narrative, either by removing all sorts of items that might seem to interrupt it, or else by reordering them. The people do not return to the Jordan for commemorative stones, they bring them with them; the booty taken from Jericho is described along with Achan's theft and what he took all in one sequence; and so forth.[10] Where possible each event or sequence of events is narrated from start to finish and left there. The 'order' Josephus claims is thematic, one theme at a time, one narrative sequence at a time. And I certainly cannot recall any instance where Josephus himself interrupts a given sequence with a distinct but thematically related incident.

Lucian, in the next century, would seem to indicate much the same attitude to avoidable interruptions, digressions, in a historical narrative, however vivid and interesting in themselves. In a battle the narrator will describe initial deployments and plans in turn and completely; only when battle is joined will he switch attention between the two sides, and then only when the turn of events demands it. Thematic order and clarity seem to be the overriding aim. 'Let the clarity of the writing be limpid, achieved, as I have said, both by the diction and by the inter-connecting of events (*tē sumperiplokē tōn pragmatōn*).' The historian 'will make everything distinct and complete, and when he has finished the first topic he will introduce the second, fastened to it and linked with it like a chain, to avoid breaks and a multiplicity of disjointed narratives'.[11]

I do not claim to have read widely among the historians for this study. However, a brief skim through Dionysius of Halicarnassus and through Thucydides afforded no obvious counter-examples. What we seem to find are strings of individually coherent events arranged in sequences; we may well switch from one sequence to another as we follow different protagonists in turn. But there is nothing here at all like the intercalation discerned in Mark, the cutting from within one apparently self-contained account to another as complete in itself and back again, yet so that each resonates with the other.

Although Mark was clearly not writing history in Lucian's sense of

10. Downing, 'Redaction Criticism'; citing here Josephus, *Ant.* 5.1-33.
11. Lucian, *How to Write History* 28 and 49-50, and 55 (LCL, with slight emendation).

the term, Richard Burridge has cogently described and analysed a wide range of analogies between Mark and the other Gospels on the one hand, and contemporary Lives on the other. Important for the present discussion is the observation that apart from often very brief chronological notes, Lives seem to be made up of anecdotes (with or without utterances), usually arranged topically. As is often pointed out, there is little or no sense of development of character to trace. Instead, character is revealed by individual sayings and incidents.[12] So here the logic of events, an ascribed explanatory chain of cause and effect, is not important, and one thing just seems to happen after another, albeit illuminatingly, as in Mark. We might then expect to find a similar freedom in writers of Lives to intercalate one narrative meaningfully into another. However, Burridge does not include any such phenomenon in his list of possible characteristics of the genre; and a search through ten of Plutarch's *Lives* was not very rewarding.

Between Theseus deciding to take the perilous land route to Athens and the dissuasions of Pitthaeus comes a brief account of Herakles dealing with similar threats; but this is really only an explanatory aside, similar to others before and later, and itself prepares for Theseus's ambition to repeat Herakles's achievements. We may compare a second comparison with Herakles a few chapters later.[13] If we contrast Plutarch's *Romulus* with Dionysius's story, then the single combat with Akron (taken from Livy?) might seem to interrupt the account of the Sabines as a whole marshalling their forces; but the episode may better be read as the first of three campaigns, each more dangerous than the last. It does not 'interrupt' a specific incident.[14] In an account of the feuds in Athens with which Solon had to deal, Plutarch includes a note of a visit from Epimenides of Phaestus; but he is following as his cue the themes of 'pollution' and cleansing arising from the massacre of Kylon and his followers, and that sequence ends before Epimenides arrives. It is really just another thematic aside involving a different character. Perhaps the incident of his friends' insider-dealing within the account of Solon's ultimately succesful cancellation of debts might at first sight seem a slightly stronger example; yet it clearly presupposes

---

12. Burridge, *What are the Gospels?*, p. 121, citing Aristotle, *Rhetoric* 1.9.33, 1367b; but cf. also Plutarch, *Alexander* 1.2.

13. Plutarch, *Theseus* 6.4-6 and 11.1–12.1.

14. Plutarch, *Romulus* 16–17 and Livy, *History* 1.10 with Dionysius of Halicarnassus, *Roman Antiquities* 2.32-34.

the start of the main account, which Markan intercalations do not.[15]

Much more to the point is the exchange with Aesop in the middle of the narrative of Croesus's encounter with Solon. Solon has refused to be dazzled by Croesus's opulence, and has warned that none can be adjudged happy until their life is complete.

> When he had said this, Solon departed, leaving Croesus vexed, but none the wiser for it. Now it so happened that Aesop, the writer of fables, was in Sardis, having been summoned there by Croesus, and receiving much honour at his hands. He was distressed that Solon met with no kindly treatment, and said to him by way of advice, 'O Solon, our converse with kings should be either as rare or as pleasing as is possible.' 'No, indeed!' said Solon, 'but either as rare or as beneficial as possible.' At this time, then, Croesus held Solon in a contempt like this, but afterwards, when he encountered Cyrus...[he acknowledged the truth of what Solon had said, invoked Solon by name; and this occasioned his release from death by fire...].[16]

We here at last do have (1) a distinct character (Aesop); (2) a different but nearby location (Solon has left Croesus before he meets Aesop); (3) an a1-b-a2 time-sequence; (4) a contrast (the worldly wise Aesop honoured by Croesus admires the still wiser Solon whom Croesus fails at the time to honour); and perhaps there is (5) irony (we know, or will discover, that Croesus comes to acknowledge Solon and find his unflattering wisdom as beneficial as Solon had insisted in his counter to Aesop's conformist prudence).

Not quite so striking is an episode in the *Publicola*: the 'miraculous' delivery of Tarquin's terracotta chariot to Rome from Veii interrupts the tale of the consecration of the temple for which it was originally intended, and has no link with the completion of the temple's dedication by Horatius in the place of Publicola. It is difficult, though, to discern any ironic (or other) comment on the main story, the consecration as such.[17] Also, into his account of the mixed reception accorded Cicero when exiled by Clodius, Plutarch inserts a note of an earthquake and the response of local soothsayers; but the theme of exile remains continuous throughout.[18]

A secondary source, Chares, presents Plutarch with a tale of yet

15. Plutarch, *Solon* 12.1–13.1; 15.3–16.3.
16. Plutarch, *Solon* 28.1 within 27–28 (LCL).
17. Plutarch, *Publicola* 13-14.
18. Plutarch, *Cicero* 32.4.

another brave solo exploit of Alexander against Arab foes, and this is recounted in the midst of the siege of Tyre, with no other link but the implicit relative proximity of the sets of adversaries. So we have again (1) some distinct characters (the Arabs, and Lysimachus, the elderly tutor protected); (2) a distinct geographical situation; (3) an a1-b-a2 time sequence. We should perhaps also note something of a contrast (4) (as elsewhere in this Life) between Alexander the powerful leader for whom others fight, and Alexander the audacious individual at risk in the midst of the fray. Just possibly there is also an intended irony (5) in the comparison between the calculating general and the impetuous young man, yet if so it is very understated; much more obvious is Plutarch's unqualified admiration for Alexander's all-round greatness.[19]

As announced at the outset, the results of this investigation of ten of Plutarch's *Lives* are not very encouraging.[20] A scholarly writer such as Plutarch is obviously able to create occasional intercalations here of a sort that share some features with those in Mark; but just as clearly they are far fewer proportionately. In both writers' work the interruptions may well seem designed to enhance the hearers' interest as well as emphasize a point; but whereas in Mark suspense is created by the break in the flow of the outer tale, in Plutarch at best a rather lengthy sequence may in this way be marginally enlivened. It is worth looking a little further, a little wider, for possible analogies for Mark's practice, both in kind and in frequency.

Theatre and Discourse

One further possibility is the theatre, and especially comedy. Unfortunately we seem not to have preserved for us any examples of what would have been certainly available for Mark and his contemporaries, any extended account of popular mimes in particular. It seems that the surviving (Latin) plays of Plautus and Terence, derived extensively from the Greek works of Menander, seem only to have been read, not performed, in the first century CE. However, it is worth noting the extent to which dramatic (and comic) effects are produced by these two playwrights precisely by interrupting one sequence of events with an-

---

19. Plutarch, *Alexander* 24.10-14 within 24.1–25.3; cf. the apologia for Alexander as self-disciplined, *Alexander* 23, and even more, *de alexandri magni fortuna aut virtute*.

20. In addition to those cited in the text, *Lycurgus, Numa, Demosthenes* and *Caesar* were scanned.

other, so that the outcome of the first remains for the time being unsure—and the 'intervening' actions of fresh, or remaining and fresh actors, suggest further possibilities to the audience. We are told that the long and narrow Roman stage with two or three house-fronts, and perhaps an intervening alleyway readily allowed for such changes of focus.[21] In Plautus's *The Two Bacchides*, for instance, a young man finds a girl who is sought by a friend of his, but is persuaded by her sister to pretend to court her, herself, so as to protect her from an unwanted suitor in whose power she is; but before this can happen, the young man's tutor and the slave of the girl's more welcome suitor see parts of the action and of course misinterpret it, while yet other encounters complicate their responses.[22] Such complications become even more convoluted in some of the plays of Terence. The Markan intercalations are certainly 'dramatic' in a theatrical sense; it must remain possible, but no more, that these conventions, or similar stage devices contemporary with Mark, could have had some influence on Mark's way of telling his stories.

Yet another genre worth considering, and one perhaps having rather more in common with Mark, is the kind of discourse storytelling with which Lucian entertained his audiences. In his *True Story* Lucian certainly strings amazing episodes together rather as Mark seems to, with no causal link between one and the next.[23] Yet quite otherwise than in Mark, there appear to be no structural devices either, no anticipations of later events, nor any allusions to those that have gone before; and neither do we seem to find here anything like Mark's 'sandwiches'.

However, the main narrative of *Lucius or the Ass* (quite likely an abbreviation of a longer tale by Lucian himself) and the body of the often very similar tale from Lucius Apuleius, *The Golden Ass*, do both

21. G.E. Duckworth (ed.), *The Complete Roman Drama* (2 vols.; New York: Random House, 1942), pp. xxv-xxvi, xxix. On Mark and the theatre, compare Beavis, *Mark's Audience*, pp. 31-35. However, intercalation is not discussed.

22. Plautus, *The Two Bacchides* (trans. E.H. Sugden) in Duckworth (ed.), *Roman Drama*, I, pp. 158-221.

23. Cf. the brief note on the novels and Mark in Berger, *Formgeschichte*, p. 369. Similarities include: 'Reihung von Szenen und Episoden, kaum komplexe und gleichzeitige Handlungen (in den Evv nur in der Passionsgeschichte). Die kurzen Szenen werden oft durch das Mittel der Reise aneinandergereiht.' ('A succession of scenes and episodes with only the simplest plot and time-sequence [the latter, in the Gospels, only in the Passion narratives]. The short scenes are often linked together by means of a journey.')

comprise what amounts to a series of 'interruptions' of a sort, frustrations of the quest for the roses that will turn the disgraceful ass into a proper human being. Apuleius's version also contains three quite unrelated tales introduced by other protagonists (Aristomenes, Thelyphron, the brigands' cook); another (of Thrasyllus) is told as a self-contained narrative by a fresh narrator, though with a link to the ass's fortunes at the end; and yet a fifth (the murderous step-mother) is told by the ass, but has no bearing on his lot. Though none of these 'intercalations' are at all like Mark's in detail (they do not cut from one otherwise self-contained account of an incident to a second and then cut back again), it still seems quite clear that simply interrupting a main narrative with lesser and often quite independent ones is a device readily available to storytellers in late antiquity.

In his *The Carousal*, however, Lucian does include just one 'intercalation' that more closely resembles our Markan ones. 'Lucinus' introduces us to a rowdy Cynic gatecrasher called Alcidamus, and tells us that the climax of the tale will involve a drinking bowl the host has ordered to try to pacify the nuisance. Always postponing the climax, Lucian proceeds to tell of disputes among other guests as tension mounts, but also inserts a quite self-contained story from a further guest, a physician, who has just escaped from a crazed patient. So here we have (1) one distinct character (the patient), as well as the physician who only reappears very much later; (2) a house elsewhere in the same town; (3) the encounter that had taken place at the time at which the other guests were arriving (contemporaneity); and (4-5) the violence the physician had escaped ironically both echoes a fight he has just missed and anticipates the fracas with which the dialogue ends, as well as contrasting with the apparent peace of the supper when the delayed guest arrives. Yet even so, the physician and his tale come at the end of one incident and before the next, without splitting any.[24]

Romances

The closest analogies that I can discern both to the frequency, the kind and the effect of the Markan intercalations are to be found in the Hellenistic romances. There are still very significant differences; but the similarities seem worth considering.[25]

---

24. Lucian, *Carousal* 20.
25. I could find only one discussion of intercalation in R.F. Hock, J.B. Chance and J. Perkins (eds.), *Ancient Fiction and Early Christian Narrative* (Atlanta:

The romances have two main actors who are newly wed or about to wed or very likely to wed, only to be separated as they journey through the east Mediterranean world, suffering various perils before finally being reunited. Mark, obviously, has only the one main character, and there is no amorous interest discernible.

Attention is engaged and maintained in the romances, and their themes of devotion and loyalty, misfortune and suffering are emphasized by cutting between the two main protagonists, but also from them to subordinate characters and back again. It is this cutting between incomplete scenes that seems to me to afford the closest analogy in effect to the Markan intercalations.[26]

So, early in Chariton's *Chaereas and Callirhoe*, we cut from Callirhoe's tomb to the piratical Theron who has been watching the costly preparations, and then back to Callirhoe coming out of a coma, back again to Theron who is all the while approaching, and yet again to Callirhoe hearing the robbers breaking in.[27] This illustrates something of the rapidity of the cross-cutting (compare Mk 11.11-25). Had he wanted to, Chariton could have offered a much simpler narrative: we could have stayed with the comatose girl until a tomb-robber arrived (compare, in fact, Callirhoe's own account, 2.5).[28] The analogy is still only partial, though, for these incidents in the novel are interrelated in the narrative, rather than independent but resonating, as in Mark.

We then spend quite a long time with Callirhoe illegally sold to be a slave, cutting to and fro between her installed in a country house with Dionysius its owner, until the ceremony of her wedding to him, when we cut abruptly over to Chaereas, and a series of events contemporary

Scholars Press, 1998)—W.T. Shiner, in his 'Creating Plot in Episodic Narratives: *The Life of Aesop* and the Gospel of Mark', pp. 163-92 (172-73): Mark's is an 'adaptation of the technique' of simple retardation. The data from the romances seems to have been overlooked.

26. The commentators I have read do not seem to find this feature particularly remarkable. G. Anderson, in his *Ancient Fiction: The Novel in the Graeco-Roman World* (London: Croom Helm, 1984), p. 123, notes 'Achilles and Longus both have plots in which hero and heroine move from crisis to crisis, with one not usually solved before the next can begin', cf. p. 125, 'a "Jack and Jill" plot', but he seems to argue as though this intertwining were only incidental, p. 31.

27. Chariton, *Chaereas and Callirhoe* 1.6-9, first century CE/BCE (trans. B.P. Reardon), in *idem* (ed.), *Collected Ancient Greek Novels* (Berkeley: University of California Press, 1989), pp. 17-128.

28. And that in Xenophon's *Ephesian Tale* 3.8.

with the foregoing but that have no bearing on the wedding as such at all. We leave Chaereas himself now enslaved and in bonds, and return abruptly to Callirhoe, who dreams of him in chains. But while their circumstances display similarities and contrasts (we cut ironically from Callirhoe holding a requiem for Chaereas to Chaereas about to be crucified), and are linked through third parties, and through dreams and through reports received (true and false), they run in parallel with no direct connections, even—or especially—when they are geographically close. (There is one exception, when the two do encounter each other at the Persian court; but they meet only to be separated yet again.) Each series has its own (fictional) causal logic, but each narrative interrupts the other sequence with distinct characters and events engaged in variations on common themes. The scale is much larger than Mark's; many of the formal characteristics are similar.[29]

Xenophon of Ephesus's *An Ephesian Tale* is constructed in a very similar way, though more lurid.[30] 'Meanwhile' is probably as frequent as is 'immediately' in Mark; the cutting from one strand to another is very frequent. 'Meanwhile (1) Habrocomes's tutor…' drowns nearby (2) while trying to rejoin his kidnapped charge: a quite separate incident sandwiched (3: a1-b-a2) within the account of Corymbus's relationship with young Habrocomes, but affording a comparison and a contrast between tutorly and erotic attachment (4). From 2.9 we mostly switch in turn between the plight of Habrocomes and his young bride, Anthia; we leave him in prison to find Anthia given in spite to a goatherd who in fact respects her, and then back to her husband in gaol. As soon as Anthia is captured by Hippothous we cut back to Habrocomes going to seach for her and then immediately return to Anthia in fresh peril from her new captors. She is rescued, only to face a forced marriage; 'meanwhile' Habrocomes meets up with Hippothous, before we return to the wedding. Anthia, like Callirhoe, is entombed in a coma and then also captured by pirates; between their decision to sell her and her actual sale Habrocomes hears the story of her death and of the grave-robbers. Later, leaving Anthia thrown to the dogs we find Habrocomes meeting Aegialeus, a kindly fishermen, and we hear the latter's life story in brief; it has no link with either strand of the main story, apart from

29. We may note again, in passing, that the incognito of the protagonists, and recognition scenes, as in Mark, are also important motifs.

30. Xenophon, *Ephesian Tale*, 2nd century CE(?) (trans. G. Anderson, in B.P. Reardon, *Greek Novels*, pp. 125-69).

affording a further reminder of marital devotion; but only then do we see Anthia emerge from her peril. (We also cut from time to time to the fate of the faithful slaves of the couple who return at the end to help reunite them in prosperity.)

The cuts to and fro are not quite as frequent in Achilles Tatius's novel *Leucippe and Clitophon*, as it is narrated by Kleitophon himself, the male of the pair; but interruptions still occur, as he gathers from others (or simply 'knows') what is or has been happening elsewhere, and to Leukippe in particular.[31] The episode of Charikles, boy-lover of Kleitophon's cousin and confidant, Kleinias, affords an opportunity for an early disquisition on erotic arousal, homosexual and heterosexual; but the account of Charikles's death as Kleinias's lesson in love continues, 'suddenly' intrudes (1.12) without any direct effect on the action that follows: Kleitophon goes straight from the funeral to practice what he has been told. The incident may well, however, be meant to presage the perils that will beset the young lovers. We switch from a delay to an arranged wedding with the wrong woman, step-sister Kalligone, to Kallisthenes's prior plot to kidnap her, and back to the resumed nuptials; and then comes the kidnapping itself. Kleitophon's campaign of seduction is simply prolonged by some interplay between a compliant servant, Satyros, and a suspicious domestic, Gnat. The lovers flee, the happy start of their sea-voyage divided from the storm that follows by a meeting with a stranger, Menelaos, who occasions a second monologue on homosexual and heterosexual love. The lovers' recovery after shipwreck is interrupted by a lengthy description of a temple mural of Andromeda. They are parted, then reunited: but this is interrupted by a flashback to events involving Satyros and Menelaos, and the reported arrival of a phoenix. Achilles Tatius also intrudes into his narrative other descriptive passages, *ekphraseis*, though these do set the mood[32] (pictures, gardens, the origins of wine, a dress, a dye-stuff, water stories, philosophical psychology, and the like). By book six it is time for a parting that Kleitophon assumes is final, and then finds is not, and from this point we cut constantly between him and Leukippe, with as frequent 'meanwhiles' as in Xenophon (without being told till 8.15 how the narrator knows what is happening to Leukippe in his absence).[33] (It

31. Achilles Tatius, *Leucippe and Clitophon* ('third quarter of the second century' CE [trans. J.J. Winkler], in Reardon, *Greek Novels*, pp. 170-284).

32. T. Hägg, *The Novel in Antiquity* (ET; Oxford: Basil Blackwell, 1983), p. 48.

33. Longus, *Daphnis and Chloe*, second century CE (simpler, with two main

is perhaps worth noting our further evidence for early Christian awareness of the romance genre, in *Paul and Thecla*, in the Clementine
Recognitions, and in other apocryphal *Acts*.)[34]

Conclusions

Some of our New Testament commentators have insisted that intercalation in Mark is more than a device to engage and hold interest, it
also focuses our attention on important themes, while the element of
irony enhances our involvement. Can we discern any similar intention
or effect in the other writings we have here briefly surveyed? Certainly
themes of constancy in captivity and suffering, of loyalty and betrayal,
and suchlike, are common among them,[35] and are emphasized by the
cutting to and fro between the characters. But further, many of the
romances make explicit reference to a hidden divine providence, and
each story encourages the hope that things will come out well in the end
for those who display constancy and loyalty. More than that, the ironies
in the narratives encourage the hearer to seek for and perceive meaning—and even purpose—in what the characters can only experience as
coincidence. Life is not, perhaps, just one damn thing after another, for
the novelists any more than for Mark. Simply that.

As was insisted at the outset of this discussion of the romances, there
is still no very close analogy with Mark. In the entire survey we have
noted only a few 'intercalations' that include the first four features we
discerned, and even fewer with all five. We have to allow still that
Mark's predilection for this device may have been idiosyncratic,
although the device as such is clearly not his invention.

But furthermore, it seems to me that we need to allow for the possibility that Mark had learned the narrative value of cutting from the middle of one scene to another and back, from the contemporary stage,
perhaps, but more likely from the widespread popular storytelling of
which the romances are simply our few remaining survivals, and that

characters), and Heliodorus's probably much later *An Ethiopian Story* (much more
complex) both maintain this system of breaking an account involving one character
with (part of) a tale of another.

34. Again, cf. Hock, Chance and Perkins (eds.), *Ancient Fiction*, for a survey of
many other resonances; esp. R.I. Pervo, 'A Nihilist Fabula: Introducing the *Life of
Aesop*', pp. 77-120.

35. Compare P.J.J. Botha, 'Mark's Story of Jesus and the Search for Virtue', in
Porter and Olbricht (eds.), *The Rhetorical Analysis of Scripture*, pp. 156-84.

there is a fair chance that his hearers would be prepared to respond to it through their familiarity with the storytellers' art. What may have been original could be Mark's practice of deploying such cutting quite frequently in a Life of one individual, imposing it on a number of the items of the (oral) traditions he shared; and very effectively. It is, of course, only one intertextual strand, not the only sign of Mark's awareness of stories circulating in the world around him. Tales told about Romulus form our next topic.

Chapter 7

A RIVAL TO ROMULUS

1. *Introduction*

In the previous chapter we saw Mark apparently deploying a repeated narrative structure—intercalation—with which he and his audience(s) may well have been familiar; on the evidence available, most likely from an acquaintance with 'romantic' storytelling. We also noted in passing Vernon Robbins's earlier study of 'three-step progressions' in Mark. Robbins points us to elements such as the passion predictions, but also the contexts in which they are placed, themselves marking the structure of the Gospel as a whole: yet another narrative device that Mark seems to have acquired from his Graeco-Roman cultural environment (as instanced here by Xenophon's *Memorabilia* in particular).[1]

This investigation takes it for granted that the basic content of Mark's narrative is drawn from the traditions of his young Christian communities, and that the literary 'palette' from which Mark draws extra colours for his telling of his story is for the most part provided by the Jewish Scriptures as perhaps already deployed in the tradition (for instance, in the passion narrative). But, it will be argued, these strands did not always on their own determine the inclusion, position, shape or detail of all the elements of Mark's story. At times, and especially in the passion narrative itself, further formative stimulus may have been provided by the non-Jewish Graeco-Roman world, and especially by

---

1. Robbins, *Jesus the Teacher*, pp. 53-73. For comparisons with the romances, C. Hedrick, 'Representing Prayer in Mark and in Chariton's *Chaereas and Callirhoe*', *PRS* 22.3 (1995), pp. 239-57; and Hock, Chance and Perkins (eds.), *Ancient Fiction*, esp. D.R. MacDonald, 'Secrecy and Recognition in the Odyssey and Mark: Where Wrede went Wrong', pp. 139-53; and Shiner, 'Creating Plot in Episodic Narratives', pp. 154-85.

the rival narrative traditions of imperial Rome: more threads for Mark's intertexture.[2]

Other studies of varying lengths also try to set Mark in this wider cultural context,[3] but without detailed comparison with individual contemporary narratives or traditonal narrative clusters (and those who attempt to analyse Mark's narrative as such tend to treat it as a self-contained 'world' for today's readers).[4] In his *What are the Gospels?* R. Burridge (following P.L. Shuler, and noting an earlier argument of mine), briefly considers common typical motifs, but attends to no specific comparable incidents, let alone sequences of them.[5] M.A. Beavis notes some very general analyses of Mark in terms of Graeco-Roman tragedies, but, again, without close comparisons. She also, but still only in passing, ventures that 'Mark and the Greek romances share certain themes and motifs: mistaken identities, dangerous sea-voyages, forensic debates, religious and didactic elements, foiled executions'.[6] We shall return to a consideration of motifs, briefly, in what follows.

2.   The issue is more often raised in discussion of Revelation, but those discussions indicate the likely extent of awareness of imperial ideology among early Christians; cf. e.g., P. Barnett, 'Polemical Parallelism: Some Further Reflections on the Apocalypse', *JSNT* 35 (1989), pp. 111-20; A. Brent, 'John as Theologos: The Imperial Mysteries and the Apocalypse', *JSNT* 75 (1999), pp. 103-14.

3.   E.g. Beavis, *Mark's Audience*; see further below. Other studies I have noted include W.T. Shiner, *Follow Me! Disciples in Markan Rhetoric* (SBLDS, 145; Atlanta: Scholars Press, 1995); R.L. Merritt, 'Jesus Barabbas and the Paschal Pardon', *JBL* 104.1 (1985), pp. 57-68. C. Myers, *Binding the Strong Man: A Political Reading of Mark's Story of Jesus* (Maryknoll, NY: Orbis Books, 1988), stresses the Roman context but ignores the imperial ideology.

4.   Cf. D. Rhoads and D. Michie, *Mark as Story: An Introduction to the Narrative of a Gospel* (Philadelphia: Fortress Press, 1982); E. Best, *Mark: The Gospel as Story* (Edinburgh: T. & T. Clark, 1983). R.H. Gundry, *Mark: A Commentary on his Apology for the Cross* (Grand Rapids: Eerdmans, 1993), leads us to expect close attention to original audiences, Introduction, passim), but echoes that they might pick up are seldom noted; compare also B. van Iersel, *Mark: A Reader-Response Commentary* (JSNTSup, 164; Sheffield: Sheffield Academic Press 1998), which sets the work's origins in Rome, offers pages on 'the foreknowledge of the Roman Readers' (ch. 2, pp. 30-57), but also ignores the imperial ideology.

5.   Burridge, *What are the Gospels?*, pp. 94-95, 122-23, 207-209; cf. Shuler, *A Genre for the Gospels*; and Downing, 'Contemporary Analogies'; C. Bryan, *A Preface to Mark*, pp. 12-14.

6.   Beavis, *Mark's Audience*, pp. 31-37, citing p. 36. What in Mark counts as a 'foiled execution' is not made clear.

Mark's passion narrative has been compared in very general terms with Jewish accounts of martyrs, and with 2 Macc. 6.18–7.42, and *4 Maccabees* 5–17 as the prime examples, but also with the later *Acts of the Pagan Martyrs*.[7] Individual motifs are significantly similar (for instance, the atoning effect expected from the Jewish martyrs' deaths),[8] but much is very different. The martyrologies focus on trials and the Jewish ones also on death agony, with extended speeches, while Mark has much more incident, apparently 'unparalleled', but Jesus on trial quite laconic and his death surprisingly soon over. The occasional modern explicit comparison with Socrates is usually framed to afford a contrast, for Jesus in Gethsemane and then crying out in abandonment on the cross does not go forward with calm nobility, as Celsus disparagingly noted.[9] The many examples of *exitus* ('departure, ending') *teleutē* ('ending, death'), instanced by A.Y. Collins are certainly of interest, and relevant; but none present themselves to her as so close to Mark as to deserve detailed comparison; and any such concentration on trial (or arrest and trial) and death (if narrated) together with speeches, can make us miss other elements in Mark's total narrative that could well have seemed significant to early listeners. Collins accepts anyway that 'From the point of view of genre, Mark altered the narrative of the *teleutē* of Jesus in several significant ways', while still insisting that the pre-Markan passion narrative she discerns belonged to that genus.[10]

7. Accepting that the term 'martyr' as such, for one witnessing faithfully up to and including death is a later Christian coinage (*Martyrdom of Polycarp*). See, for instance, H.A. Musirillo, *The Acts of the Pagan Martyrs* (Oxford: Clarendon Press, 1954); H. Hendrickx, *The Passion Narratives of the Synoptic Gospels* (London: Geoffrey Chapman, 1977); Mack, *A Myth of Innocence*, pp. 249-68; A.Y. Collins, 'The Genre of the Passion Narrative', *ST* 47 (1993), pp. 3-28.

8. See the study by my brother, J. Downing, 'Jesus and Martyrdom', *JTS* NS 14.2 (1963), pp. 279-93, comparing Mk 10.45 with 2 Macc. 7.37-38; *4 Macc.* 9.23-24, among other passages.

9. Origen, *Contra Celsum* 2.24; R.E. Brown, *The Death of the Messiah* (2 vols.; London: Geoffrey Chapman, 1994), I, pp. 217-18 and notes. This is not to ignore Jesus' final acceptance of the 'cup', Mk 14.36, nor to exclude the possibility that Mark expected his audience to imagine Jesus reciting all of Psalm 22; yet even so there is a contrast with Socrates as usually portrayed; contra Collins, *The Genre*, p. 14; cf. *eadem*, 'From Noble Death to Crucified Messiah', *NTS* 40.4 (1994), pp. 481-86; *eadem*, 'Finding Meaning in the Death of Jesus', *JR* 78 (1998), pp. 173-92 (181). Luke's Jesus is perhaps a little closer to Socrates (and his Paul still closer—see Alexander, 'Acts and Ancient Intellectual Biography', pp. 57-63).

10. Collins, *The Genre*, pp. 18 and 20.

Confronting Rome

Trials and executions involve us in local and imperial administration and political ideology, and the importance of this wider context for early Christianity as a whole has been argued by, among others, D. Georgi and H. Koester, demonstrating the challenge to contemporary Jewish and Christian beliefs and expectations of 'imperial realized eschatology' as set out by Roman poets such as Virgil (*Fourth Eclogue*) and Horace (various *Odes*, and the *Carmen Saeculare*; one might add the opening of Philo of Alexandria's *De Legatione*), and point to the response in, for example, the Jewish and Christian *Sibylline Oracles* and in Revelation.[11] As Koester explains, 'Once Augustan Rome had adopted these eschatological and utopian ideals and domesticated them for its own purposes, every movement of liberation would naturally confront the state-sponsored realized eschatology of the Caesars'.[12]

One episode in particular in the Markan passion has been accorded a detailed Graeco-Roman political setting (if others have, they have so far escaped my notice). P.B. Duff has compared Mark's entry of Jesus into Jerusalem with 'the advent' of a king-emperor. 'It is our suggestion that the text...draws its readers' [better, hearers'] attention to their knowledge and/or experience of typical Greco-Roman entrance processions in order to highlight [its] allusions to the divine warrior [of Zech. 14]'.[13] Citing various examples, Duff explains, 'The political entrance processions of the Greco-Roman world were an outgrowth of Greek epiphany processions'.[14] The entering ruler or conqueror, accoutred and attended to emphasize his power and authority is met at the gates and escorted in with hymns and/or acclamations, and brought to a central temple to offer sacrifice—and so seal his possession of the city. A Roman triumph for a

11. D. Georgi, 'Who is the True Prophet?', in G.W.E. Nickelsburg and G.W. MacRae (eds.), *Christians among Jews and Gentiles: Essays in Honor of Krister Stendahl* (Philadelphia: Fortress Press, 1986), pp. 100-126; H. Koester, 'Jesus the Victim', *JBL* 111.1 (1992), pp. 3-15; *idem*, 'The Memory of Jesus' Death and the Worship of the Risen Lord', *HTR* 91.4 (1998), pp. 335-50; see also n. 2 above.

12. Koester, 'Jesus the Victim', p. 10.

13. P.B. Duff, 'The March of the Divine Warrior and the Advent of the Greco-Roman King: Mark's Account of Jesus' Entry into Jerusalem', *JBL* 111.1 (1992), pp. 55-71, citing p. 56.

14. Duff, 'The March', p. 59, citing O. Nussbaum, 'Geleit', *RAC* 9 (1969), pp. 963-78 (965).

returning conqueror has much in common—procession, hymns, acclamations, sacrifice and a feast in the temple; and the entry with his army and the sharing of a feast there emphasize the victor's power for the moment in the city (although he is to be reminded he is still a 'mere human'). Echoing these rituals, and besides more or less clear allusions to Zechariah 14, Mark thus has as additional features: Jesus escorted by disciples and followers, accompanied by acclamations, ceremoniously honoured by being seated on others' clothing (branches perhaps constituting a further local symbol); and so Jesus (but a day later) takes over the Temple (momentarily). Yet, Duff himself then argues, Mark's narrative shows Jesus not taking possession of the Temple for renewed use but rather to 'disqualify' it and abandon it to future destruction.

My point for now is to emphasize that a knowledge of ritualized Graeco-Roman imperial ideology seems to be taken for granted in the account as presented, to the extent of enabling an ironic variant (so, Duff). This perception then tallies, of course, with other clear reminders that Mark's hearers will have been very much aware of the power of Rome and its puppets. Mark begins with 'the beginning of the gospel about Jesus Christ, Son of God'. Stanley Porter commented a while ago,

> What has been overlooked is how the use of 'gospel' introduces a controlling Markan theme, carried forward by the absolute use of the word on the lips of Jesus…it helps to reinforce the Markan emphasis upon Jesus as the son of God, introduced at 1.1, developed in the Gospel, and explicitly reiterated by the Roman centurion at Jesus' death in 15.39. The conjunction of the two concepts of 'good news' and 'son of God' is also found in Hellenistic inscriptions with reference to Caesar as son of God…at least it provides evidence for one who consciously crafts his Gospel in terms of religious and political terminology of the day, replacing Caesar with the genuine son of God, Jesus Christ.[15]

With these points in mind it is worth looking to see whether further echoes (incidental, positive, ironic, polemical) of Roman imperial ideology figure in Mark's narrative. Be it said, this search does not necessitate a Roman setting for the composition of Mark, for some knowledge of Roman tradition can by now be taken for granted at least among

---

15. S.E. Porter, 'Literary Approaches to the New Testament: From Formalism to Deconstruction and Back', in S.E. Porter and D. Tombs (eds.), *Approaches to New Testament Study* (JSNTSup, 120; Sheffield: Sheffield Academic Press, 1995), pp. 77-129, quoting from p. 122. Porter is arguing for literary and historical interpretation to be undertaken together.

Greek speakers in all the centres proposed for the Gospel.

The Roman imperial ideology had by the first century itself gathered items from other sources—in particular, legends of Herakles/Hercules, and together with versions of that figure, echoes of Alexander the Great but also Cyrus, and others.[16] There are individual motifs from these wider fields that may be significant here in Mark (for instance, Jesus like Heracles tested in the wilderness).[17] But, as the title of this piece indicates, I am primarily proposing a significant comparison and contrast between Jesus, his people and their city of Jerusalem on the one hand, and Romulus and his people and Rome on the other, and our concentration is most fruitfully focused on the passion narrative. The account will take Plutarch's *Romulus* as its basis, and it is to the latter that the simple references in brackets will refer.[18] Other references will be given in the footnotes. Plutarch was writing later than Mark, of course, but much of Plutarch's account occurs also in Dionysius of Halicarnassus's apologetic for Rome, his *Roman Antiquities*, from around the beginning of the Common Era, and much also appears in other sources, as noted below; and still further sources are discussed by Plutarch and by Dionysius. We have no way of knowing what variants would be available to Mark and his communities, but from the matter surveyed so far we seem assured that some were.

Prior to the passion, be it said, we seem at best to find only individual motifs, and most of these are as readily instanced in other narratives. However, 'ominous' birds are significant in both cases: a dove for Jesus, eagles for Romulus and Remus (an eagle picks out Tarquin I by landing on his head).[19] Jesus spends time with wild beasts, Romulus and Remus with birds of prey and wild beasts (including the she-wolf; 7.6).[20] We the listeners to the recitation (but not the actors in each story) know that Romulus and Remus are of divine origin, as is Jesus, although both they and he have a lowly upbringing, suffering discord in the family (while responding quite differently; 3–7).[21] Recognition in

16. Cf., e.g., Dio of Prusa's four kingship *Discourses* 1–4; Plutarch, *Romulus* 5 and 9; Dionysius of Halicarnassus, *Roman Antiquities* 1.34-36, 38-44; 2.1.4.

17. Dio, *Discourse* 1.66.

18. Plutarch, *Romulus*, in *Plutarch's Parallel Lives* I (trans. B. Perrin; LCL; London: Heinemann; Cambridge, MA: Harvard University Press, 1914).

19. Dionysius, *Roman Antiquities* 1.86; cf. 3.47.3.

20. Dionysius, *Roman Antiquities* 1.79.6-8.

21. Cf. Plutarch, *Comparison of Theseus and Romulus* 4.1; Dionysius *Roman*

each case depends on divine initiative (7.4).[22] The founding of Rome begins with grief, repentance and the expiation of guilt; the inception of Jesus' ministry with a message of repentance and forgiveness. People do realize early that Romulus is born to command (6.2), just as Jesus' authority is soon recognized (Mk 1.16-20, 27—but see below), and fame follows rapidly in both accounts, as both gather adherents, and a riff-raff at that (6.2; 7.1; 9.3).[23] The careers of neither were lacking 'great marvels' (8.7).[24] Among Romulus's most signficant acts, according to Plutarch, were his honouring of his mother and grandfather (cf. Mk 7.10-13);[25] enacting a law consolidating lifelong marriage (22.3; cf. Mk 10.1-12);[26] and ensuring that the dispossessed had 'territory, country, kingdom, clans, marriages and relationships' (cf. Mk 10.29-30).[27] Dionysius includes the protection of children (*Roman Antiquities* 2.15.1-2; cf. Mk 9.36-37, 42; 10.13-16).

However, it is only when looking back from the end of the story (or on a second or third hearing) that such minor motifs as these might possibly 'ring bells', and resonate with the Romulus story in particular.

The Passion of the Leader

It is, then, as indicated, in the final chapters of Mark that the most significant parallels and apposite contrasts are to be found. Many of the popular figures in Roman tradition seem to be suffering heroes, 'who gave their lives to save their country', as Cicero makes clear,[28] and the founding fathers of Rome set the stage: Remus is to be killed by his brother, Romulus is to die at the hands of his people, despite his record of rescuing the oppressed.[29] Only so can the sequence of Roman history

Antiquities 1.77-84; Ovid, *Fasti* 2.395-99.

22. Dionysius, *Roman Antiquities* 1.81.4.

23. Assessed rather differently by Dionysius, though he acknowledges the open welcome, *Roman Antiquities* 1.89.1.

24. As well as Plutarch, *Romulus* 8.7; *Comparison of Theseus and Romulus* 6.5.

25. Cf. Plutarch, *Comparison of Theseus and Romulus* 5.1; Dionysius, *Roman Antiquities* 2.26.

26. Cf. Plutarch, *Comparison of Theseus and Romulus* 6.2-3; Dionysius, *Roman Antiquities* 2.24-25

27. Cf. Plutarch, *Comparison of Theseus and Romulus* 4.2; Dionysius, *Roman Antiquities* 2.15.4.

28. Cicero, *De Finibus* 5.63-65.

29. Plutarch, *Romulus* 6.3; Dio Cassius, *Roman History* 1 in *Dio Cassius, Roman History* (trans. E. Cary; LCL; London: Heinemann; Cambridge, MA: Harvard

begin. Jesus, too, 'must suffer' at the hands of the leaders of his own folk (Mk 8.31; 9.31; 10.33), he must give his life 'a ransom for many', (Mk 10.45); and so set the pattern for others to follow (Mk 8.34-38).[30]

However, while Romulus places first those with most wealth and noblest family tradition (13.3),[31] Jesus puts in first place a child (Mk 9.33-37); and Jesus himself is specifically *not* like other great men and rulers, lording it over people, Mark insists (Mk 10.42-43), drawing attention to his comparison, *sunkrisis*: not harsh and dictatorial—like Romulus or his modern successors. Although Mark may well have local governors and other powerful men in mind, they only represent the power of Rome (cf. Mk 12.13-17), and the current Caesar, Nero or Vespasian, could but be in mind. In fact a contrast between Romulus's harshness and an acceptable exercise of authority seems to be commonplace.[32] So Jesus comes to serve, not be served, in clear contrast with Romulus, born to command, not obey, just as Rome was itself to be free but rule others.[33] This dismissive comparison between the ethos of their rulers on the one hand and the humble service offered by Jesus on the other acts as Mark's prologue to Jesus' approach to Jerusalem and his entry.

In between comes the restoration of sight to Bartimaeus (Mk 10.46-52). It has no parallel in the Romulus complex, but scholars often compare it with the tale (given in three sources) of Vespasian, just *after* his triumphal entry into Alexandria and acclamation as emperor in 69 CE, curing a blind man (and someone with a crippled limb). Mark's and

University Press, 1925), 'When at the risk not only of his safety but even of his life, he encountered danger in your behalf'.

30. See A.Y. Collins, 'The Significance of Mark 10.45 among Gentile Christians', *HTR* 90.4 (1997), pp. 371-82; one of a number of examples where individual passages are better explained in terms of other contexts: the Romulus traditions here afford no telling parallels.

31. Cf. Dionysius, *Roman Antiquities* 2.8.1.

32. Plutarch includes a discussion of patronage by the great in his *Romulus* 13, as had Dionysius, *Roman Antiquities* 2.9-10. On Romulus's harshness, Plutarch, *Comparison of Theseus and Romulus* 2; Dio, *Discourse* 25.8. Plutarch has earlier in his main narrative characterized Romulus as bellicose and a constant threat to his neighbours, and haughty and overbearing (26), compared with Numitor; cf. Dionysius, *Roman Antiquities* 1.85.5-6; 2.56.3, 60.1-2; Dio Cassius, *Roman History* (in John of Antioch fr. 32. M).

33. Plutarch, *Romulus* 6.2; Dionysius, *Roman Antiquities* 2.3.6, 4.1; but cf. Dionysius's Romulus at 2.4.8, 'ready to obey' the will of the people.

these other accounts share some specific if commonplace features (urgent request, delayed response, involvement of onlookers, faith and doubt). The healings by Vespasian confirm him as divinely chosen and empowered.[34] If the Gospel was written later than the early propaganda circulation of a version of this story (and especially if it was composed in Rome, or in Alexandria itself) that could have afforded one telling reason (though by no means necessarily the only reason) for placing the healing of Bartimaeus at this juncture, just before Jesus' own entry into into his city of Jerusalem.

In his study of entry processions, summarized above, Duff notes without comment one account of a triumph for Romulus, but otherwise concentrates on rather more recent instances. In fact both Dionysius of Halicarnassus and Plutarch agree that it was with Romulus that the Roman triumph originated: 'This procession was the origin and model of all subsequent triumphs', (16.6; though Plutarch notes that later victors rode in a chariot, where Romulus and his immediate successors walked).[35] But Romulus provides an important precedent, having celebrated four triumphs, and being one of only three victors to have gone on to dedicate an item in the temple, in his case a huge log which he carried himself. In Duff's analysis, as we noted, we are pointed not only to the 'Graeco-Roman' motifs additional to ones that appear in Zechariah 14, but also to the divergencies in Mark from what both complexes might lead us to expect. Certainly the sequence in Mark is broken, and that fact may have some of the ironic significance Duff argues. But it is also worth noting that others of the standard motifs do appear in variant forms later in the ensuing narrative, not least a feast of sorts, and an imperial robe, a heavy baulk of timber, and a death that has been designated a sacrifice.

One of the 'disruptions' noted in the entry sequence is, of course, one of the 'intercalations' we listed in the previous chapter, the cursing of the fig-tree. The split episode itself has been discussed in depth by W. Telford, drawing to our attention echoes from a range of scriptural and other Jewish sources, and these might seem sufficient. While no one verse seems to have afforded the main stimulus, 'we suggest that *in*

---

34. Suetonius, *Vespasian* 8.7; Dio Cassius, *Roman History* 65.8; Tacitus, *History* 4.81. Cf. B. Blackburn, *Theios Anêr and the Markan Miracle Traditions* (WUNT, 2.40; Tübingen: J.C.B. Mohr, 1991), p. 87 and all of his ch. 2, pp. 13-96.

35. See all of Plutarch, *Romulus* 16.5-8, citing 6, and 24.3 25.5; Dionysius, *Roman Antiquities* 2.34.1-2, 54.2, 55.5.

toto they [the set selected] may have exercised a formative influence',
and indicate 'a *solemn judgment* upon the nation…and *against a cor-
rupt Temple cultus*'.[36] There is, however, no particularly significant
actual fig-tree on or on the approach to the sacred mount, in Jewish
tradition.

There was one such in Rome: the *ficus rumina* or *ruminalis*, the
erineos rōminalios (the golden Rumina's fig tree), in front of the Senate
House, mentioned by a large number of Greek and Roman authors:

> A fig-tree growing in the actual forum and meeting-place of Rome is
> worshipped as sacred because things struck by lightning are buried there,
> and still more as a memorial of the fig-tree under which the nurse of
> Romulus and Remus first sheltered those founders of the empire on the
> Lupercal Hill… And it is also a portent of some future event when it
> withers away and then by the good offices of the priests is replanted…[37]

For Christians in Rome, or aware of Roman traditions, the cursing of
a fig-tree at this juncture in the disjointed entry might well have still
more significance than Telford discerns for us.

Though the traditional title 'cleansing' does not really suit Jesus'
action in the Temple, he certainly seeks to reform it, expelling those
whose activities seem to prevent its proper functioning, which is, he
insists with a scriptural text, for prayer. The action is often interpreted
as itself a symbolic destruction by Jesus; but in Mark's narrative this
can hardly be so, as Jesus goes on to commend a poor widow for her
generous devotion to the Temple service. Romulus, too, is said to have
been 'eminently religious' (*theosebēs diapherontōs*, 22.1), 'rejecting all
the traditional myths about the gods that contain blasphemies or calum-
nies',[38] piously prayerful (18.6), concerned with holy places ('no one

---

36. W. Telford, *The Barren Temple and the Withered Tree* (JSNTSup, 1; Sheffield: JSOT Press, 1980), pp. 161, 163 (Telford's italics).

37. Pliny the Elder, *Natural History* 15.20.77 (LCL; London: Heinemann; Cam-
bridge, MA: Harvard University Press, 1923); cf. Livy, *History* 10.23; Plutarch,
Romulus 4.1; Dionysius, *Roman Antiquities* 3.71.5; Ovid, *Fasti* 2.412; Athanaeus,
Deipnosophists 3.6.7; cf. Pausanias, *Description of Greece* 1.37.2; *Anthologiae
Graecae* 3.24.3; (though only Pliny mentions significant withering). We might also
note the cornel said to have sprung from Romulus's staff, whose well-being seems
to have been significant, until it was damaged and withered in the reign of Gaius
(Caligula); Plutarch, *Romulus* 20.5-6; Ovid, *Metamorphoses* 15.560-64. (I am
grateful to Lloyd Pietersen for helping find some of these references.) Suetonius
also tells of trees that portended the future of the Flavian family: *Vespasian* 5.2, 4.

38. Dionysius, *Roman Antiquities* 2.18.3.

could name any other newly founded city in which so many priests and ministers of the gods were appointed from the beginning'),[39] and with rites and purity (9.3; 11.1; 14.4; 24.2); and these are special concerns for him specifically when he makes a triumphal entry. When Mark's Jesus comes again to the Temple, he goes on to insist that God be given what is his own, and Caesar his (Mk 12.13-17); and in Mark's scriptural tradition, if God has what is his, there is nothing left (cf. Ps. 24.1; 50.12; 89.11—and 1 Cor. 10.26). Mark's Jesus, in temporary command in the Temple makes clear his opposition to all that prevents God receiving his due through the Jewish cult, *but also* his opposition to the cult inaugurated and sustained by the divine Romulus, the cult and service of Caesar, Romulus's deified successor, and of Roma herself, as represented by the Roman coin.

The question of the coin is one of a series of six dispute stories following the second part of the fig-tree incident and some brief teaching on faith, prayer and forgiveness. For the latter brief items and for the sequence itself there is no formal parallel in the received Romulus tradition, although disputes certainly abound, in the story and among the storytellers (as Dionysius and Plutarch make clear). It is perhaps worth acknowledging, nonetheless, that some similar or related themes do occur. The discerning of divine support (Mk 11.27-32) is of course a recurrent strand in the Romulus legends.[40] A dispute over land among herdsmen, a dispute that escalates from blows to armed force to a threat to the life of Remus provides the occasion for the brothers' recognition and the end of the tyrannical reign of their usurping uncle (7.1-7; 8.6).[41] Mark's clearly scriptural parable of the mounting wickedness of the vinedressers is in similar vein, and threatens the end of the usurping 'chief priests, scribes and elders' (Mk 12.1-12, with Mk 11.27). The issue of God and Rome's Caesar (Mk 12.13-17) we considered just above. Physical ascension is at issue at the climax of the story of Romulus, and that leads Plutarch into a discussion of the quasi-divine state of departed souls (28.4-8), just as the conception stories had led Dionysius to debate the appropriateness of talk of sexual relations among divine beings; and he returns to a discussion of quasi-divine beings in commenting on Romulus' death (compare the debate in

39. Dionysius, *Roman Antiquities* 2.21.1, and all of 2.21-23; cf. 1.87.

40. Plutarch, *A Comparison of Theseus and Romulus* 6.4; Dionysius, *Roman Antiquities* 1.79.7-9; 2.63.3.

41. Dionysius, *Roman Antiquities* 1.79.12-14; 83.3.

Jewish terms over similar issues, Mk 12.18-27).[42] Piety and *philanthropia* were central to the self-image of the Flavian dynasty, care for 'things divine and human';[43] and Mark's Jesus affirms the similar but stronger traditional Jewish ethical summary demanding love for God and neighbour (Mk 12.29-31).

For the generous widow's donation there is not even a distant equivalent in the available Romulus and Remus legends, though the generous poor herdsman, Faustulus, and his wife, do have an admired role there.

The various forms of the Romulus legend and Mark's Gospel are addressed to hearers around the time of composition. 'Let the reader apprehend' (Mk 13.14). Mark 13 sketches an explanation of important events in the hearers' recent past, and looks to their still open future with reassurance. The talk of cities being destroyed, of wars and of celestial phenomena are as much at home in non-Jewish as in Jewish writings of the time, as I have demonstrated elsewhere.[44] The equivalent Roman eschatologies are also expressed in speeches in Dionysius and in Plutarch. In the former Aeneas (Romulus's ancestor) hears a divine voice that tells him,

> to stay there [where an escaped sacrificial victim had stopped] and build a city immediately, and not, by giving way to the difficulty occasioned by his present opinion, just because he would be establishing his abode in a barren country, to reject his future good fortune that was all but actually present. For it was fated that, beginning with this sorry, and, at first, small habitation, he should in the course of time acquire a spacious and fertile country, and that his children and posterity should possess a vast empire which should be prolonged for many ages. For the present, therefore, this settlement should be a refuge for the Trojans, but after as

---

42. Dionysius, *Roman Antiquities* 1.79.3; 2.56.6.

43. S. Dill, *Roman Society from Nero to Marcus Aurelius* (London: Macmillan, 1905; repr. New York: Meridian, 1956), p. 536, 'restorer of temples and public ceremonies'; Suetonius, *Vespasian* 8.5–9.1 and 13–14, 17–19.

44. Downing, 'Common Strands'; *idem*, 'Cosmic Eschatology'; cf. E. Adams, 'Historical Crisis and Cosmic Crisis in Mark 13 and Lucan's *Civil War*', *TynBul* 48.2 (1997), pp. 329-44 linking the language of both. B. van Iersel, 'The Sun, Moon and Stars of Mark 13.24-25 in a Greco-Roman Reading', *Bib* 77.1 (1996), pp. 84-92, would discern a reference to individual deities; but the fall of individual gods would only be significant if all the rest perished with them, in the cosmic *ekpyrōsis* ('conflagration'). The cosmic order which Rome saw as focused on itself is here under sentence, as the passages in my studies amply illustrate.

many years as the sow should bring forth young ones, another city, large and flourishing, should be built by his posterity.[45]

Aeneas himself responds a little later with the assurance

that the colony would become illustrious and an object of wonder and would gain the greatest renown, but that as it increased it would be envied by its neighbours and prove grievous to them; nevertheless it would overcome its adversaries, the good fortune it had received from heaven being more powerful than the envy of men that would oppose it.[46]

Plutarch's ascended Romulus picks up some of the same themes:

It was the pleasure of the gods...from whom I came, that I should be with humankind only a short time, and that after founding a city destined to be the greatest on earth for empire and glory, I should dwell again in heaven. So farewell, and tell the Romans that if they practice self-restraint and add to it valour, they will reach the utmost heights of human power. And I will be your propitious deity, Quirinus (28.2).[47]

With this we may compare Mark's 'do not be alarmed...' 'do not be anxious beforehand...' 'I have told you all things beforehand...' 'the news must be preached to all nations...' 'whoever endures to the end will be safe...' 'and then they will see the Son of Man coming in clouds with great power and glory; and then he will send out his angels, and gather his elect from the four winds...' 'my words will not pass away...' 'watch therefore...' (Mk 13.7, 23, 10, 13, 26, 31).[48]

It would seem appropriate to emphasize here my initial careful qualification. It is most definitely *not* being argued that the Rome–Romulus traditions provided major content for Mark's story, nor even that potential parallels with it provided a decisive reason for the inclusion of important elements in that narrative. But it has been argued already that Mark quite explicitly has the Roman imperial ideology in view, and it would seem much more likely than not that as he shaped his account over time among friends at least some of the 'echoes' here indicated would have become obvious to him and to them; and the fact that so

45. Dionysius, *Roman Antiquities* 1.56.3-4; cf. Virgil, *Aeneid* 8.42-48.
46. Dionysius, *Roman Antiquities* 1.59.5.
47. Cf. Livy, *History* 1.16.6-7; Ovid, *Fasti* 2.505-508.
48. Marcus Teretius Varro, famous polymath, 116–28 BCE claimed to have determined *eis hēmeran kai horan*, 'to the day and the hour' the birth of Romulus (11.4); Mark's Jesus specifically denies such knowledge of the birth of the new age, 'the day or the hour'.

many apparent echoes remain suggests he and they were at least content with them, and perhaps intensified them, even if he had not designed their resonances from the start. (I have elaborated and defended above the foregoing picture of collaborative composition.)[49]

There is nothing like an anointing for burial in the Romulus tradition, but there are plots and betrayals and trials, as well as the feasts and sacrifices we earlier remembered to expect, as the climax to the triumphal entry. So Jesus holds a Passover feast with his friends, and dedicates himself as a sacrifice.[50]

Romulus's life is often at risk, but in armed conflict. He expects to be told 'the will of heaven', and to comply.[51] His prayer for divine protection is answered (18.6). According to Livy he himself became 'King and Father' of the city of Rome, and could be addressed as such in prayers. The contrast with Jesus in prayer in Gethsemane is both pointed and marked.

There is plotting at Romulus's birth, and a sort of (quite unfair) arrest and trial for Remus still towards the start of the story:

> After blows and wounds given and received on both sides, the herdsmen of Numitor prevailed and took Remus prisoner, who was then carried off to Numitor and denounced. Numitor himself did not punish his prisoner, because he was in fear of his brother Amulius, who was severe, but went to Amulius and asked for justice... Amulius was therefore induced to hand Remus back to Numitor himself, to treat him as he saw fit (7.2-3).

Remus complains that this hardly counts as a fair trial (7.5). Dionysius, however, says Remus went to the punishment he expected from Numitor 'not turning to lamentations and entreaties...but with a becoming silence going to his fate' (*Roman Antiquities* 1.81.3). The encounter leads, of course, to Remus being asked who he (and his brother) really are, and the truth emerges. Betrayal—by night—comes later (by Tarpeia, 17.2-5).[52]

There are elements in common with Mark:

---

49. Downing, 'Word-processing in the Ancient World: The Social Production and Performance of Q', ch. 4 of this volume.

50. Collins, 'Finding Meaning in the Death of Jesus'; as I insist in conclusion, many individual *pericopai* in Mark are individually more richly illustrated from other sources.

51. Dionysius, *Roman Antiquities* 2.6.1.

52. Ovid, *Metamorphoses* 14.776-77; Dionysius, *Roman Antiquities* 2.38-40.

They laid hands on him and seized him. But one of those who stood by drew his sword and struck the slave of the high priest and cut off his ear...and they led Jesus to the high priest... Jesus was silent and made no answer... 'Are you the Christ, the Son of the Blessed?' and Jesus said, 'I am...' ...and they bound Jesus and led him away and delivered him to Pilate, and Pilate asked him, 'Are you the King of the Jews?' ...and delivered him to be crucified (Mk 14.43–15.15).

(Quite why we are told of the naked fugitive at the arrest of Jesus continues to be debated.[53] One of the main Roman rituals, attributed to or associated with Romulus and Remus, the purificatory Lupercalia, involved young men running round naked [21.4-8]).[54]

Ultimately, many forms of the tradition have it, Romulus became a threat to the power of the senate that he had himself instituted, in particular in arbitrarily allowing a killer to go free (so, Plutarch, only, 23.3).[55]

He changed to the way of a monarch, made hateful and vexatious first by the state which he assumed. For he dressed in a scarlet tunic, and wore it over a toga bordered with purple and sat on a recumbent throne when he gave audience (26.1-2).

Jesus is forced to accept just such a cloak, together with a wreath parodying that for a triumphator, in a mock homage that says more than it knows (Mk 15.16-20).[56] And where Romulus carried his own wooden trophy, someone else carries the cross-beam for Jesus.

Like Jesus in Mark (as we have already recalled), Romulus, according to many accounts,

was killed by his own people... He seemed now to be harsh and arbitrary and to be exercising his power more like a tyrant than a king. For these reasons, they say, the patricians formed a conspiracy against him and resolved to slay him... Others say that while haranguing the people he was slain by the new citizens of Rome...[57]

Jesus is executed as a self-appointed King of the Jews.

---

53. See, recently, H.M. Jackson, 'Why the Youth Shed his Cloak and Fled Naked: The Meaning and Purpose of Mark 14.51-52', *JBL* 116.2 (1997), pp. 273-89.

54. Dionysius, *Roman Antiquities* 1.80.1; Ovid, *Fasti* 2.379.

55. Different in Dionysius, *Roman Antiquities* 2.53.1

56. On the mocking, see further below, the concluding paragraph.

57. Dionysius, *Roman Antiquities* 2.56.3-5; cf. Plutarch, *Romulus* 27.2-3.

In both sequences women figure in dangerous circumstances, though they are not noted as present at the death of Romulus.[58]

The deaths of Jesus and of Romulus occur in similar circumstances, as is often noted (but in isolation from other common features of the stories).

> Suddenly strange and unaccountable disorders with incredible changes filled the air; the light of the sun failed, and night came down upon them, not with peace and quiet, but with awful peals of thunder and furious blasts of driving rain…(27.6)

Dionysius has a shorter account, 'sudden darkness rushed down out of a clear sky and a violent storm burst (*Roman Antiquities* 2.56.2)'. 'And when the sixth hour had come, there was darkness over the whole land until the ninth hour' (Mk 15.33). (However, there is no cry of dereliction, nor earthquake nor disturbance to a temple, in the departure of Romulus).[59]

Our authors then discuss whether Romulus was assassinated by the conspirators under cover of the storm and his (dismembered) corpse concealed, or whether he was taken bodily to heaven, for no remains were found. The people are persuaded of the latter explanation, and accept Romulus as a divine being (27.7-8).[60] 'They succumbed to some supernatural influence, like divine possession' (28.3; cf. Mk 13.11, 'it is not you who will speak, but the Holy Spirit'). Livy has the acclamation of Romulus as a god come from the assembled soldiers.[61] Mark has such an acclamation for Jesus from the lips of a centurion.

There is no burial related for Romulus, but his physical disappearance leads Plutarch into a long excursus on tales (with two examples) of

---

58. Mark 15.40-41; 16.1-8; in the Romulus sequence especially the abducted Sabine women ending the battle between their Roman spouses and their Sabine kin.

59. Gundry, *Mark*, p. 963, lists these and other darknesses, but, as with most commentators, *seriatim*, with no reference to context or to links with further similarities in individual sources. Similarly, P.G. Bolt, 'Mark 16.1-8: The Empty Tomb of a Hero?', *TynBul* 47.1 (1993), pp. 27-37, dismisses the possible relevance of tales of 'the empty tomb of a hero' as irrelevant for our understanding of Mark by the same 'divide and rule' method. The place of such an account within a possible *series* of closer or more distant resemblances is ignored; so, too, Brown (of prized memory), *The Death of the Messiah*, I, p. 1043.

60. Dionysius, *Roman Antiquities* 2.56.3-6; Cicero, *De Republica* 2.17-20; cf. Dio Cassius, *Roman History* 1, in John of Antioch, fr. 32.

61. Livy, *History* 1.16.

empty tombs (though he himself, as we noted above, cannot credit the idea of physical bodies being taken to the realm of the gods, 28.4-8). M.A. Levi notes a gold aureus of 69–70 CE, with the verso inscription ROMA RESURGENS.[62]

No appearance of Romulus is directly related, just as there is none in Mark. Reassurance comes from a third party, Iulius Proculus, and that (according to some versions) only after some time, during which the people remain in doubt as to what has happened.[63] Iulius is sent off with a message from the deified Romulus, to the effect that he will be Rome's propitious deity, and Rome will rule (28.2-3). The popularity of this sequence in the legend may be gauged from its frequent quite incidental repetition, for instance by Quintilian; much the same tale has then to be told of current deified successors of Romulus, as in Seneca's parody on Claudius, and even in Justin Martyr ('you produce someone who swears he has seen the burning Caesar rise to heaven from the funeral pyre').[64]

Livy tells us that the loyal soldiers' initial response to the senators' reassurances was that they remained for some time sorrowful and silent, as if filled with the fear of orphanhood ('velut orbitatis metu icta maestum aliquandiu silentium obtinuit'), a little like the reaction to the words of the young man in Mark, from the women who 'said nothing to anyone, for they were afraid' (Mk 16.8).[65]

Conclusion

There are, to be sure, individual episodes, in other sources, that resonate still more forcefully with individual pericopai in Mark than most if not all those noted above. There are more vivid trials, more closely related discussions of the actual topics in Mark 11 and 12, more conventional forecasts of cosmic change. To mention two particular examples; there is Philo's well-known account of the mocking of Agrippa I, sig-

---

62. M.A. Levi, 'I Flavi', *ANRW* II.2 (1975), pp. 177-207 (192).

63. Dionysius, *Roman Antiquities* 2.63.3-4; Ovid, *Fasti* 2.491-512; *idem, Metamorphoses* 14.806-27 (directly related, but as seen by the gods).

64. Quintilian, *Institutes* 2.4.19; 3.7.5; Seneca, *Apocolocyntosis* 1 on Drusilla as well as on Claudius; Justin, *Apology* 1.21.

65. Livy, *History* 1.16.2 (LCL). There is sufficient discussion elsewhere of the 'dramatic aposeiopesis' at Mk 16.8: W.L. Knox, 'The Ending of Mark's Gospel', *HTR* 35 (1942), pp. 13-25; P.W. van der Horst, 'Can a Book End with ? A Note on Mark XVI. 8', *JTS* NS 23 (1972), pp. 121-24; F. Kermode, *The Genesis of Secrecy* (Cambridge, MA: Harvard University Press, 1979); Magness, *Sense and Absence*.

nificantly on an official visit to Alexandria, by the homage offered to another Syrian, 'Carabas' decked out as a king; and there is Dio of Prusa's account of the Persian festival when a prisoner is allowed royal privileges before being stripped, scourged and hanged.[66] Both of these have more potential relevance for our understanding of the mocking of Jesus than anything in the surviving Romulus legends. And, furthermore, while a handful of sequences do seem to relate explicitly to the Roman imperial ideology, for most of the items adduced above there is no possibility of showing one way or the other whether Mark and his associates and eventual hearers would have picked up the particular similarities suggested, for any given one of them. Yet the fact remains that the discussion of rulers, the entry, the references to Caesar and to kingship and the execution articulate inescapably a response to Rome's self-image, and if we allow these then to point us to the Romulus traditions we find a much greater number of resonances with it in Mark's story than, it seems, we could find in any other contemporary extended narrative source. For the time being, at least, no such tally of resemblances with any other sequential narrative seems to have been suggested.

The trouble with most searches for significantly repeated motifs in writings from the ancient world is that instances are considered as examples in isolation from the sequences in which they appear. A common sequence of motifs—whatever the genre of the work in which they appear (history with Livy, Dionysius, Dio Cassius, biography with Plutarch, essay with Cicero, poetry with Ovid)—has a force that demands recognition.[67]

I repeat in conclusion what I urged at the start and again on the way through. It has *not* been argued that the Rome–Romulus traditions furnished any major episodes for Mark's story, nor even that potential parallels with Roman tradition decided the issue of inclusion of any particular item that lay to hand or came to mind. But it has been argued that Mark quite explicitly had the Roman imperial propaganda in view, it is part of his intertexture, and it would seem much more likely than not that as he shaped his account over time among fellow Christians at least some of the 'echoes' here indicated would have become obvious

---

66. Philo, *Flacc.* 36-39; Dio, *Discourse* 4.67; discussed by Robbins, *Jesus the Teacher*, pp. 189-91. Still more are listed by Gundry, *Mark*, p. 942; but the context is ignored, and the additional ones are not 'royal'.

67. See, again, Downing, 'Contemporary Analogies'.

to him and to them. Then the fact that so many apparent resonances remain suggests he and his associates were at least content with them and may even have intensified them, even if he cannot be shown to have arranged these harmonics from the start. They are an important element in the production and an important facet of the message of the Gospel.

Mark in effect and probably in intention presents Jesus as a thoroughgoing rival to Romulus and so to all his successors. That is not all he had to say, nor even the most important conclusion he conveyed; but it is an integral part of what he had to share with his first collaborators-and-hearers.

In the foregoing the priority of Mark and the Q hypothesis (Matthew and Luke both independently used Mark and a further source) have been assumed, with occasional cautions offered. But I have over the years joined in efforts to establish these positions more securely, and now include two of these studies, examining literary production, and especially the use of sources, in the wider world of the evangelists.

Chapter 8

COMPOSITIONAL CONVENTIONS AND THE SYNOPTIC PROBLEM*

The Synoptic Problem

There is a 'literary' relationship, it is widely (if still not universally) agreed, between the Gospels of Matthew, Mark and Luke. That agreement is presupposed here (though it may incidentally emerge from this discussion further strengthened).

Quite what this literary relationship is remains in contention. Although many would accept, even take it for granted, that Mark wrote first and was used by Matthew and by Luke, independently of each other, while the latter two shared, but also independently of each other, a further common source, 'Q', there are those who would strenuously disagree. Among them some would argue, for instance, that Matthew having used Mark, both these works were themselves used by Luke, unpicking and reassembling the Matthaean additions and changes.[1] Others, again, would urge that, yes, Luke 'rewrote' Matthew and then Mark 'conflated' both (and that also after a measure of 'unpicking' of some of Luke's adaptations of his Matthaean material).[2] However, in the light of the inconclusiveness so far of the debate, others again would argue that we have insufficient data and must leave the issue open.[3]

*   Reprinted from *JBL* 107.1 (1988), pp. 69-85, with kind permission.

1.   For instance, M.D. Goulder, *Midrash and Lection in Matthew* (London: SPCK, 1974); *idem*, *Luke, a New Paradigm* (JSNTSup, 20; Sheffield: JSOT Press, 1989), discussed in more detail in the next chapter; J. Drury, *Tradition and Design in Luke's Gospel* (London: Darton, Longman & Todd, 1976).

2.   W.R. Farmer, *The Synoptic Problem* (New York: Macmillan, 1964); also in Bellinzoni (ed.), *The Two-Source Hypothesis*.

3.   For instance, H. Palmer, *The Logic of Gospel Criticism* (New York: Macmillan, 1968); J.B. Tyson, 'The Two-Source Hypothesis: A Critical Appraisal', in Bellinzoni (ed.), *The Two-Source Hypothesis*, pp. 437-52 (449). E.P. Sanders and M. Davies, *Studying the Synoptic Gospels* (London: SCM Press; Philadelphia:

Considered in the abstract, the suggestions indicated are all equally possible. The second two seem to involve much more difficult procedures of 'unpicking' prior to the fresh composition, as I have argued elsewhere, and will urge again in what follows.[4] But, even if that be agreed, it may be argued that with a powerful enough theological aim in view, a writer might well have undertaken the task, complex and laborious though it were. How can we possibly tell, it is asked, what might have seemed a proper or sensible or feasible compositional procedure to a follower of the Christian way in the first century? We are in no position to decide that one rather than another would have seemed the more logical, let alone the only logical procedure. So Joseph B. Tyson has insisted, 'What Luke did with his sources may have made perfect sense to him but not to us. Or, what is more likely, we may not be able to discern the sense that things made to an ancient author'.[5]

The present chapter intends to argue to the contrary. We are in a position to tell with a considerable degree of certainty what compositional procedures for making use of existing writings would have been readily available in the first century. We can tell on the basis of many examples of practice and some indications of theory: even the most highly literate and sophisticated writers employ relatively simple approaches to their 'sources'. We are also able to take into account the sorts of compositional exercises people are likely to have been taken through in their elementary education. On this basis, the Two-Document hypothesis (Mark and 'Q' used independently by Matthew and by Luke) fits snugly in the known cultural context of the time. The other suggestions presuppose a quite gratuitous invention of a complex new procedure, where there was no indication at the time that any such innovation was called for and every indication that effective composition on the basis of prior 'sources' could be achieved with complete success following known and time-honoured procedures prepared for from school days.

No one in or around the first century CE seems to have considered 'unpicking' a source that showed signs of being or even admitted having been itself 'conflated', before reusing it in their own composition.

Trinity Press International, 1989), argue for a still more complicated solution; see ch. 9 below.

4.   Downing, 'Towards the Rehabilitation of Q'; and in *idem*, 'Redaction Criticism'.

5.   Tyson, 'The Two-Source Hypothesis', p. 449, again.

Conflation in any detail was itself only rarely attempted, and then very simply effected.

In fact, the long debate on the sources of the synoptic Gospels seems to have been conducted without paying much or any attention to this issue, of whether any indications of 'sensible' compositional procedures in the first century CE are available.[6] It may still, of course, be possible to argue that the synoptic Gospels were written in a cultural vacuum or that such other information as we may have comes from a different intellectual milieu at the time. But, clearly, neither conclusion ought to be taken for granted without supporting argument. A number of studies in the past three decades have stressed the parallels between the Gospels as they stand and other writing of the period,[7] and would seem to have strengthened the case for such a comparison with the use of sources in contemporary literary composition. Particularly important are discussions of elementary education and examples that have survived of elementary exercises. The procedures are always so similar that it would be absurd to suppose without massive supporting evidence that the New Testament evangelists could have learned to read and write Greek and cope with written source material at all while remaining outside the pervasive influence of these common steps towards literacy.

Composition among Classicists

Recent scholarship on this 'compositional' aspect of literary activity outside of the New Testament field points in a significant common direction. In his study of Livy, T.J. Luce noted first, by way of contrast, that a modern historian of ancient times will split his sources up into what he believes are their constituent parts: 'The twin processes of breakdown and restoration seem natural and self-evident to modern students of history.'[8] But, Luce would claim, such a course would not have suggested itself even to the most sophisticated and well-served writer in the centuries around the beginning of the common era. Mostly

---

6.   W. Sanday considers the physical setting, though not the literary context, in his 'The Conditions under which the Gospels were written, in their Bearing upon some Difficulties of the Synoptic Problem', in *idem* (ed.), *Studies in the Synoptic Problem* (Oxford: Clarendon Press, 1911), pp. 16-19. Even the physical setting seems thereafter to be ignored; see further below, and Chapter 9, here.

7.   E.g., Talbert, *What is a Gospel?*; Shuler, *A Genre for the Gospels*; Robbins, *Jesus the Teacher*; since this was written, Burridge, *What are the Gospels?*

8.   T.J. Luce, *Livy* (Princeton, NJ: Princeton University Press, 1977), p. 143.

Livy will alternate intact but paraphrased blocks of Polybius with blocks of his (now lost!) Roman source, 'now composing with great care and concentration, now adapting the source in front of him rapidly and mechanically'.[9] Such conflation of parallel accounts as does appear is occasional and ad hoc, lacking, as just noted, any sign of any prior analytical 'unpicking'. Even such conflation as this is rare, and, in Luce's judgment, so clearly unsuccesful ('an appalling pastiche') as obviously to have been found very difficult to achieve.[10]

Since the 'Roman' source is lost, there is no possibility of Luce's presenting a detailed 'synoptic' study; but this present chapter will shortly attempt one for some Hellenistic material where parallels have survived for us to consider, and which strongly bear out his general conclusions.[11]

D.S. Russell also discerns a similar compositional simplicity, when analysing Plutarch's *Coriolanus* as based on Dionysius of Halicarnassus's *Roman Antiquities*. Russell is presupposing a widespread agreement that in this instance Plutarch is (unusually) employing only one source. Nonetheless, there are clear signs that he does not even have that source unrolled in front of him: witness his 'confusion over the names of Coriolanus' women-folk', and others. Russell asks,

> Did Plutarch forget or make a mistake in his notes? I will only say that it seems to me prudent to come down on the side of memory. The process of composition is likely to have involved much less 'paper-work' than a modern scholar likes to think. Even a very bookish ancient, like Plutarch, enjoyed what would nowadays be a phenomenally good memory. No doubt he made notes on Dionysius, or had them made for him, but their scale is something we cannot guess and should be careful not to exaggerate.[12]

9. Luce, *Livy*, p.140.

10. Luce, *Livy*, p. xix.

11. For further confirmation of Luce's contentions one may note the unreserved agreement of C.B.R. Pelling, 'Plutarch's Method of Work in the Roman Lives', *JHS* 99 (1979), pp 74-96: 'Everything here supports Luce's conclusion: Livy read widely, but nevertheless followed a single source for a single section; within these sections he would occasionally add supplementary items from other sources, but he would not use a number of sources to weave together a coherent and independent account of his own' (p. 92).

12. D.S. Russell, 'Plutarch's Life of Coriolanus', *JRS* 53 (1963), pp. 17-35 (22). Compare also F. Millar, *A Study of Cassius Dio* (London: Oxford University Press, 1964). Both refer to work by E. Gabba, in Italian, and not accessible to me.

The question of 'memory' (as contrasted with the 'literary' relationship presupposed for the synoptic Gospels) we shall revert to briefly later. For the moment the point being stressed is simply the rough-and-ready simplicity of the methods used by 'even a very bookish ancient', at least as seen by another specialist in late classical studies. There is certainly no sign of any detailed preliminary analysis.

In her monograph on Hieronymus of Cardia, J. Hornblower includes a short review of the history of classical studies in our area of concern, 'composition', and concludes that hypotheses involving complex composition have been largely abandoned as unfruitful.[13] Diodorus Siculus, writing in the reign of Augustus, is her main source for Hieronymus, and he 'merely paraphrased or extracted, without addition or interpretation, except of the simplest kind... He followed his single main source, supplemented by additions which could, in principle, be distinguished' (as opposed to any notion that he might have 'spliced his sources together...into a framework of his own construction').[14] This is demonstrated from the few instances where Hieronymus's passages in Diodorus are quoted independently in another surviving source. The sort of procedure envisaged by, for instance, B.H. Streeter, in his *The Four Gospels*, is of this kind.[15] The procedures imagined by those suggesting other orders of composition are quite different and quite without contemporary exemplar.

A fourth introductory illustration is drawn from some of C.R.B. Pelling's studies of Plutarch.

> Plutarch drew on a fairly wide range of material. Yet...it is still clear that the greatest portion of these [later Roman] Lives is based on the [lost] Pollio source alone: even on those occasions (such as Caesar's murder) where Plutarch has other sources, it is still Pollio's account which provides most of the facts. The extraneous material is not more than one quarter of the whole of Plutarch's narrative... This is undeniably odd: if a modern researcher had read so widely, he would weave these items from all these sources into a composite and independent narrative... Plutarch has no hint of this... Time and again, we find Greek and Roman historians claiming a wide range of reading, and deserving to

13. J. Hornblower, *Hieronymus of Cardia* (London: Oxford University Press, 1981), pp. 3, 21.

14. Hornblower, *Hieronymus*, pp. 280-81.

15. B.H. Streeter, *The Four Gospels: A Study of Origins* (London: Macmillan, 1924), esp. pp. 192-95.

be believed; yet, time and again, we find them demonstrably basing their narrative of individual episodes on a single source.[16]

It is worth, then, noting Pelling's sketch of an author at work:

> A writer would not normally refer back to [earlier] reading to verify individual references, and would instead rely on his memory, or on the briefest of notes... Stray facts and additions would be recalled from the preliminary available reading, but it would be a very different matter to recall the detail of an episode's presentation... Such a procedure seems less perverse in view of the physical difficulties of working with papyrus rolls...[with] non-existent or rudimentary...indexing, chapter-headings, line- and column-numbering... Even if, for example, a slave held a second roll for an author to compare accounts, or the author himself used a book-rest, combining versions would still be awkward.[17]

If this general picture be accepted for a fairly sophisticated and wealthy writer's preparations for writing, then the implications for the study of the synoptic Gospels is clear. Even had one of our evangelists wanted to emulate the well-staffed and well-equipped compositional procedures of a sophisticated literary figure, nothing would suggest that he should begin by analysing his source material, nor on that or any other basis that he should plan some complex conflation of his sources. Only the 'Streeterian' model fits at all in the first-century scene.

These classical scholars' reconstructions of compositional conventions in late antiquity are entirely borne by Lucian of Samosata's critical essay, *How to Write History*. In assembling his facts the historian should allow for favour or malice in the witnesses, and remain impartial if a 'myth' has to be related. But what Lucian really cares about is arrangement and proportion and style and ethical integrity.[18] There is no suggestion of any further (or prior) analysis of source material, oral or written. There are no instructions at all about using—or even avoiding—conflation. There is nothing to suggest any other model for our evangelists to follow than what we have already found in a range of classical scholars' conclusions.

The only first-century author for whose use of sources we have at all extensive controls is Flavius Josephus. The use he makes of Jewish

16. Pelling, 'Plutarch's Method of Work', pp. 91-93; compare his 'Plutarch's Adaptation of his Source Material'.

17. Pelling, 'Plutarch's Method of Work', pp. 92-93; compare W. Sanday (ed.), *Studies*, pp. 16-19: the accounts are very similar.

18. Lucian, *How to Write History*, 46-51 (LCL).

Scriptures (as I have myself tried to show elsewhere[19]) looks very like the procedures suggested by the classical scholars cited (and which I only met after my own study was in print). Josephus's use of a single source (the *Letter of Aristeas*) had been analysed in much more detail by A. Pelletier and affords further support to this conclusion.[20] Josephus produces paraphrases, précis, expansions and omissions (but nothing more complex). As Vernon Robbins in particular reminded us, this is exactly what we would expect from our knowledge of elementary education in Quintilian, Ps.-Cicero's *Ad Herennium*, and from Theon.[21]

Children learned to retell 'the same' story from varying points of view, for varying purposes, in varying styles—and writing freely. Theon in particular suggests that they should learn to 'weave' a narrative context into the telling of a 'myth' (or 'fable') and, later, that a narrative may be enriched by 'weaving' a fable into it. That is the closest anyone seems to come to anything that may be called an exercise in 'conflation'. He instances telling the fable of the camel that wanted to gain horns and lose its ears. Then one might say, There seems some similarity between that camel and Croesus of Lydia, and so continue on into the whole narrative of Croesus.[22] To our way of thinking this would be more like 'inlaying' than 'interweaving'; and nothing in any way more complex is suggested when Theon considers

19. Downing, 'Redaction Criticism', I.

20. Pelletier, *Flavius Josèphe*.

21. V.K. Robbins, 'Pronouncement Stories and Jesus' Blessing of the Children', in *SBLSP 1982* (ed. K.H. Richards; Chico, CA: Scholars Press, 1982), pp. 407-30; and in *idem*, 'The Woman who Touched Jesus' Garment', *NTS* 33 (1987), pp. 502-15 (503); and in other discussions of *chreiai* in particular, listed in Robbins, *Jesus the Teacher*. See Quintilian (late first century), *Institutes* 1.9; 2.4.12-15, especially, for elementary education; also 3.6-7, on sorting out 'the facts' so as to be able to offer a clear account of them. *Ad Herennium* is usually dated in the first century CE, Theon in the first part of the second century: in C. Walz, *Rhetores Graeci* (repr. Osnabruck: Otto Zeller, 1968); some of the text is available in Hock and O'Neil (trans. and eds.), *The Chreia*.

22. Theon, *Progymnasmata* 3.12 (Walz, p. 175, 1-10) and 3.13 (Walz, p. 177, 10-17), where the word used is *sumplekomen*; compare also 3.22 (Walz, pp. 192, 13-16). The discussion of narrative (Theon, *Progymnasmata* 4, Walz pp. 182-85), suggests similar elements to those in Quintilian, *Institutes* 3.6: a balance is to be struck in the final result between simplicity and complexity. But nothing is said about the use, let alone the analysis of sources. For further discussion of education at the time, see still Marrou, *A History of Education in Antiquity*; Clarke, *Higher Education in the Ancient World*; Bonner, *Education in Ancient Rome*.

narrative as such. In these kinds of exercises in retelling tales and suchlike, other versions the student knew might well influence the result. But at no point is there any suggestion of practice in combining variants, let alone in analysing received variants with a view to (re-) conflating them. Neither is there, presumably, any call for learning or teaching such procedures. No one needs or wants to learn to compose that way.

All the studies so far cited would still warrant the judgment that the synoptic Gospels display a 'literary' relationship to one another. Matthew and Luke might just possibly have been relying on memory (as Russell and Pelling both suggested Plutarch might). But that would have had to amount to a recalling of Mark as a memory available only in one form, a finely memorized document, to allow for the often very close reproduction of one synoptic writer by another, both in wording in distinguishable passages and in the order of such passages. Memory would not seem impossible; but, for the frequent verbatim and near-verbatim identity that obtains, the presence of the actual document before the dependent writer is still more likely.

The issue of visible over memorized (or perhaps visualized) source document(s) does not have to be decided in advance of the next step in the present discussion. Either way, the Gospel writers must be taken to have been rather unadventurously bound by their sources, with less skill (or less interest) even in paraphrasing, than we find among our more sophisticated authors. Yet every attempt at a 'literary' explanation of the relationship between the first three evangelists (as said, whether working from sight or from memory) does, nonetheless, imply the somewhat unusual and not a little adventuresome process of conflation of some kind. Either Mark has complicatedly part-unpicked and then (re-)conflated Matthew and Luke (Griesbach);[23] or Luke has complicatedly unpicked and (re-)conflated Mark and Matthew (Farrer);[24] or Matthew and Luke in a much simpler fashion, without any prior 'unpicking', have independently conflated Mark and Q.[25] It is worth looking to see if we can find examples of such 'simple conflation', since more

---

23. E.g. in Farmer, *Synoptic Problem*; and various contributors in Bellinzoni (ed.), *The Two-Source Hypothesis*.

24. E.g. Drury, *Tradition and Design*; Goulder, *Luke*; and various contributors in Bellinzoni (ed.), *The Two-Source Hypothesis*.

25. Streeter, *Four Gospels*; and others, again, in Bellinzoni (ed.), *The Two-Source Hypothesis*.

complex procedures seem precluded in the pervasive culture of the age. (It is worth stressing that it is only 'simple' conflationary composition, assembly, that is now at issue, the interspersing of items from two sources. Individual items may well be rewritten by the second author, but freely: even if the rewriting is influenced, consciously or unawares, by one or more other known versions of an episode, there is not likely to be any attempt deliberately to interweave in detail sequences of words from two versions of it. Nothing of that sort is being looked for or is expected.)

Returning to Josephus (having just above referred to Pelletier's study of his treatment of the *Letter of Aristeas*), it is entirely clear that he does himself practice conflation of a kind when he is faced with obviously parallel accounts of 'the same' incident. I quote from my own earlier study (focusing here on *Ant.* 6.368-77).[26]

> For instance, I Chronicles 10.1-12 gives us almost word-for-word I Samuel 31.1-13, and Josephus renders almost every phrase, adding only a note on the valour of Saul and his sons, and a massacre when these heroes fall. However, at II Samuel 1.6 he has a second account of Saul's death; and although this may represent a deliberate deception by the Amalekite, Josephus conflates both versions. He follows I Samuel 31.7 where it differs from I Chronicles 10.7; but uses the more plausible order of I Chronicles 10.8-9 for what ensues. He returns again to I Samuel, save for the unlikely 'burnt' in v. 12, to which he prefers the Chronicler's 'buried'.[27]

Most of this parallel material is very similar, and, where that is so, Josephus usually treats minor divergencies as supplementary or as corrective. Where similarities are very close, Josephus seems happy to use most of what is jointly available, with only stylistic changes. However, on two occasions he is in fact confronted with two accounts widely differing in detail and yet still clearly of 'the same' series of events (2 Sam. 5 and 1 Chron. 11—the crowning of David and the capture of Jerusalem—and 2 Sam. 24 together with 1 Chron. 21—the census, the plague,

26. Downing, 'Redaction Criticism', I, p. 61. L. Alexander has cogently drawn our attention to the importance of 'middle-brow', largely technical literature, as a context for our appreciation of Luke in particular: L. Alexander, 'Luke's Preface'; and *eadem, The Preface to Luke's Gospel*. Cf. Lucian's note of a war history by a military surgeon, *How to Write History* 16; and the note at the end of this chapter appended below.

27. The conflation here in Josephus extends much further than do any of the passages from Plutarch referred to in this chapter.

and the purchase of the site for the Temple). Here Josephus seems simply to lose his patience, and writes his own third version, making no attempt to focus on common details, let alone disentangle the later account of the Chronicler from its [presumed] earlier source in Kings.[28] Recognizable conflation does seem to have been a possibility, but clearly, only of the very simplest kind. When the going gets difficult, the easier procedure of a fairly arbitrary rewriting is adopted.

So far as I am aware there is only one other likely and at all extensive instance of such conflation available to us in classical literature from around the first century, to afford us a further test case.[29] Livy, Dionysius of Halicarnassus and Plutarch all have accounts available to us of Camillus's siege of the Etruscan town of Veii. There are, unfortunately, apparent lacunae in Dionysius's text, but it remains extensive. Its obvious parallels with Livy suggest to scholars a dependence of both on a still earlier (now lost) source. There are also divergencies.

Plutarch, I suggest, writing a century or more later, conflates these two earlier accounts, following most of their close parallels quite extensively, preferring now one, now the other version in differing tellings of subordinate incidents. But on the few occasions when his sources clearly conflict with each other, or display perhaps a deficient narrative logic, he simply creates a fresh sequence of his own.

That he is using both seems to me quite clear. Plutarch refers explicitly to Livy at *Camillus* 6.2. At 5.5-7 he includes an account of a prayer, placed on Camillus's lips.[30] It is very similar to one in Dionysius (*Roman Antiquities* 12.14.1-2),[31] both in structure and in the (Greek) words and phrases used.

---

28. Downing, 'Redaction Criticism', I, pp. 62-64.

29. Pelling refers to other, much briefer passages: in his 'Plutarch's Method of Work', and 'Plutarch's Adaptation'.The material quoted here seems to be the most extensive potential example extant.

30. 'He stretched out his hands to heaven and prayed to Zeus and the other deities that, if possible, his present good fortune might not prove a cause of hatred against either him or his country; but that if any calamity was to befall the city of Rome in general, or his own life, as counterbalance to things at present going so well, it might be the least and the most limited' (LCL).

31. 'He lifted up his hands to the gods and prayed, saying, "O greatest Zeus, and you deities who see men's good and evil deeds...if," he said, "as counterpoise to this our present good situation, some retribution is due to come upon us, spare, I beseech you, the city of the Romans and their army; and let it fall upon my own self, though with the least possible harm" ' (LCL).

Roman Antiquities 12.14.2	*Camillus* 5.6
διατείνας εἰς οὐρανὸν <u>τάς χεῖρας</u> <u>εὔξατο τῷ Διὶ καὶ τοῖς</u> ἄλλοις ἄλλοις <u>θεοῖς</u>, μάλιστα μὲν ἀνεπίφθονον ἑαυτῷ τε καὶ τῇ πατρίδι γίνεσθαι <u>τὴν παροῦσαν εὐδαιμονίαν</u>... <u>εἰ δέ</u> <u>τις</u> ἔμελλε κοινῇ συμφορὰ τὴν Ῥομαίων πόλιν ἢ τὸν <u>αὑτοῦ</u> βίον καταλαμβάνειν <u>ἀντίπαλος</u> τῶν <u>παρόντων</u> ἀγαθῶν, <u>ἐλαχίστην</u> γενέσθαι ταύτην καὶ μετριωτάτην.	ἀνέσχε <u>τὰς χεῖρας</u> τοῖς θεοῖς καὶ προσ<u>ευχόμενος</u> εἶπε· ʻ<u>Ζεῦ</u> μέγιστε <u>καὶ θεοὶ</u> χρηστῶν ἐπίσκοποι καὶ πονηρῶν ἔργων... <u>εἰ δ᾽ἄρα τις</u>ʼ, ἔφη, ʻκαὶ ἡμῖν <u>ἀντίστροφος</u> ὀφείλεται <u>τῆς παρούσης</u> νέμεσις εὐπραξίας, εὔχομαι ταύτην ὑπέρ τε <u>πόλεως</u> καὶ στρατοῦ Ῥωμαίων εἰς ἐμαυτὸν <u>ἐλαχίστῳ</u> κακῷ τελευτῆσαιʼ.

There are more verbal coincidences here than are usually found when Josephus, for example, can be seen quite clearly to be paraphrasing one of his sources;[32] they are more than the 'exact and frequent echoes' that Russell finds when Plutarch elsewhere uses Dionysius for his *Coriolanus*, and more considerable than the 'synoptic' parallels displayed by Hornblower.[33] However, there seems to be considerable resistance among classical scholars to any admission that anything even as detailed as this would have been attempted, and a strong preference for ascribing the parallels to the influence of the 'lost' common source of Dionysius and Livy, rather than supposing that a first century author might have written with his eye on two texts.

I shall nonetheless argue in what follows that the phenomena are such as to point much more clearly to genuine conflation. But the implication is that even if Plutarch did here decide on a procedure somewhat more complex than the conventional one and his own custom, it was nonetheless still quite a simple one. And if I do not make a case for a genuine 'side-by-side' conflation here, then the argument for supposing that a first-century use of sources was very simple and rough and ready indeed is in fact even stronger than my study of Josephus would suggest.

---

32. Pelletier, *Flavius Josèphe*, p. 29, finds one broken sequence of 12 words and another of 10, in common between Josephus and the *Letter of Aristeas*, his source.

33. Russell, 'Coriolanus', p. 21; Hornblower, *Hieronymus*, pp. 280-81.

Three Accounts of the Siege of Veii

For any reader without ready access to one or more of the relevant texts, a summary of the sequence may be of some help: (1) While Veii is invested by the Roman armies, the Alban Lake inexplicably rises, and this is taken as a portent. (2) A Veiian citizen has or seems to have important information on the question of the lake and is lured into Roman hands. (3) The Romans deal with the lake so as to obtain a favourable result for themselves. (4a) Camillus mines the city, having made vows to Juno; the Romans turn another omen to their own advantage; or (4b) the Veiians send an unsuccessful peace mission. (5) The city is taken, and Camillus utters a deprecatory prayer. (6) He fulfils his vow to Juno, whose statue signifies her acquiescence.

(1) *The lake.* Dionysius (*Roman Antiquities* 12.10-11) begins with a discussion of the season of the year, leaving the 'miraculous' nature of the rise in the water-level implicit. Livy (*History* 5.15.1) says that there had been no rain, without concerning himself with the season, but tells us outright that among 'prodigies' it was indubitably a *miraculum* (a 'wonder'). Plutarch both discusses the season and talks of *thaumata* ('wonders').

Livy then mentions the occurrence of many prodigies, but adds that solely the one concerned with the lake was sufficiently well attested to be taken seriously; and, anyway, the Romans were deprived of their own *haruspices* ('interpreter of omens'), being entirely dependent on those from Tuscany. Dionysius makes no mention of any other portents at this juncture, and the Romans have plenty of soothsayers of their own to refer to. Thus they present Plutarch as supposed reader with at least two apparent contradictions: many prodigies or only one, a lack of seers or plenty of them. And even though both Livy and Dionysius go on to agree that an immediate embassy is sent to Delphi, in Livy the mission arises from the lack of other interpreters for the omen of the lake, whereas in Dionysius it stems from the (plentiful) Roman seers' failure to offer any clear explanation.

In the face of this disagreement, perhaps, Plutarch omits all reference to other soothsayers, Roman or Etruscan (just as Josephus will often bypass conflicts between his sources).[34] Plutarch also postpones any account of an embassy to Delphi, having lost his sources' respective

---

34. Downing, 'Redaction Criticism', I, pp. 62-64.

motives for the mission. In fact, it is also possible to discern a certain tension between the theme of consulting Delphi, on the one hand, and the narrative significance accorded the incident of the loquacious Veiian's revelation, on the other, in both the earlier accounts. Plutarch produces a much tauter story line: the Veiian discloses the significance of the unprecedented rise in the water level, but it is the Delphic oracle that is then asked for guidance on how best to respond. (Josephus—and Luke—can both be seen to be creating an enhanced narrative logic out of the texts before them.)[35] Yet, if Plutarch is taken to be following the sequence already in the lost 'common source' it is hard to imagine Livy and Dionysius diverging so pointlessly from what they would have found there.

(2) *The Veiian soothsayer.* Plutarch again offers a more plausible narrative sequence than either of the others, with the soothsayer merely dropping hints that he has an encouraging secret, so making his capture worthwhile (rather than his having already revealed all). For most of the episode of the capture, there are minor differences but no major contradictions between Livy and Dionysius, and Plutarch seems content to conflate them. He takes the longstanding friendship of the Veiian and his Roman captor from Dionysius, as well as the former's knowledge of ancient oracular tradition and his happy laughter prompted by the news of the rise in the level of the lake; but his note that such conversations often occur in long sieges is in Livy, as is the Roman's request for advice on some private affair of his own.[36] Dionysius has the much less plausible device of the Roman tempting the Veiian with hints of intelligence reports from the Roman army, and Plutarch ignores these; but he does include from Dionysius the Roman's reference here to other recent signs. He adopts from Livy an explanation of how the Roman was able to carry off the soothsayer bodily, and also Livy's excuse for the Veiian's betrayal of his city's secrets as willed by the gods (Livy), 'inevitable' (Plutarch).

(3) *Dealing with the lake.* In Livy the lake must be artificially emptied (5.15.4; 16.9), whereas in Dionysius the water must simply not be

---

35. Downing, 'Redaction Criticism', I, pp. 51-52, 54-55, 56-57, and II, pp. 40-41.

36. Dio Cassius provides yet another attempt to make sense of this story, *Roman History* 6.20: The Etruscan has to be captured because the Delphic oracle has provided no practical instructions. Dio offers no indication of a source that might 'explain' any of our three.

allowed to continue flowing out to sea (12.11.1-4). Plutarch conflates the two: the water is to be kept in its ancient banks, away from the sea, or, failing that, is to be drained into the plain (*Camillus* 4.1-3). Again, just such simple conflation can be found in Josephus, and, I would argue, in Luke: where distinct details can be added together, they are.[37]

Plutarch now has the embassy go to Delphi and return, making one single episode; Josephus (and Luke) both display a similar preference. Livy has a consultation with the now highly respected seer, who commands new Latin games and sacrifices 'to expiate the Alban prodigy'. Plutarch has these instructions provided from Delphi, so (with Dionysius) keeping the Romans independent of any positive advice from the Etruscan seers. Livy recounts the draining of the lake in an ablative absolute clause of eight words; Plutarch seems to prefer the longer treatment in Dionysius, again echoing a considerable amount of Dionysius's vocabulary ('sea', 'ancient course', 'others', 'channels', 'into the plain', 'the operations', 'the water', 'diverted')[38] while still retaining Livy's offering of sacrifice.

(4a) *Mines, vows and a second portent.* (4b) *Peace overtures.* Here Livy and Dionysius go entirely separate ways, with the latter suggesting that the Romans' refusal of a negotiated settlement sought by the alarmed Etruscans brought on them the invasion by the Gauls in punishment. The author of the *De Fortuna Romanorum* would perhaps be reluctant to agree (he goes on to explain that Veii deserved its fall and that its deity preferred to dwell in Rome [*Camillus* 5.6; 6.2]). Instead, Plutarch offers us an account similar to Livy's, with other magistracies abolished, Camillus appointed dictator, and Cornelius Scipio master of horse; omitting the punishment of deserters, he takes us (with Livy) to vows to the goddess, promising a temple. In his account, the Veiians are unalarmed and unawares, as in Livy; in both the city is mined, and the defenders distracted by an assault on the walls. Both have the story of the Veiian priest's sacrifice being captured by the Romans, along with its beneficial effects. (And both include a note of incredulity.)

(5) *A deprecatory prayer.* Part of the text of the prayer is displayed above. Plutarch does include prayers with a similar motif elsewhere,

---

37. Downing, 'Redaction Criticism' I, pp. 56-57; II, pp. 34-35.

38. *Thalassa, archaias…hodou…heteras, horygmasi, eis to pedion, ta erga, to hydor, exetrepen.* Some of the words would be hard to avoid, though not impossible. Together they may seem significant.

but the language here is much closer to that of Dionysius than to Plutarch's own at other points.

There follows the episode of Camillus's stumble, in all three. Plutarch (summarizing drastically) follows Dionysius in linking it to Roman custom in prayer, and in interpreting the mishap as the minimal counterweight to his good fortune for which Camillus had prayed.

(6) *The moving statue*. Plutarch then returns to Livy for the following episode. (Dionysius has a version, but, as the text stands, only much later, at 13.3.) It is here that Plutarch explicitly refers to Livy (*Camillus* 6.2), as saying that Camillus touched the statue, whereas in our texts of Livy (5.22.5) he refers only to the reluctance of the young men to touch the statue at all. If (as I am nonetheless arguing) Plutarch is using both sources, and has both to hand, he is not doing so with close attention. On the other hand, he does also seem to be aware of Dionysius's account here, too: with the latter, Camillus is directly in charge of operations; his vow is recalled; and we are told of the goddess's response in similar words. In Livy the response is said to have been a later addition to the story; Plutarch correctly notes that Livy supposes the only words spoken to have come from bystanders. (With Livy, Plutarch then recounts Camillus's ostentatious triumph, which is not in Dionysius; but our texts are deficient here, anyway.)

In this brief survey of the three accounts, I have concentrated on the issue of conflation, with only occasional reference in the text and in the notes to the apparent tendencies of Plutarch's changes. I hope that this has been sufficient to show that they are very similar to those I have suggested for Josephus; for the latter they seem quite sufficient to account both for his changes to a single predecessor and for his very occasional use of twin parallel sources: narrative coherence, interest and clarity, religious piety and propriety, and (informal) 'political' apologetic.

It would seem to me quite clear that Plutarch is conflating, but very simply and quite arbitrarily, without much very close attention to the texts in front of him. He certainly shows no signs of any interest in 'unpicking' the changes Livy and Dionysius may have made to their common (lost) source, and in fact, no sign of having laid them at all closely side by side. Where they agree, he follows (unless the story line is particularly weak); where they can be taken as supplementing each other, he allows them to; where they go their separate ways, he simply follows one; and where they contradict each other in detail in what nonetheless seems to be 'the same' episode, he makes up his own version. All of this matches precisely (as we have already noted) what we are told about the exercises in writing that Plutarch is likely to have undertaken as a lad.

Conflation, although of this simple 'off-the-cuff' kind, does seem much more likely than the other, 'one lost common source' hypothesis preferred by contemporary classical scholars—simpler still though that might at first sight seem to be, both in terms of the actual technique and in terms of its closeness to what we otherwise gather concerning contemporary compositional convention.

If Plutarch were using the 'lost common source' fairly faithfully, then, of course, when the other two 'agreed' in their use of it, Plutarch would be in agreement with them, too. Where one or other diverged, Plutarch (on this hypothesis) would agree with the one who had not differed. Plutarch would be on his own 'against' the other two either where both the others happened to diverge, but in different ways, from the 'lost common source'; or, of course, at any point where he abandoned his own (hypothetical) faithfulness to it, albeit for good narrative reason (without either of the others chancing to make in advance of him a similar alteration).

Then, if the 'strong narrative logic' I suggested is there in Plutarch itself reproduced a similar strong narrative logic in the 'common lost source', it means that time and again the other two preferred, quite independently, to disrupt that strong story line and in fact to diverge, in advance, again and again, at the same juncture (but quite without collusion); or Plutarch has frequently made 'improving' changes and did not, in the event, keep faithfully to his original. The former (independent and differing divergencies from a clear story line) seems very unlikely; and the latter contradicts the hypothesis of which it is a part.

On the other hand, if Plutarch is taken to have made the kinds of 'improvements' here that, for instance, Russell takes him to have made in his *Coriolanus*,[39] we have to imagine him nonetheless and quite by chance (or by distant and *ex hypothesi* unprompted) memory choosing to follow now this, now that item, which either Livy or Dionysius (but not both) quite independently chose to include in recognizable form. So Dionysius chooses (but Livy omits) the Veiian's long-standing friendship with his captor and his knowledge of ancient oracular tradition

39. Russell, 'Coriolanus', pp. 22-28.

(and Plutarch chooses this, too); whereas Livy chooses (while Diony-sius refuses) conversations in a siege and a request for private advice (and now Plutarch makes the same choice). Livy ignores the offer of military secrets, and Plutarch does too; but with Dionysius, accepts a reference to other recent signs, refused by Livy, while (as now Livy does) explaining that the Veiian was light enough, the Roman burly enough for the abduction; and so on, through the detail recounted above (and more). One has to accept a lot of coincidences—not least that Dionysius and Livy never seem to agree together against Plutarch in their use of the common source, save where Plutarch judges its narra-tive weak; he has otherwise never happened to go his own way where they agree. And if, as we argued above, all the details Plutarch is sup-posed to have reproduced from the lost source made the coherent story we seem to find in his *Coriolanus*, it is again hard to imagine why the other two should have made such unsatisfactory selections where they fail to agree. Pursued closely, the 'single lost common Roman source' hypothesis is very difficult to sustain (recalling, also, that the Greek of Plutarch and of Dionysius can at times be very similar).

Yet, however the reader decides on this issue, the overriding point is that even if the somewhat more difficult procedure of conflation seems to afford the more plausible hypothesis in this instance, it is still *a very simple*, rough-and-ready process of conflation that is being proposed. There is no contemporary analogy at all for anything more complicated still.

Either Q or Total Novelty in Compositional Procedures

Only with the 'lost source Q' hypothesis can we avoid supposing that an early Christian author stepped intellectually, technically and even technologically right out of his contemporary culture, without the least precedent to guide him and with every indication that his intended aim (a new narrative based on earlier ones) could be readily produced by tried and tested means that were part of the education of anyone who could read and write.

The simplest seeming alternatives to the Two-Source hypothesis (Mark and Q) have whoever is placed third (Mark for Griesbach, Luke for Farrer) initially unpicking and then reassembling material in the earlier two. Other theories are more complicated still. Even when such unpicking and reassembly might seem relatively easy (say, in whole narrative units), there is no contemporary analogy. No other writer of the time runs backwards and forwards in two sets of materials in the way the hypothetical third of the Gospel writers must be supposed to have done (on these two competing hypotheses).

In my early study 'Towards the Rehabilitation of Q', some 35 years ago now, I suggested that there are 4 synoptic passages in particular where the process for 'the third writer' would have been particularly difficult.[40] They are the Baptism and Temptation narratives (Mt. 3.1–4.11; Mk 1.12-13; Lk. 3.1-22; 4.1-13), the Beelzebul Controversy (Mt. 12.22-45; Mk 3.20-29; Lk. 11.14-26 with 12.10 and 6.43-45); the Mission Charge(s) (Mt. 9.35–10.6; Mk 6.13-19 with 6.6, 7, 8-11; and Lk. 9.1-5 with 6.13-16 and 10.1-12); and the synoptic Apocalypse (Mt. 24.4-26; Mk 13.5-37; Lk. 21.8-36, and other scattered passages). Here the 'third' writer would be confronted with accounts of 'the same' complex event (action/teaching) where some accounts of utterances or other actions are very similar in each, in sense, wording, syntax and order; some accounts are unique to one or the other; and other accounts display verbal similarities but perhaps rather different order and/or syntax.

We would expect a contemporary writer to choose 'the common witness' both for ease and for security. It is what Josephus and Plutarch (by my account) both do, for ease at least, and what Tacitus says he

40. Downing, 'Towards the Rehabilitation of Q', pp. 169-81; repr. Bellinzoni (ed.), *The Two-Source Hypothesis*, pp. 269-85. It is probably apposite to note that in his 'Conclusion' to the latter collection, J.B. Tyson suggests, p. 447, that in this *NTS* article I may have wrongly analyzed some of the similarities and differences between one Markan and one Matthaean verse. In terms of a word count, his sole criterion, he clearly has a point; but my original argument was in terms of all three of 'words, syntax, order' (*NTS*, p. 171; Bellinzoni, p. 272). On that triple basis, I think my analysis ('fairly close' *not—pace* Tyson—'verbatim') still stands. But it would not much affect my case there—and here!—were that one verse (Mk 2.38// Mt. 12.31) to fall from my 'largely the same' into my 'fairly similar' category. Luke (on the hypothesis in question) would still be ignoring the ready-made conflation and preferring the 'single witness'. The only other rejoinder to my article of which I am aware comes in R.T. Simpson, 'The Major Agreements of Matthew and Luke against Mark', *NTS* 12 (1965/66), pp. 273-84, also reprinted in Bellinzoni (ed.), *The Two-Source Hypothesis*, pp. 382-95. In a footnote, 18 (*NTS*, p. 283; Bellinzoni, p. 394), Simpson finds assertions in my article that are 'at variance with each other'. He is right, of course; he has just failed to note that (in my intention at least) these are entailments of the case made by A.M. Farrer, to whose self-contradiction I was myself drawing attention.

does for safety: 'Where the authorities are unanimous, I shall follow them...'[41] The third Gospel writer (on this alternative hypothesis, and whoever it is thought to have been) almost always (I think with only one exception)[42] actually refuses the most fully common witness. Instead, he adopts, almost word for word, much of what is unique to one or the other. And then, from what is similar he chooses material not to reproduce, but now to re-cast.

Thus, if we take Luke as our imagined third, with Matthew and Mark before him, for the Baptism and Temptation, he includes (often very precisely) the material of Mt. 3.7-10 and 4.3-10, which are not in Mark at all; he has variants of much else, including perhaps the one bit of Mt. 3.4-6 that differs noticeably from Mk 1.5-6; but the closest parallels in Matthew and Mark, John's baptism of those confessing their sins, and—even more significant—John's dress, are not reproduced by Luke at all.

This does not just seem an odd procedure (anyway, as Tyson points out, 'oddness' can be very culture-specific).[43] It is, for anyone, quite a difficult procedure. For the best-equipped writer in the first century CE intending to use source material, it is a *very* difficult procedure, as already noted above. But it is also, so far as we can tell, a totally un-precedented procedure among literate people whose education already gave them well-tried ways of using source material. A Luke who had had anything approaching a normal education, and wanted to 'use' Matthew and Mark would have learned plenty of techniques that he and much more sophisticated writers would have deemed entirely adequate and appropriate. There would have been nothing—nothing at all—to suggest the possibility, let alone the need, to develop some complicated new technique and apply it with such novel criteria for selection and rejection.

The procedure as described would have had to be employed by Luke in the three other passages listed, still refusing all really clear and ready-made conflation, preferring the unique and paraphrasing the merely similar. If Mark were third, the same phenomena would recur: in the Baptism and Temptation narrative, for instance, he would reject John's

41. Tacitus, *Annals* 13.20 (LCL).
42. The quotation from Isaiah (Mk 1.3/Mt. 3.3/Lk. 3.5), 13/14 words, appearing slightly differently in Jn 1.23 (and 1QS 8).
43. Tyson, 'The Two-Source Hypothesis', in Bellinzoni (ed.), *The Two-Source Hypothesis*, p. 449.

preaching and the encounters with the Adversary, where an extensive conflation is ready-made (or all-but); he would reproduce most closely the account of John's dress and his baptism of those who confessed, from Matthew only (while omitting the one phrase there that Matthew and Luke share); but then make his own version of much of the rest. This Griesbach hypothesis (with Mark third), in fact takes him as a con-flater focusing on the common tradition in Matthew and Luke:[44] yet he seems to refuse every ready-made conflation he finds (save the one biblical quotation). In fact, if we pick out in Matthew and Luke passages of 20 words or more with 75 per cent of those in each shared with the other, Mark 'refuses' every one. Not only does he refuse them, but in the four sections here noted, he overcame considerable difficulties in doing so.

It is no answer to imagine possible theological motives for the end result: theologically similar results could readily have been achieved using conventional methods of paraphrase, excision, addition and re-arrangement. Nor is it now appropriate to insist, on the other hand, that we cannot know what someone then might have felt it was worth doing. It would make as much sense to suggest such a procedure at the time as it would to propose the use by an evangelist of a computer. It is simply not an available technique, among those who had a commonplace set of techniques judged adequate, as the evidence here adduced shows.

Of course, it is possible simply to assert that Mark or Luke or Matthew 'simply did' invent a new and unprecedented compositional technique of a sort that intellectually satisfies some of our own contemporaries: this is the way they would have produced this result, so it must be the way it was done back then. Not every assertion is equally plausible, and the case for such unwarranted novelty on the part of one supposedly culturally isolated early Christian with far less skill as a

---

44. Farmer, *Synoptic Problem*, p. 211, 'concurrent testimony'; p. 236, 'deviated from his sources as little as possible'. Farmer seems so mesmerized by the 'minor agreements of Matthew and Luke against Mark in Markan contexts' that he fails to note let alone attempt to account for the many 'major agreements of both against Mark in Markan contexts'—to wit, the passages here listed; but also the other major Q passages, where, on his Griesbach hypothesis Mark refuses every piece of unmistakable 'concurrent testimony', refuses every ready-made conflation, even though conflation is his aim. (This seems still to be so in the second edition of *Synoptic Problem*, not available to me, but partly reprinted in Bellinzoni (ed.), *The Two-Source Hypothesis*, pp. 164-203.)

paraphraser than had, say, Josephus, has very little to commend it.

A Matthew and a Luke using Mark and (lost) Q are behaving very much as someone with a contemporary elementary education would be expected to. The procedure fits, snugly.[45] Unless and until some first-century or thereabouts parallel is found for, say, a Mark or a Luke as third, unpicking and reassembling the other's use of the first, rejecting close parallels, preferring the unique, and paraphrasing mostly the similar, then I would suggest that there should be a moratorium on the elaboration of any such theory. The Griesbach and Farmer theories (and others more elaborate still) fly in the face of all the specific evidence we have, and in the face of all our insights into language, culture, society and individuals. So far from the various theories being all so lacking in evidence as to leave the issue insoluble, none but the Two-Document hypothesis has any initial plausibility at all.[46]

However persuasive I may find the foregoing, it is not a knock-down argument. It certainly has not proved so. W.R. Farmer still maintains Matthaean priority, M.D. Goulder has gone on to argue in great detail his conclusion that Luke used Matthew as well as Mark. In the next chapter we try to discern what the latter process could have meant in first-century practice.

Appended Note

Very little new work in this area has since in fact come to my attention. The most significant has been S.L. Mattila's 'A Question Too Often Neglected', *NTS* 41.2 (1995), pp. 199-217. Mattila emphasises more strongly than I have done the two anomalies in the work of the synoptic

---

45. Downing, 'Redaction Criticism', again; but also 'Contemporary Analogies', pp. 51-65; and 'Ears to Hear', pp. 97-121; and, of course, most of the remainder of the present volume.

46. That the issue may be insoluble is canvassed by Bellinzoni, in his 'Introduction' to *The Two-Source Hypothesis*, p. 15; and cf. Tyson, again, on the inconclusiveness of the argument as it appeared to him, 'The Two-Source Hypothesis', p. 449, as noted above; and also Palmer, *Logic*. I am suggesting that this conclusion can be drawn only when the contemporary cultural context's literary practices are ignored, along with an important selection of the synoptic evidence. Objectors to one or both of Markan priority and of Q will presumably want to check on the account here sketched of that contemporary scene, and more work in this area would be welcome.

evangelists to which I draw attention: the closeness of reproduction at times (but she further emphasises the unevenness); and the greater complexity of Matthew than might be expected. However, just as she allows that Tatian's technique 'while being an innovation, is not *sui generis*... It stems from methods that have already been in use but it *stretches these to new limits*', p. 205 (Mattila's emphasis), so it seems to me that the two document hypothesis indicates a similar flexibility deployed by the evangelists in the application of contemporary literary convention, in any posited spectrum of approaches very much closer to evidenced examples than any rival reconstructions appear. Mattila's further 'preliminary suggestion', that the implications here of L. Alexander's work, *The Preface to Luke's Gospel*, be taken into account, seems also cogent: in (technical) 'school' settings, close reproduction is more likely than among the style-conscious literati, pp. 216-17. I am also grateful for Mattila's drawing my attention in correspondence to the notion of 'living texts'—texts in constant use, and so subject to constant revision, as one possible way in which such sequences as Matthew's and Luke's Sermons may have diverged; Mattila is drawing on a discussion of texts of Galen by A.E. Hanson, 'Papyri of Medical Content' (YCS, 28; Cambridge: Cambridge University Press, 1985), p. 45. We should look forward to more investigations and proposals along these lines.

Chapter 9

A PARADIGM PERPLEX: LUKE, MATTHEW AND MARK*

Introductory

In their 1989 survey of the synoptic problem, E.P. Sanders and M. Davies argue that a complicated solution must be held to be the most likely, and conclude,

> Mark probably did sometimes conflate material which came separately to Mathew and Luke (so the Griesbach hypothesis), and Matthew probably did conflate material which came separately to Mark and Luke (so the two-source hypothesis). Thus we think that Luke knew Matthew (so Goulder, the Griesbachians, and others) and that both Luke and Matthew were the original authors for some of their sayings material (so especially Goulder). Following Boismard, we think it likely that one or more of the gospels existed in more than one edition, and that the gospels as we have them may have been dependent on more than one proto- or intermediate gospel.[1]

In his own lengthy discussion of Luke, published around the same time, M.D. Goulder refuses to countenance any such complex solution, dismissing anything of the kind as a forlorn attempt to patch up an outworn hypothesis. Instead he urges what he terms 'a new paradigm', one that provides a perspective on the material that contrasts with the 'contradiction, error, muddle and circular argument' with which the 'old' is riddled.[2] He quotes Karl Popper and T.S. Kuhn on the demand for such new insights when a scholarly community is employing more and more complex ingenuity to defend an old perspective that has outworn its usefulness and is no longer able to provide an effective approach to the data to which it is being applied: such, he insists, are the explanations

*   Reprinted from *NTS* 38.1 (1992), pp. 15-36, with kind permission.
1.   Sanders and Davies, *Studying the Synoptic Gospels*, p. 113.
2.   Goulder, *Luke*, p. 5.

currently on offer to explain the 'Minor Agreements' against Mark in Markan contexts of supposedly independent Matthew and Luke. Goulder's positive argument, which occupies most of his two volumes, consists in showing how Luke's mind could have been working with Mark and Matthew and Scripture to produce the result we find. Sanders and Davies urge an acknowledgment of complexity, Goulder claims warrants for a simple solution.

It is argued here that there is a major defect in both approaches, albeit one quite widely shared. Both proposals, as well as the previous ones of Boismard, Farmer, Schramm and others are vitiated by anachronistic assumptions concerning available compositional techniques in the first century.[3] I shall for simplicity concentrate on Goulder's essay, as the most recent [still] full-scale assault on the Two-Document hypothesis here preferred. But I shall refer from time to time to implications for some of the other proposals.

I shall first try to piece together from the hints that Goulder drops, something of the implicit picture he has of Luke at work 'reconciling' Mark and Matthew, although this is never written out for us. (There is still less in our other authors.) We shall compare and contrast our results with what our surviving ancient sources suggest that a writer at the time attempting to 'reconcile' such works as Mark and Matthew (or Luke and Matthew, or suggested earlier editions of these) might have been expected to do, on the basis of common education and common literary practice. But we shall also note some possible incoherences underlying Goulder's account which both render it self-contradictory and also in detail even more at odds with contemporary practice than his overt asides suggest. Other hypotheses that suggest much more elaborate compositional techniques (Farmer, Boismard) are equally or still more implausible.

Goulder's Luke's Procedure

For Goulder Luke is 'harmonising' (p. 382), 'reconciling' (pp. 201-203, 207, 311, 328, 341, 407) Mark and Matthew, and is 'no amateur when it comes to reconciling his sources' (p. 410). So far, so good. Such a

---

3.   M.-E. Boismard, 'Commentaire', in P. Benoit and M.-E. Boismard, *Synopse de quatre évangiles*, II (Paris: Cerf, 1972); Farmer, *Synoptic Problem*; T. Schramm, *Der Markus-Stoff bei Lukas* (Cambridge: Cambridge University Press, 1971). None of these works considers the details of ancient compositional techniques.

programme, simply undertaken, would have been entirely credible in the first century, although no instances are adduced, let alone examined. We may for our part note, however, how Josephus conflates Chronicles with 2 Samuel/1 Kings, or how Plutarch conflated Livy and Dionysius of Halicarnassus; or how Tatian in the next century may have worked to conflate all four Gospels.[4] Both the intention and relevant procedures are evidenced.

Yet present-day classical scholars seem unanimous in agreeing that any conflation, if done at all, would most often have been done simply, using just one author at a time, in blocks.[5] Any close conflation of, say, two parallel accounts of 'the same' event would be very uncommon: there would be very little if any precedent to suggest it as a procedure to Goulder's Luke (or to Boismard's Luke or to Farmer's Mark). Even if the analyses of Josephus and of Plutarch just referred to are valid,[6] we would still expect that any conflation of parallel accounts of incidents (colloquy or other activity) that was achieved would have been very simply effected. If, as Goulder supposes, Luke was 'no amateur' harmonizer, but an educated historian (p. 270) this is the sole 'professional' model that would have been available for him to follow: and the conclusion, as will be argued in detail, is inconvenient for Goulder's thesis, for his Luke seems to follow a very complex (and so, amateurish?) procedure indeed, one for which no available precedent prepares us. We otherwise know of no comparable undertaking before Tatian in the next century, producing his Diatessaron, 'harmony ' of all four Gospels; and Tatian was obviously sure that Luke had made a pretty poor job of it, paying least attention to the order Luke imposed (and adopting a 'block procedure' of the sort Luke does on the Two-Document hypothesis, but quite different from Goulder's Luke, as we shall see).

---

4.   For this and the next three paragraphs see the much fuller discussion in Downing, 'Compositional Conventions and the Synoptic Problem', *JBL* 107.1 (1988), pp. 69-85, ch. 8 above; and S.L. Mattila, 'A Question Too Often Neglected', *NTS* 41.2 (1995), pp. 199-217; and the extended note to Chapter 8 above.

5.   See Downing, 'Redaction Criticism'; *idem*, 'Compositional Conventions and the Synoptic Problem', Chapter 8 above; for Tatian, Appended Note, below, and Mattila, 'Question', pp. 203-206.

6.   E.g. Luce, *Livy*, pp. 140-43, and other references in Downing, 'Compositional Conventions'.

As well as conflating pre-existing material Goulder's Luke at times also creates fresh matter on the basis of suggestions sparked by Matthew and by the Jewish Scriptures. For the acceptability of such invention from the hands of contemporary writers, on the basis, often, of very exiguous hints in their sources (but not *ex nihilo* [pp. 78, 383]) Goulder has plenty of evidence (pp. 123-28). It is quite conceivable that the author of the third Gospel could have used Mk 14.3-9 and both repositioned it and elaborated it to form 'The Anointing' we now find at Lk. 7.36-50, as Goulder and I both argue,[7] and we may compare as further examples, say, Lk. 3.10-14; 5.1-11; 14.7-14. What seems much less likely on the basis of our available examples is that 'real' Luke would do other than dash such items off spontaneously. There might well be incidental echoes of his other major sources, or of other writings familiar to him. But there is no precedent for the deliberate and elaborate collage from widely separate sectors of the sources used that Goulder (or, for that matter, Boismard) so often proposes.

There is no difficulty in allowing Goulder's Luke in general to rely on memory (pp. 389, 428, 549), as other contemporaries seem to have done, though I shall question the way in which he is said to have used it.[8] In those places where close visual attention to a single source seems discernible the result from other contemporaries will often be a paraphrase rather than word-for-word quotation.[9] Thus Luke's freer renderings (especially in the Passion narrative)[10] would be not at all unexpected. Indeed, we might be rather surprised at Luke's so often including so much of Matthew's wording as exactly as on this hypothesis he does. However, exact copying is clearly a possibility in the first century, and presents us with no technical problem. (I would draw attention again to S.L. Mattila's suggestion that the model of 'middle-brow' technical writing may provide some instances of closer copying combined with freer adaptation.[11])

---

7.   Goulder, *Luke*, pp. 367-406; Downing, 'Redaction Criticism', II, p. 37.

8.   E.g. Russell, 'Coriolanus', p. 22; and C.R.B. Pelling, 'Plutarch's Method', pp. 92-93.

9.   E.g. Pelletier, *Flavius Josèphe*, p. 29.

10.   Goulder, *Luke*, ch. 8, pp. 719-99; Downing, 'Redaction Criticism', II, pp. 40-41.

11.   See the reference to proposals by Mattila, 'Question', referring to L. Alexander in particular, in the note appended to Chapter 8 above.

Physically, how does Goulder's Luke set about his task? We only receive from time to time such incidental comments as 'Luke rolls up his scroll of Mark, with a marker at 3.19' (p. 346; cf. pp. 197, 291), and, 'So the Matthaean scroll is rolled up and Mark is resumed on the table' (p.410). The case for the use of the codex form as early as Mark has been argued,[12] but does not seem to have persuaded many, and Goulder does not adopt this easy path for his Luke, who is firmly restricted to scrolls. What sort of 'marker' is intended, and on what evidence, is not said. The scroll could well have remained with either end rolled up to the column in question; the place could certainly have been marked with ink or a pricked hole or in some other way. We seem to have no surviving texts that have been at all obviously marked for excerpting; but we cannot argue much from such a lack. Rather more significant is the fact that no one ever describes or mentions in passing such a procedure, even if we suppose that Tatian at least in the next century must be supposed to have used (and even invented) one. Goulder's '3.19' we can of course allow as a shorthand for 'where AYTONKAI divides'—although this shorthand does conceal the fact that in *scriptio continua* ('writing with no breaks between words') there would be little space or ease for any such mark to be made. The 'table' is perhaps a conventional reading desk, taking one scroll at a time; the scroll not in use seems to have been put somewhere else for the time being.[13]

Is Luke doing his own writing, or is he dictating? Mostly we have terms that are ambiguous on this score, 'adds', 'continues', 'inserts'. On I think quite a rare occasion, 'Luke writes' (p. 303), but I suppose that could still mean 'has the following words written for him;' it is not clear whether the absence of a 'scribe' from his church (p. 300) consitutes also the absence of a stenographer.

So, then, Goulder's Luke may be standing by a small desk and dictating his version of the text on the scroll before him to a scribe seated nearby, cross-legged, or on a chair or a stool, with a blank scroll on a

12. C.H. Roberts, 'Books in the Graeco-Roman World and in the New Testament', in P.R. Ackroyd and C.F. Evans (eds.), *Cambridge History of the Bible*, I (Cambridge: Cambridge University Press, 1970), pp. 53-56.

13. S.L. Mattila cites doubts about the use of reading desks in this period, suggesting rather a seated reader using his or her lap or one thigh as a rest; and making things more difficult still for Goulder's Luke; Mattila, 'Question', p. 215, citing G.M. Parássoglou, 'A Roll upon His Knees' (CS, 28; Cambridge: Cambridge University Press, 1985), p. 273.

board across his or her knees.[14] This would leave Luke's hands freer to manipulate his scrolls. On the other hand, the detailed collage of items perhaps implies a visual control of both source and product, as Luke implants in a Matthaean sequence, say, reminiscence from Mark, from Matthew elsewhere, or from Scripture (e.g. pp. 316-28, 528-45). So Luke could of course be doing his own writing, himself seated; and his source could then be on a low stand beside him. (Placing it more securely still on the ground would put the text well outside most people's optimum focal distance.[15])

It would be possible to use two scrolls on stands either side of the writer (or the one dictating), or in the hands of two assistants. Goulder only once, I think, suggests that two scrolls are consulted together (pp. 299-300). Usually he indicates a fairly simple procedure, as already noted: 'So Luke rolls up his scroll of Mark…and opens Matthew again…' (p. 346; cf. pp. 197, 291, again). However, there are clear indications of Alexandrian scholars somehow having compared and collated classical texts, of Homer and others, so we can certainly allow the use of two scrolls in some circumstances. Tatian, later, will have to cope with three together quite often, and on occasions, four. But Luke, as we shall argue, is doing almost the exact opposite of what was done by the only scholars whose practice could have afforded him a model. As did Tatian later, they collated scrolls to minimize divergencies. Goulder's Luke is actually vastly increasing them. They concentrated on one stretch at a time of their two (or possibly more) scrolls, (and so, later, did Tatian). Goulder's Luke in practice runs backwards and forwards, sometimes from memory, sometimes (apparently) rolling his main current scroll to and fro, especially for the sections we label Luke 11–14, and this in order to create fresh complexes of material.

We have no indication of anyone else having behaved this way. Tatian (who could afford Goulder his most promising comparison) turns on or back in, say, Luke or Mark to 'the same' pericope as he is reading in Matthew. He shows no sign of exploring for innovative connections. If one is defending Markan priority and the Q hypothesis along

---

14. Turner, *Greek Manuscripts*, pp. 6-9; rather less detail in J.H. Greenlee, *Scribes, Scrolls and Scripture* (Grand Rapids: Eerdmans, 1985), pp. 1-20; other references in Downing, 'Compositional Conventions', Chapter 8 above; Mattila, 'Question', pp. 215-16.

15. Turner, *Greek Manuscripts*, p. 7, it is 'not easy to visualize satisfactory copying from an open scroll placed on the ground beside the writer'.

conventional lines one does have to allow for Matthew reordering early chapters of Mark, and also much of Q, thematically.[16] But this is on a very significantly smaller scale than Goulder suggests for his Luke: Matthew would be dealing with perhaps 35 columns at most of Q (or 18 codex pages) and about as much of the early chapters of Mark. Matthew's detailed conflation (on this view) for the Baptism–Temptation, Beelzebul, Mission Charge and Eschatological Discourse is similar to, though rather simpler than, Tatian's procedures later; and far simpler than that of Goulder's Luke, or any of Boismard's final three authors. A Farmer-Griesbach Mark is similar enough to Tatian in the way he collates, physically, quite simply: but then elaborately eccentric in the way he refuses all the closely similar material and enhances the divergencies of what he does accept.[17]

But when Goulder's Luke 'opens up his Matthew again', apparently so simple an action, we seem to lose all touch with first-century reality: '...before him stands Matthew's Great Sermon, as majestic in its structure and as soaring in its eloquence as the mountain on which it is preached' (p. 346). Book-stands (where used) seem to be designed for normal use, that is, for reading one column at a time,[18] mostly containing around four or five hundred characters. Matthew's 'Great Sermon' contains around 9500 characters, 19 average columns' worth. In a small proportion of surviving manuscripts we do find columns that vary enormously, both vertically and horizontally. Some are a lot smaller, with far less than four hundred characters. Turner reproduces the largest he seems to have been able to find, a text of Aristotle, with around 3200 characters in a column.[19] It would, I think, be quite difficult to lay such a column out open satisfactorily on a conventional book-stand, with both the rolled ends safe from falling. (The second copier of the scroll resumed a more normal module.) Even at this size Matthew's Sermon would need a nominal three columns, more likely four (unless it happened to begin or end with the start or finish of the Sermon). On the ground that would mean around 700 millimetres of very cramped text. In the more likely configuration of around 19 columns it would spread for nearly three metres. Yet Goulder really does seem to want his Luke

16. See, again, the appended note to Chapter 8. above.

17. On Farmer, see again Downing, 'Redaction Criticism', II; and Chapter 8 above.

18. E.G. Turner, *Greek Papyri* (Oxford: Clarendon Press, 1968), p. 7.

19. Turner, *Greek Manuscripts*, p. 108.

to have the whole thing in view, so that he can, for instance, run forward from Mt. 5.42 to 7.12 and back again to 5.46 and then to 5.7 and then on again to 7.2 (pp. 363-66), planning (it seems) what to include in his Plain Sermon, what to omit altogether, and what to save for various other occasions. Goulder's Luke's copy of Matthew must now be on the ground to be so wide open...with its ends probably out of reach for anyone seated, and the writing at either end certainly very much further away than the 500 millimetres presupposed for normal reading. (Goulder's Luke is certainly himself doing the reading, rather than relying on someone else to read to him.)

If Luke is doing his own writing, rather than dictating, he is balancing a springy new scroll on a board on his knees, together with a pen; and somewhere to hand are his scroll of Mark, and a pen-sharpener, a pricker or other line-marker, ruler, dividers, sponge, bowl of water, pumice and ink (perhaps some sand?)...[20] It is not the sort of circumstance to encourage the invention of a complex new way of composing a text from sources.

As noted, Goulder's Luke could avoid some difficult manipulation if he were to use an amanuensis, even if that were more time-consuming. The Luke we are imagining then has two texts on two stands, and reads out aloud from the one in front of him, or rehearses out loud a passage recalled from memory.[21] He then indicates each time when his scribe is to start recording. Perhaps Luke or his scribe or a second scribe has a wax tablet for Luke's initial musings as he assembles bits and pieces from here and there. Maybe he has a fine audio-visual memory.

It is tempting to adduce further difficulties in imagining any of these suggested procedures as an argument against accepting each in turn. But our difficulty in imagining may turn out to be quite relative to our own experience of reading or writing, and someone else may be able and willing to show that a result like the one we find in our Luke can be produced out of predecessors analogous to our Matthew and Mark in just this way, at dictation. The really important difficulty remains: nothing we are aware of would seem to have been likely to suggest such a toing and froing procedure to Luke, whether dictating or doing his own writing; nor to any of Boismard's three final authors. And, on the other hand, there were plenty of quite simple examples available for tackling the task of reconciling sometimes similar sometimes very divergent

20. Turner, *Greek Manuscripts*, p. 8.
21. Turner, *Greek Manuscripts*, p. 19.

accounts into new narrative, models of composition well prepared for in any literate person's education.[22]

What we would expect from our knowledge of normal education in late antiquity is an ability to paraphrase, précis, expand—and simply omit. One of the *Progymnasmata* (Theon) does talk of learning how 'we weave' (*sumplekomen*) one piece of text into another: but it is simply a matter of giving a fable a historical reference, or illuminating a historical incident with such a fable.[23] When Lucian reflects on writing history, there is no instruction on splicing sources, let alone unravelling them first. Livy, Polybius, Dionysius, Josephus, Plutarch and the rest just go ahead and write, mostly on the basis of a single prior text in front of them, paraphrasing, précising, expanding, omitting, while relying otherwise for the most part only on unchecked memories of other sources and even of the one in front of them.[24] On the (very) rare occasions when they conflate two similar accounts of one event or of one sequence of events, it is done very simply, as we have already noted. In particular, it is worth repeating that we have no evidence whatsoever for even the most erudite of our surviving authors bothering to unpick interrelated sources from one another, prior to a new assembly.[25]

The criteria for change, for what counts as improvement, are narrative coherence, plausibility, interest, clarity, religious piety and propriety, and informal 'political' apologetic.[26] Plausibility is gained where sources agree, as Tacitus notes.[27] One may suspect that such agreement in the sources is also welcome because work is then that much easier. Where we can check, first-century writers certainly do choose to follow 'the common witness', and a Luke attempting to 'reconcile', to 'harmonize' Matthew and Mark would be very conventional in emphasizing what they had in common, and in reducing any (apparent) inconsistencies between them. And this is what Goulder tells us his Luke intends. Unfortunately for the most part his Luke actually does

22. E.g. Pelling, 'Plutarch's Method of Work', pp. 74-96; and Chapter 8 above.

23. Theon, *Progymnasmata* 3.12 (Walz, p. 175 ll. 1-10); Chapter 8, p. 158 and n. 22, above.

24. Chapter 8 above.

25. Luce, *Livy*, p. xix; Hornblower, *Hieronymus*, pp. 3, 21; and Chapter 8 above.

26. Downing, 'Redaction Criticism', I and II; and Chapter 8 above, again.

27. Tacitus, *Annals* 13.20; Mattila cites in addition Arrian, *Anabasis Alexandri Pref.* 1-3, 'Question', pp. 211-12.

the exact opposite. He produces what is in effect a third and discordant narrative. It emphasizes the divergencies of its sources by following now one, now the other, just where they are *most* distinct; and almost every time they do agree, it goes off on its own, as we shall see. (Farmer's Mark is even weirder, as noted earlier.)

In his discussion of Luke's *Proem*, Goulder argues that his author is chiefly concerned to reconcile the *order* of Mark and Matthew, rather than their detailed texts. But even here what Goulder's Luke does is produce by and large a third order, mostly disagreeing with both his predecessors, and doing nothing to reduce the perplexities of his puzzled Theophilus (or, for that matter, of Tatian, who sees Luke as offering no worthwhile base on which to structure a harmony). It may be worth noting that when later Christian 'Fathers' start to discuss discrepancies between the Gospels, it is in divergencies between individual episodes, not their relative order, that interest lies.[28] Even if Goulder's Luke does produce some kind of chronological resolution that persuades Michael Goulder himself, and others, he does it at the expense of any of the kind of harmonizing with which other contemporaries of Luke concerned themselves (or that Tatian did, later).

A First-Century Luke in Action

A first-century Luke who had read Matthew and Mark, and perhaps got to know them thoroughly, might well have decided to produce his own combined version of them; and he might on a few occasions have produced the results we find, as I have already allowed, and even for some of the reasons Goulder suggests. But overall a first-century Luke would have worked very differently with these sources and would have produced a book very different from our third Gospel.

To try to substantiate this further, I shall attempt briefly to imagine at least the first few steps that might have been made by a first-century writer, positively convinced of the value of Matthew and of Mark, but far from satisfied with either.

For a useful comparison we have to imagine that he brings with him not only a form of early Christian faith, but also a number of the spec-

---

28. John Chrysostom, *Homilies on Matthew* 26.3; 27.1; 67.1, presupposing wide awareness of discrepancies between the Gospels. Luke's contemporary, Josephus, clearly prefers thematic order above his sources' indications of chronology (Downing, 'Redaction Criticism', I).

ific concerns we do find in our actual third Gospel. Our list might well include at least an interest in the wider Roman world, and in people outside the author's own circle and its enemies (if only as people whose opinions his own hearers might care about); and we might also include attention to oppressed groups, with women high on that list; and we would expect an emphasis on piety, prayer and good works, especially among the more eminent; but also on repentance and forgiveness; together with notes of human emotions (joy, amazement, sorrow). We could substantiate the plausibility of this list from a reading of Josephus, or of the model he seems to have adopted, Dionysius of Halicarnassus. We shall allow our Luke to be influenced by Jewish Scriptures, but also to display something of the manner of a popular Hellenistic historian (even if his own background is more in technical literature).[29] We would thus permit the practices suggested above, paraphrasing, précising, expanding, omitting, in the interests of narrative coherence, plausibility, interest, clarity, religious piety and informal 'political' apologetic. And we would bear clearly in mind the factor already noted, that any first-century writer working with more or less 'parallel' sources would be more than likely to welcome the closer parallels he found, where his splicing was already done for him. But since 'reconciliation' is so important a part of Goulder's thesis, we should perhaps expect our Luke to display an even stronger than normal interest in 'harmonizing'. He will do little to cross-examine his witness (despite Lk. 1.2-3), apart from noting agreement and disagreement in keen appreciation of the former: two witnesses saying the same thing afford both reassurance and a simpler task.

We have already noted the kind of freedom in rewriting and in creating, if not entirely from scratch, that our author would naturally exercise. Speeches he would certainly expect to create, but not individual authoritative teachings (even though mis-ascriptions might well get through).

If we were working this imaginary reconstruction out in detail we might well also take on board many of the further Lukan traits discerned by Goulder and displayed by him under 30 headings with further sub-headings (pp. 89-128), as well as agreed Lukan preferences in vocabulary and syntax. We could indeed, I think, allow all this—and

---

29. As argued by L. Alexander, *The Preface to Luke's Gospel*; compare Lucian's surgeon-historian, *How to Write History* 16.

still expect our Luke to produce a very different result from what we find in our third Gospel.

On the other hand I think we might do well to pay a lot less attention than does Goulder to hypothetical reconstructions of Luke's mind as he works with Matthew, Mark and Scripture. In the light of the ready diversity of readers' responses very little warrant for a particular reconstruction is afforded by such comments as 'It was Mt. 7.16a which was in Luke's conscious mind, for it is to 7.16b that he immediately proceeds...' (p. 371). Goulder is not alone, of course, in supposing that most if not every word retained in common, as well as echoes and divergencies among linked authors, are to be interpreted as intentionally significant in ways we may readily discern. But this kind of supposition is badly out of tune with first-century literary composition, which at its most sophisticated had detailed concerns only with syntax and vocabulary, however open it may have been to un- or half-conscious resonances.[30] Deliberate allusion is clearly signalled. A great deal of space and, one must assume, intended force of Goulder's argument depend on this kind of minute analysis of Luke's mind, but it can only appear persuasive to those who share this mistaken approach.

Our Luke, then, has copies to hand of Mark and of Matthew and has come to know them both quite well. He is therefore aware that there are areas of quite close, even very close overlap between them, both in individual instances of purposeful activity, and in some sequences of events. He respects both works, but is sure he can improve things by combining them as well as by altering them along the lines just sketched.

There is one very important issue we shall have to imagine our Luke having decided at the outset. With less of an interest in harmonizing than we have allowed him we might well have expected him only very rarely to refer to his scroll of Mark at all. He could easily have relied on his memory to supply the few incidental items worth recalling that were not also in Matthew. As the churches quickly decided, almost everything of importance in Mark is there in Matthew in some recognizable form and measure already, as well as a great deal more of as much or of more importance. (Tatian uses very little of 'pure' Mark.) But with the extra interest in 'reconciling' that we have allowed him, our Luke will indeed from time to time have to consult his text of Mark as well as that

---

30. See 'Words and Meanings', Chapter 3 above.

of his major source, Matthew. And once we have allowed him to consult the text of Mark as well as having Matthew open in front of him we have ensured a very different result from the one in our New Testament collection. Our Luke will, *ex hypothesi*, show a marked preference for stretches of narrative (including discourse) where his sources already agree, rather than omit them or radically alter them—in the way that Goulder's Luke does.

Our First-Century Luke in Action alongside Goulder's Luke

So to our Luke in a little detail. We can happily allow him a prologue like the one in our third Gospel: we find much the same in Josephus and in Dionysius, as well as in technical *Fachprose* ('technical writing').[31] He will claim accuracy in the use of sources, comprehensiveness, painstaking research (perhaps more than two predecessors have been tapped), and promises good order (logical rather than factually chronological).[32]

Our Luke could well discern the symbolic import of Matthew's genealogy and decide to include it, or something like, but a bit later in the story. Genealogies do appear in other Hellenistic histories, though they do not introduce them. Perhaps our Luke has done his own scriptural research in the past, or someone in his congregation has, and he might prefer that version. He is unlikely, *ex hypothesi*, actually at this point to create a discordant tradition if all he already has is what he finds in Matthew.

The same applies a fortiori to the birth and infancy narratives. It would be no 'reconciliation' to create a quite other, and discrepant, account. Unless he is embarrassedly sure on the basis of still more authoritative information also known to his potential readers that Matthew is largely 'wrong', he will use Matthew here extensively. Popular first-century historians are well aware of discrepant infancy traditions accorded to their characters, and Luke would very likely feel free to embroider (as Goulder and many others note), or to condense and add from other stock (if such he has). In this free rewriting he would readily express theological and imply 'narratalogical' motifs that are important to him. He could introduce likely further links with ancient tradition

31. Downing, 'Redaction Criticism', II, pp. 30-31; L. Alexander, *The Preface to Luke's Gospel*.

32. See n. 28 above.

and the Jewish holy city, and could portray the ascetic piety of main and attendant characters, and delineate in advance the kind of 'well-being', 'salvation' that his chief character will enable; and so on. But in all this we will expect to find more of Matthew in our Luke than a few names of people and places and oddments of obvious scriptural phrases (pp. 208-209, 221-25, 237-42, 246-53, 255-61). Even someone not aiming at harmony as such will show more signs of respect for his original than we discover in actual Luke.

It is clear, then, that our Luke could—plausibly—have readily adapted as well as, if need be, augmented Matthew's nativity sequence to convey his vision of what God intended, maintaining at least his normal minimal signs of dependence. Goulder is able to argue persuasively for Luke's ability to rewrite the passion to convey his intended interpretation of it, while retaining clear signs of his Markan original. If he had had Matthew 1–2 in front of him, we would have expected to find roughly the same signs of dependence here at the Birth as we do at the Death. Even if Luke had other traditions that he valued more highly than he did Matthew's at this point, we would have expected at least the ackowledgment we find at Lk. 3.19 (John's imprisonment) in compensation for the omission of Mk 6.14-29. The upshot is, we do not find 'harmony' with Matthew 1–2. In fact we do not so far find any of the signs we would expect in a first-century author of any clear awareness of these chapters at all.

However, we could very readily allow our first-century Luke to write an infancy narrative for his hero pretty well from scratch if he had found none in his two sources. He would include a selection of standard motifs, and very likely echo stories from the sacred traditions of his hero's people. He would very likely include a tale of his hero as a precocious 12-year old. Without Matthew 1–2 to confuse him, our Luke could readily have produced the first two chapters of our third Gospel.

For his next sequence our imaginary Luke knows and has to hand his copies of Mark and Matthew. To his delight he will have realized—or he checks and finds—that both texts are very similar for some distance: agreed witnesses. Matthew then has some words of John not in Mark, so these can be omitted or condensed or otherwise adapted. The detailed Temptations that follow in Matthew are quite powerful, the motif of the testing of the hero is very acceptable, Mark agrees that something of the sort is to be narrated, and so we shall expect Luke to include a version of Matthew's narrative, more or less drastically re-cast.

Again, little of our expectation is realized. Now, we may well allow the third Gospel we know to guide our imagining of this Luke as already agreed, and so may decide that any presentation of John as an Elijah figure will be dropped, even if it is word for word in both witnesses. But the fact is that apart from scriptural texts (as here and as in a small number of other instances) our Luke hardly reproduces *any* passage where Matthew and Mark are word for word the same, and none where they are in agreement for more than 20 words at a stretch.[33] He will reproduce quite a number of Matthew-only passages of perhaps 30, even 60 words, very closely indeed.[34] But *common* witness he manages to avoid, indeed he actually seems to go to great pains to obviate it. We have to imagine him running against every available procedural convention. He is using two quite long texts, side by side, and that, as we have seen, is difficult enough. But he is collating them, not to find common witness to include—he is looking for it, and very carefully, to excise. And if we are expecting to find someone intent on reconciling divergencies between two known texts, what we find instead is someone going to unprecedented pains to produce a text that omits the existing harmonies, and produces yet another narrative, a third one, with yet more divergencies all of its own. This is starting to look very much less 'simple' than Goulder promised (pp. 24-25). (It in fact resembles rather closely the eccentricities of Farmer's Griesbachian Mark's procedures, as I have argued in the previous chapter.)

Our Luke might well feel that the bare summary of Jesus' proclamation in Matthew and in Mark was inadequate, and so prefer to provide Jesus with a fuller statement (Lk. 4.16-30). And when he came to the call stories, we might again agree with Goulder that a writer like Luke (we could compare Josephus) would quite likely feel that an instant response from those summoned was psychologically implausible, and prepare a summons with its own preparatory stage, to be placed a little later in the main narrative. Our author might even have had such an elaborated tale to hand, based on a resurrection encounter narrative, as some have thought. The fact remains that in the call stories, it is again closely similar common witness that Goulder's Luke rejects. We also might well not be surprised if our Luke brought forward the tale of Jesus being rejected in his homeland. But the Matthaean and Markan

33. Lk. 7.27; 20.28, 42-43 (quotations); 5.23-24 and 9.23c-24 are otherwise the longest.

34. E.g. Mt. 3.11b-12, Lk. 3.17; Mt. 3.7b-10, Lk. 3.7b-9.

accounts are still clearly common tradition, even if the respective context of each is not the same. A less than convincing story in a single witness may well be 'improved', that we allow; but joint witness we would expect to be afforded more respect.

Matthew 7.29 has 13 words of which 12 are in Mk 1.22 exactly; Mark then goes off on his own into an exorcism. Goulder's Luke again omits the common witness, but includes the exorcism, using much of the Mark-only wording as it stands. So our author is not averse to reproducing some of Mark fairly precisely: a run of 29 words recurs exactly. It makes it even more striking that he so rarely cares to copy Mark exactly just where Matthew also chooses to.

Mark continues with a series of further healings. Matthew's equivalents come 'later' in his narrative. Where sources disagree over 'the same' matter other contemporaries will often in fact produce a third account.[35] However, if our Luke really wants to harmonize he can do so quite readily. For instance, he could go on to the last of Mark's present series (the Paralytic, Mk 2.1-12) and then bring the rest of the Matthaean series forward; a far simpler device than Goulder's Luke adopts (and much closer to what Tatian later produces). The result would then resemble both his sources quite closely and enhance Theophilus's impression of the extent of their accord.

On the other hand, if our Luke is not particularly concerned with reconciliation at this point, where his sources tell of the same/similar events but in a different order, he may simply stay with one of them. Well, he stays with Mark, apart from inserting his own version of the call of Peter, already mentioned. Then we shall not be so surprised if our Luke rejects the common witness to Preaching throughout Galilee (Mk 1.39//Mt. 4.23). Following Mark only, he may not have discerned it as common witness. But what may well surprise us is what we then discover in Luke's version of the immediately following item in Mark, the Cleansing of a Leper. We here find what could be seen as some quite unexpected faint echoes of Matthew, both in omissions and in substitutions. Goulder is quite pleased to come upon his Luke at last displaying his double-dependence, 'a heaven-sent opportunity for reconciling his two authorities' (pp. 328-30). Agreed, the apparent echoes (or 'significant Minor Agreements' as Goulder prefers to call them) may seem embarrassing to a Streeterian view of Luke. But there are also at

35. See Chapter 8 above.

least as severe anomalies on Goulder's view. If his Luke is aware of both sources, is using both, and concerned to reconcile them, why has he just refused one equally 'heaven-sent' ready-made harmony (preaching throughout Galilee)? And why does he go on to omit some words Matthew and Mark have in common, while including others that come in Mark only? Of course, it could just be 'accident', although Goulder thinks that is a weak suggestion. Once one allows for coincidence on this scale one has conceded too much to the opposition (p. 50). However, if Luke is freely paraphrasing (as on my hypothesis we would expect) then these coincidences would be very difficult to avoid. If he is working deliberately, either from memory of, or still more, if from sight of both texts, the resulting scant reconcilation is very strange indeed.

In fact, Goulder's Luke can do better than this. He does so, just once, in his version of the next pericope in Mark, the Healing of the Man Sick of the Palsy. Our Luke is here presented (from memory, or by rolling on his scroll of Matthew) with a sequence where, of 47 words in Mark, Matthew reproduces 38, including one identical run of 17. Luke manages 33 of Matthew's 38, including the 17. *If* just as much amalgam as this is what he wants here, and *if* he is able here to achieve it deliberately, it is very strange that he does as much as this just this one time and (barring scriptural quotations) never again. (We may contrast Tatian, once more.)

From the next six Markan episodes (Levi, Fasting, Plucking Grain, Withered Hand, General Healing, and the Call of the Twelve, reversing the order of the last two) Goulder's Luke now includes no more than odd phrases of common tradition, omitting others, including bits of solo Mark, and now just the odd possible echo of Matthew-only. Or, of course, he could perhaps be coinciding with Matthew's use of Mark while working independently, as others have argued.

Our Luke has now assembled a following for Jesus, and is aware that there is a lot of teaching for them to receive, much of it in Matthew only (or perhaps also in other sources to hand or to mind; but not in Mark). Using Matthew only he is under no great pressure to follow Matthew's positioning or Matthew's construction. He is likely to organize the material thematically. If he is going to disperse what he finds in Matthew 5–7, he is likely to do it in blocks (just as Tatian, later, worked in blocks). If there is already thematic order in front of him, he is very likely to reproduce it as he finds it. We have already seen that while a 'speech' can be constructed freely, 'sayings' of a teacher are to be transmitted more faithfully.

Yet again, in the event we do not find things working out quite as we are by now rather unrealistically expecting. Our Luke certainly disperses the material; but he also omits a lot, and reorders much else, sundering many of Matthew's thematic links. He rolls to and fro in this section of Matthew, but also quarries much further afield, in 'our' chs. 10, 12 and 15. We might allow Goulder's conviction that actual Luke would not want to press the disparagement of ancient tradition in the form of the Matthaean antitheses (p. 347). But since Luke can, on Goulder's hypothesis, readily remove content from its interpretative framework, it is odd to have him omit such eminently respectable injunctions as those against anger and lust and recourse to oaths, let alone those against ostentatious piety. Although our imagined Luke will later reproduce quite carefully some of the Matthaean matter now omitted, here where he first has Matthew open before him, only 6.41-45 (Mt. 7.3-5; 12.33, 35) remain at all extensively in touch. Why just some scattered words of Jesus in Matthew get this precise treatment it is hard to tell, even on our hypothesis; harder still with Goulder's stress on 'reconciliation' (though he does try to imagine 'reasons').

And all of this running to and fro and re-allocation of parts is so much more complex than any writer needs, any writer with the freedom of a first-century author, the freedom the real Luke seems to display in his use of Mark. He has all the liberty he requires to allow him to achieve any theological reinterpretation or narrative impact that appeals to him (and his associates), without all this scrolling forwards and backwards on papyrus or in his mind. But our Luke is also continuing to produce more and more a third entity by this rewriting and re-allocation of Matthew, rather than achieving any reconciliation of his sources. We are unearthing a great many unpredicted complexities in Goulder's 'simplest' of hypotheses.

Despite his attention to Matthew in detail, Luke did not include the Centurion's Boy in its Matthaean sequence, but kept it till the end of his second sermon from Jesus, albeit quoting some of Matthew very precisely, so that we may take it that he does still have Matthew open before him. We might well expect him to stay with Matthew. The relation of Matthew to what follows in Mark is, of course, complex; but since our Luke turns out to have been looking ahead from time to time already, we could reasonably expect him to note that the Tempest,

Gadarene Demoniac, Jairus's Daughter, and the Woman in the Crowd are in the same relative order in both, and so, again, afford a measure of ready-made harmony. (Tatian, later, shows every sign of being influenced positively by such occasional common sequences.) Instead, Luke moves a long way forward in Matthew, to material about John the Baptist, where he copies some 180 of Matthew's 210 words (while omitting one sentence to paraphrase later). Close to Matthew though he is, he is still going to some pains to create a distinctive third narrative. He prefaces his material from Matthew with a resuscitation story to prepare for a reference to raising the dead, and allows a reference to eating with sinners at the end to provide a cue for another long piece of his own, the Anointing; and follows that with a list of other women who followed Jesus.

The next sequence on in Mark from where Luke last used him is Companions' Misunderstanding followed by the Beelzebul Controversy, and Jesus' True Family, and a series of parables. Matthew has the same relative sequence. Luke yet again ignores common witness, and proceeds to a selection of the Markan parables. He does coincide with Matthew in omitting the Seed Growing Secretly, but otherwise makes his own choice, refusing any of Matthew's additions here, save one or two minor echoes. There are a few more such echoes as he continues in Mark's sequence with the Tempest, though always fewer than the agreements of Mark and Matthew, which he ignores (or avoids). He then does his own thing with the Gadarene Demoniac, and takes very little notice of Matthew on Jairus's Daughter and the Woman in the Crowd. We noted earlier that he had refused the quite close joint tradition of Matthew's and Mark's tale of Jesus rejected at Nazareth.

Luke now agrees with Mark that the Twelve are at this point to be sent out on a mission. Matthew had sent them out earlier, adding quite a bit of fresh material to what he had culled from Mark. If that suggested to our Luke that there had been two missions, we might have expected him to follow Matthew there and Mark here; instead he adds a further mission at a different point again, after the Transfiguration. But he does more. Rather than use Mark here and Matthew later, he opens both his rolls together (again) and runs through the common material, carefully avoiding some of Matthew's larger additions (the Harvest, Kingdom Come, Heal the Sick, Worker's Due, Greetings Rebound, Sodom and Gomorrah, Sheep and Wolves). However, a number of Matthew's minor changes to Markan sentences he does accept, while often at the same time refusing joint testimony, and sometimes making his own independent use of Mark. Matthew 9.36, very similar to Mark, he refuses completely. Then, later, when he narrates the Mission of the 70, he goes back to Matthew, and now carefully avoids almost everything that can also be found in Mark, apart from sending people out in twos, the begging bag (no ready synonym), and Mark's 'house' rather than Matthew's 'city'. It would not be impossible to achieve this careful sifting of Matthaean matter, but it would be quite difficult. We have no indication that anyone in the first century would have dreamed of trying. On the first run through he has his own (apparently arbitrary) mix of Mark and Matthew. On the second run he almost succeeds in separating his sources completely. This Luke is just not a real first-century writer (nor does Tatian in the second century do anything of the kind).

Matthew now, and for the first time, largely agrees in sequence with Mark, from the Reports Reaching Herod right through to the end of 'our' Mark 9, Sayings on Salt: 22 pericopes, on a conventional count. Matthew does omit the Blind Man from Bethsaida, and the Strange Exorcist, and adds the Temple Tax and perhaps an oddment about Signs. But as well as keeping in step overall, he stays particularly close to the Markan wording. But our Luke? Not a word of it. He picks one Feeding story, and then leaves out a great chunk of this closely similar tradition, only coming back in again with Peter's Confession. He even had a choice of Feeding stories, one where Matthew reproduces about half Mark's words, and one where he reproduces only a third. Luke chooses the latter, and even then (as so often) ignores much of the common wording. Of course, we could probably think of pages of reasons why Michael Goulder might have done the same had he been Luke: he is running out of space, he has had enough incidents, he wants more room for teaching, he has distinctive insights to share. But as a first-century writer who knows both works well (and who, on this hypothesis, is accustomed to rolling on ahead to plan things), he could have left the required space by omitting earlier awkwardly disparate incidents and sequences, and chosen instead the prized common tradition, handed him on papyrus. For sure, yes, he might still have chosen to omit one of two very similar Feeding stories—but column after column of agreed testimony, of which he was aware and able to remind himself with the rolls in front of him? That is quite incredible. And Goulder's Luke could have retained all this striking harmony while still adapting it to express all the distinctive things he might have wanted to convey.

Luke picks up Mark again at Peter's Confession, and on through to the Strange Exorcist, Mark only. For the most part he makes his own mix, accepting most of Mk 8.35 (word for word in Matthew) but otherwise mostly avoiding more than a few words together of joint witness. (We have agreed not to be surprised at his omission of common testimony to John the Baptist as an Elijah figure.)

From 9.51 onwards we have to imagine Goulder's Luke running backwards and forwards in Matthew, continuing his laborious construction of a third account in conflict with both the others. Sometimes he keeps quite close to Matthew, sometimes very close indeed (Answer to Prayer, Beelzebul, Against Seeking Signs, Demon Returns, Single Eye, Cares, Faithful Steward). He seems to make much the same decisions about the extent of individual *pericopai* as we do, but never preserves an unbroken Matthaean sequence of them in the way we have seen him treating Mark.

I end my present survey with a glance forward to the Beelzebul Controversy. It is one of four quite distinctive sequences where a Matthew dependent on Mark has augmented his Markan text in detail. (The other three are the Baptism and Temptation, the Mission Charge, and the Eschatological Discourse, as already noted.) Each time our imaginary Luke ignores the common witness where Matthew and Mark largely or entirely agree, Luke further changes what is similar but less extensively so—and picks out for close repetition only the solo witness afforded by Matthew's additions.[36] It would not be easy to do this; and it would be quite unprecedented, contravening all evidenced norms for workable procedures for the use of parallel sources, flying in the face of the common harmonizing aims of contemporary practitioners, not what we would expect from Goulder's Luke who is 'no amateur when it comes to reconciling his sources' (p. 410, again).

---

36. See Downing, 'Towards the Rehabilitation of Q', pp. 169-81, and also ch. 8 above. Goulder resists my conclusions here (*Luke*, pp. 502-16), insisting that the sequences Mt. 12.29, 31a and Mk 3.27-28 which I judged 'largely the same' and 'fairly close' but which his Luke must, surprisingly, be taken to have omitted, were not 'identical'. The similarities between them are so striking that the lack of total identity (which I never claimed) is hardly relevant. Here is near-identical witness, refused by his Luke. (Goulder finds much lesser similarities elsewhere highly significant, when they can be made to favour his case.)

Oddments

There are other oddities that warrant brief attention. Goulder's Luke knows his sources well, well enough to rely on memory: but not always. He puts Mark down, rolled to where he has been using that scroll, and so could readily check it for detail—but instead relies on his memory. Where he could most conveniently rely on his memory for earlier and later passages in Matthew is where he has that scroll directly in play, open at the vital columns. Yet it is precisely here that he runs to and fro in Matthew, instead of relying on memory, and so risks losing the main section of text that he is using; he must be doing this, to get some of these Matthaean passages (near) word-perfect.[37]

And when this Luke goes back to columns of Matthew from which he has already taken matter, or arrives again at ones he has plundered in advance, he most carefully avoids repeating what he has already copied, however well it fitted what preceded or followed it. At least Goulder mentions only one word that could be a counter-example.[38] This Luke has stepped in his footprints so carefully on subsequent visits that one might think he had only been once through the sources he deploys. But that, of course, would not be Goulder's Luke.

Conclusions

Goulder claims that his is a simple hypothesis—indeed, the simplest on offer. It is not. The simplicity of a hypothesis about literary interdependence cannot be assessed solely on the basis of the number of conjectural sources involved. Goulder's hypothesis has fewer documents than has Streeter's. But to justify Goulder's there are innumerable hypotheses about what was going on in Luke's mind. And, more serious still, we find an unquantifiable cluster of surreptitious hypotheses about an apparently fairly ordinary first-century writer's ability and willingness to ignore simple and rational contemporary compositional

---

37. For Goulder's Luke's knowledge of Matthew, *Luke*, pp. 371, 400, 409, 529, 539, 542, 566; relies on memory for scroll that is open, pp. 276, 282, 291, 428, 512, 622; yet checks to and fro, pp. 428, again, p. 433 and chs. 6 and 12, *passim*.

38. Goulder, *Luke*, pp. 464-76. The only 'Matthaean' phrase his Luke repeats in ch. 10 from ch. 9 is 'no pack', *mē pēran*, 9.3 and 10.4; perhaps one should add the almost identical phrase *eis hēn d'an* in 9.4 and 10.5.

conventions and scribal techniques and pioneer new, complex and self-defeating ones all of his own.

The awkward 'minor agreements' can be explained in ways that are at home in first-century practice (especially in terms of possible diverse early versions of Mark as a 'living text'), whether or not these happen to irritate a twentieth-century scholar such as Goulder. The extraordinary behaviour of Goulder's Luke, who refuses every simple and conventional way to rewrite his Matthew and Mark to suit his given purposes, is totally foreign to the first century, and no ingenious mind-reading by Michael Goulder is adequate to explain it.

I have concentrated attention on Goulder's recent and elaborately argued case; but, as indicated earlier, a careful consideration of our evidence for first-century compositional techniques seems to rule out as impossibly complex the procedures presupposed but unstated in every proposed 'solution' of the synoptic problem other than the Two-Document hypothesis.

Appended Note: Tatian [39]

If we can trust our available texts at all, Tatian's aim seems to have been to include as much detail as possible from all his sources. This is in itself quite distinctive, and obviously different from any defensible picture of any of our synoptic Gospels as produced on the basis of the others. No one of them could possibly be said to display an intention to include everything from the other two. Tatian's unusual aim means that Longstaff's comparison (in his *Evidence of Conflation in Mark*) of his word-by-word method with that of Mark as supposed conflater of Matthew and Luke is of doubtful relevance; see also C.M. Tuckett's critique (*The Revival of the Griesbach Hypothesis*), pp. 41-51. However, although there is some uncertainty about the details of the text Tatian produced, there seems to be widespread agreement that most if not all of the order Tatian created has been preserved in the various texts dependent on him that have come down to us. For order, then, we

---

39. For Tatian see H.W. Hogg, 'The Diatessaron of Tatian' (*ANF*; Edinburgh: T. & T. Clark, 1897); J.R. Harris, *The Diatessaron of Tatian* (Cambridge: Cambridge University Press, 1898); T.W.R. Longstaff, *Evidence of Conflation in Mark* (Missoula, MT: Scholars Press, 1977); C.H. Kraeling, *A Greek Fragment from Tatian's Diatessaron* (London: Christophers, 1935); C.M. Tuckett, *The Revival of the Griesbach Hypothesis* (Cambridge: Cambridge University Press, 1983), pp. 41-51; and Mattila, 'Question', pp. 204-206.

may make useful comparisons with Goulder's Luke, said to be reordering Matthew and Mark.

Tatian's procedure seems to have been to use one scroll—the Dura fragment is itself from a scroll, not a codex—one scroll at a time, inserting material from it in blocks, adding from the other three any details his current source 'omits' from 'the same' pericope. Working in blocks is what Streeter takes Luke to have been doing.

For words of the Lord in particular Tatian will roll on or back in one of the scrolls set aside (or will work from memory) for quite detailed supplements. For his main thread he tends to follow one source (mostly Matthew) consecutively, to the point where he risks repeating items he has already given when selecting from one of the others (Luke, mostly, as second main lead). He then picks up the latter as his main thread, from the point where he was last using it in sequence. He does not create fresh sequences of events or complexes of teaching of his own: quite unlike Goulder's Luke; still less does he show any signs of having pioneered disentangling fairly similar from closely similar matter in his sources, to use in different ways.

Tatian's is the most complex attempt at 'reconciliation' of sources of which we know in late antiquity, and yet the order he creates is of a quite different kind from that posited for Goulder's Luke: Tatian's is comprehensively inclusive in detail, but overall logically simple, straightforward, coherent and rational.[40]

I have tried to show how Luke should *not* be characterized. The next, penultimate, chapter invites the reader to imagine Luke among his first hearers, in the socio-cultural context that I have been trying to illustrate throughout this volume, and its companion, *Making Sense in (and of) The First Christian Century.*

---

40. In his 'Luke's Compositional Conventions', *NTS* 39 (1993), pp. 150-52. M.D. Goulder accuses the above discussion of ignoring issues that were in fact referred to in the footnotes as having been argued in detail in my 'Redaction Criticism', I and II, and in my 'Compositional Conventions'.

Chapter 10

THEOPHILUS'S FIRST HEARING OF LUKE–ACTS*

Theophilus, the Performance and the Audience

Theophilus

Theophilus may well have been the real name for a real person. Loveday Alexander tells us it was a favourite name among Hellenistic Jews, and she assures us that there is very little evidence, if any, for dedications to imaginary people.[1] Whether he was a patron of superior status, or a friend of similar standing to the author's we cannot tell, and still less whether he would have been expected to finance the further 'publication', the wider circulation of the two-volume work. We do not know for sure whether he was a committed Christian, and of course it has been argued that Luke was writing a defence of the Christian movement, directed to an important pagan Roman official. However, Alexander also argues that the preface to the Gospel strongly suggests that the work which follows is intended as a reminder for people already well aware of much of the contents. It is not an introduction for outsiders.[2] If Christian Luke has Theophilus as a friend or patron (or friendly patron), he is most likely at least a sympathizer, more likely a member of the group.

Reading—Aloud

I want us to imagine his first reading. I have to allow that someone else may have done this imagining already—and more competently. But recent studies in Luke–Acts have not pointed me to any such recent

---

*   First appeared as 'Theophilus' First Reading of Luke–Acts', in C.M. Tuckett (ed.), *Luke's Literary Achievement* (JSNTSup, 116; Sheffield: Sheffield Academic Press, 1995), pp. 91-109; reprinted here by kind permission.
    1.   L. Alexander, *The Preface to Luke's Gospel*, pp. 73-75, 133, 188.
    2.   L. Alexander, *The Preface to Luke's Gospel*, pp. 142, 188-93.

reconstruction,[3] and attempting such in this essay also allows me to survey together some (fairly) recent monographs and collections, as well as to air again one or two original studies of my own.

We may take it that the reading would almost certainly have been aloud.[4] Perhaps the author himself would have read his work, or some other competent speaker would have read for him. We have been reminded of late that silent reading was less uncommon in the ancient Mediterranean world than is sometimes supposed, but Frank Gilliard's 1993 study nonetheless accepts there is no reason to question 'the predominance of orality'.[5] Of course, not only is performance oral, composition is, too. Almost certainly some of Luke's friends—if not Theophilus himself—would have been invited to discuss his early drafts of the work with him while it was in progress.[6]

The Wider Audience (1)

The reading would have taken one or two sittings, and it would probably have been in company. In some circles, of course, men and women would have been segregated. When Pliny the Younger gave a reading of his own work, his wife Calpurnia sat behind a screen to listen (*Letters* 4.9). However, I have suggested that Luke's and Theophilus's circle will have been Christian, and all the Pauline and later deutero-Pauline letters suggest Christian men and women met together, albeit,

---

3.   There are a number of 'reader-response' analyses available. J.B. Tyson, 'The Implied Reader in Luke–Acts', in his *Images of Judaism in Luke–Acts* (Columbia: University of South Carolina Press, 1992), pp. 17-41, attempts to profile the implied reader in the appropriate cultural setting; and see the useful survey in F.S. Spencer, 'Acts and Modern Literary Approaches', in B.W. Winter and A.D. Clarke (eds.), *The Book of Acts in its First Century Setting*. I. *The Book of Acts in its Ancient Literary Setting* (Grand Rapids: Eerdmans, 1993; Exeter: Paternoster Press, 1994), pp. 381-414. The sketch that follows does not seem to have been anticipated.

4.   Cf. P. Gempf, 'Public Speaking and Published Accounts', in Winter and Clarke (eds.), *The Book of Acts*, pp. 259-304, but esp. pp. 260-62; Downing, '*A bas les Aristos*', ch.1 above; L. Alexander, 'The Living Voice'; contra P.F. Esler, *Community and Gospel in Luke–Acts* (SNTSMS, 58; Cambridge: Cambridge University Press, 1987), p. 7.

5.   F. Gilliard, 'More Silent Reading in Antiquity: *non omne verbum sunt*', *JBL* 112.4 (1993), pp. 689-94, quoting from p. 694.

6.   Cf. Downing, 'Ears to Hear', p. 98; and my 'Word-Processing in the First Century', ch. 4 above.

after the earliest days, on very clearly unequal terms. Luke himself suggests much the same conclusion (Lk. 10.39; 11.27; Acts 1.14; 12.12; 16.13-14, etc.), and perhaps the amount of apparently sympathetic attention given to women in the Gospel supports this view. Dr Alexander has argued for an adult 'school' setting for the reading of Luke–Acts.[7] We may note Luke's account of Paul in Tyrannus's lecture-hall (Acts 19.9). If we accepted that conclusion, then I do not think we would expect children to have been present. I do not think we have any accounts of children being included in meetings of adults for study, even among Christians. However, households that had been baptized together would doubtless have included any children in festival meals, and so, presumably, in the supper of the Lord Jesus, and I shall argue that a relaxed mealtime is a yet more likely occasion for the 'performance' of Luke–Acts. But at this, as at every point, further evidence of any sort would be very welcome.

Social Composition

We are assured these days of a kind of consensus among New Testament historians, to the effect that the early urban Christians mostly if not universally will have included in their number relatively prosperous fellow townspeople, able to act as patrons to local congregations, at least to the extent of affording hospitality for meetings (and perhaps bed and board for visiting missionaries). This may well be overstated for Paul, but does seem valid for Luke and his circle.[8] *Kratistos*, 'most excellent' Theophilus (Lk. 1.4) will presumably have been such a person. Certainly recent studies by H. Moxnes and by J.C. Lentz both indicate that the ideal hearer would share the attitudes of those from whom patronage would be expected.[9] The Pauline writings would lead

7.   L. Alexander, 'Acts and Ancient Intellectual Biography', expanding the suggestion in *eadem, The Preface to Luke's Gospel*, pp. 202-205.

8.   E.g. Meeks, *The First Urban Christians*, ch. 2, pp. 51-73; B. Holmberg, *Sociology and the New Testament* (Minneapolis: Fortress Press, 1990), pp. 59-60; but see now the strong counter-arguments à propos Paul at least, from Meggitt, *Paul, Poverty and Survival*.

9.   H. Moxnes, *The Economy of the Kingdom: Social Conflict and Economic Interaction in Luke's Gospel* (Philadelphia: Fortress Press, 1988), and 'Patron–Client Relations and the New Community in Luke–Acts', in J.H. Neyrey (ed.), *The Social World of Luke–Acts* (Peabody, MA: Hendrickson, 1991), pp. 241-68; J.C. Lentz, *Luke's Portrait of Paul* (SNTSMS, 77; Cambridge: Cambridge University Press, 1994).

us to expect that a number of ordinary, impoverished people would also be present at Theophilus's invitation, and Luke's own highlighting of some wealthier and more influential converts suggests that he had a similar expectation of a mixed constituency (Acts 17.12, 34).

The Setting: Public Open Space, Lecture Hall, Symposium?
As to the precise kind of occasion, as already noted, it is difficult to decide. Quite a lot of teaching in both the Gospel and in Acts takes place in the open where crowds happen to gather. People did read their works in the open, for any who would collect to hear,

> crowds of wretched sophists around Poseidon's temple, and their disciples, as they are called, fighting with one another, many writers reading aloud their stupid works, many poets reciting their poems while others applauded them

is how Dio in the late first century CE imagined the Isthmian Games in the late fourth BCE (*Discourse* 8.9; cf. 27.5-6); but he describes contemporary Alexandria and Tarsus in his own day very similarly (*Discourses* 32.9-12; 33.1-7).[10] And he himself delivered some public orations of around the same length as the Gospel or Acts (around 20,000 words). I do not think we can imagine the reading taking place in a synagogue, though our hearers could have gathered in someone's lecture hall. However, there seem to be strong indications both in his narrative and in his ethos that Luke's own preference would have been for a decorous symposium (though of course a 'school' might very well share a symposium). A large number of the occasions for teaching in the narrative are in a convivial setting (Lk. 5.29; 7.34, 36-50; 9.4; 10.7, 38-42; 11.37-52; 13.26; 14.1-24; 22.14-38; 24.13-35(?) and Acts 2.42; 6.1-6; 20.7-12).[11] Very engaging is Dio's description of a symposium:

10. *Discourse* 8.9 (LCL).
11. Luke 14.1-24 is the subject of a useful discussion by W. Braun, *Feasting and Social Rhetoric in Luke 14.1-24* (SNTSMS, 85; Cambridge: Cambridge University Press, 1995); there are some apposite references collected in C.A. Roberts, 'The Role of the Patron in the *Cena Dominica* of Hippolytus' *Apostolic Tradition*', *JTS* N S 44 (1993), pp. 170-84; and a fine if not flawless discussion in Corley, *Private Women, Public Meals*: 'the primary setting of early Christian dialogue and worship was a formal public meal' (p. 24; 'formal' should not be overstressed in the light of much of the evidence Corley herself collates!). There is further relevant matter in D. Aune, '*Septem Sapientem Convivium*', in Betz (ed.), *Plutarch's Ethical Writings*, pp. 51-105; see also D.E. Smith, 'Table Fellowship as a Literary Motif in

> Some attend for the sake of drinking, and devote themselves to that...saying and doing indecorous things...the naturally loquacious, feeling they've got their table companions for an audience, recite stupid and tedious speeches, while others are singing in tune and out of it—almost more annoying than the quarrelsome and abusive...others bore people to death by their uncongenial manner, refusing to share a drink or the conversation (Dio, *Discourse* 27.2-3).

There are also plenty more accounts of rowdy suppers which we noted above, Chapter 1 (Lucian, *The Carousel*; Petronius, *Satyricon*), with which to compare Paul's account of goings on in Corinth. Pliny the Younger, we may recall, had been intending a rather less unruly occasion when a friend let him down: 'You would have heard a comic play, a reader, or a singer—or all three if I had felt generous...a feast of fun, laughter and learning' (*Letters* 1.15; cf. 9.17.3).[12] The character of Luke's writing would fit this setting well, if it be agreed that he affords 'serious entertainment'—as I shall urge at a little more length below (following R. Pervo).[13]

The Audience (ii)

Here we might expect our most mixed audience, free and freed men and women—and children and male and female slaves. The wider evidence for their respective roles (as silent or vocal participants) is not unambiguous. Juvenal in Rome expects women and scholarly conversation at parties (and does not like the mixture: *Satire* 6.434-41). Dio's *Discourse* 61, a literary discussion with a well-read woman who holds her own, may well be relevant. Plutarch imagines the legendary Dinner of the Seven Wise Men to have included Eumetis, the young daughter (*paidos*) of Cleobulos, admired for her intelligence. She sits for the meal, while an older woman, Melissa, reclines with her partner. Here, too, of course, there are slave attendants. Eumetis is engaged in conversation initially, but none of these join in once the serious talking—and drinking—have begun (*Septem sapientem convivium*, *Moralia* 148C-150B). Diogenes Laertius (or his source) finds it noteworthy that the Cynic Hipparchia went to dinners with her man Crates, and joined in the cut and thrust of debate (*Lives* 6.97-98). Epicureans will probably

---

the Gospel of Luke', *JBL* 106 (1987), pp. 613-38.
  12. *Letters* 1.5 (LCL).
  13. R. Pervo, *Profit with Delight* (Philadelphia: Fortress Press, 1987).

have included women in their symposia. In other accounts, there are free women present, as well as the servants, flute-girls and actresses, but none of these take part in the discussions.

In Luke's narrative, Mary is there as supper is prepared, but there to listen, only (Lk. 10.38-42).[14] Luke at 7.37 seems to evince surprise that a woman should dare to be the focus of attention, and certainly no women are recorded at Jesus' last meal (Lk. 22.14-38, again). Yet the indications given above, and the Pauline and deutero-Pauline evidence, suggest Luke would have expected mixed company at Christian symposia, women for sure,[15] but also quite possibly children (though Eutychus, Acts 20.9, is a young man, *neanias*, not a child); also Jews and sympathizers with Judaism become Christian, as well as converts from 'paganism'.[16] There is, then, plausibly, quite a wide-ranging audience along with Theophilus, while only the adult males are likely to feel free to comment at the time on Luke's work. However, anyone might applaud.

The Script

The Preface—As for a Technical Treatise?
We take it that the reading starts with the preface as we find it in our texts. Loveday Alexander shows that this preface most closely resembles in style and in length the prefaces of surviving technical works on medicine, astronomy, engineering and architecture. Historians' prefaces, even when covering similar themes and using similar key words, are longer, usually very much longer, and (for instance) where dedicated do not use a second person address. The rest of Luke's work rarely even approaches the high style adopted by those historians whose writings have come down to us.[17]

Yet the company assembled round Theophilus would hardly have come expecting to hear a technical treatise; and even if the first sentence had them revising their expectations, the second would have immediately redirected them. As Alexander herself admits,

---

14. On which see L. Alexander, 'Sisters in Adversity'; Corley, *Private Women, Public Meals*, pp. 133-44.
15. Aune, '*Septem Sapientem Convivium*', p. 77.
16. Esler, *Community*, pp. 71-109.
17. L. Alexander, *The Preface to Luke's Gospel*.

may it not be asked, is not our hypothetical informed reader still going to be disappointed, or at the very least, puzzled, when the narrative which unfolds proves to be so very unlike the mathematical or medical treatises which begin with prefaces like this?[18]

She canvasses two main possible responses: 'biography . . . within the school traditions' (but most philosophical biographies are rather different, consisting in a series of didactic anecdotes),[19] and a presentation of the content of the school's tradition (but that fits Acts much less well than Luke).[20]

'Non-Professional' History-Writing

It would seem worth going back a little to consider more generally the kinds of expectations Theophilus and his Christian friends might have brought with them. They are likely to have had some awareness of the distinction of genres, *Gattungen*.[21] But even if they had some knowledge of rhetorical theory, they would have realized that in practice genres tended to overlap (as the theorists themselves acknowledged).[22] Accepting Dr Alexander's main contention—the preface to Luke most nearly resembles prefaces to technical works—Luke is unlikely to have been the first writer whose main familiarity was with works of that kind, but who had also undertaken to write a Life or a history—or both. Only one example happens to come to mind, and that is the military surgeon of whose history Lucian writes,

> he has compiled a bare record of the events and set it down on paper, completely prosaic and ordinary, such as a soldier or artisan or pedlar following the army might have put together as a diary of daily events. However, this non-professional (*idiotes*) was not that bad—it was quite obvious at the beginning what he was, and his work has cleared the ground for some future historian of taste and ability...[23]

Some further criticisms of the style of this 'Callimorphus, surgeon of the Fifth Lancers' follow, and then Lucian concludes, 'and, after beginning in Ionic, for some reason I cannot fathom, he suddenly changed to

18. L. Alexander, *The Preface to Luke's Gospel*, p. 202.
19. Cf. L. Alexander, 'Acts and Ancient Intellectual Biography'.
20. L. Alexander, *The Preface to Luke's Gospel*, pp. 202-205, again.
21. Cf. Burridge, *What are the Gospels?*, pp. 26-81.
22. Burridge, *What are the Gospels?*, e.g. pp. 68-69; and Downing, 'A Genre for Q and a Socio-cultural Context for Q', ch. 5 above.
23. Lucian, *How to Write History* 16 (LCL).

the vernacular...taking the rest from the language of everyday, most of it street-corner talk'. The coincidence with the tradition of 'Luke the beloved physician' is not to be pressed, but it does seem unlikely that Luke and Callimorphus were the only two amateur writers of histories or biographies in the ancient Mediterranean world whose styles may have been influenced by technical treatises—and Callimorphus does not appear to have been writing for the use of a 'school'. Furthermore, as Dr Alexander herself notes, and as I have myself pointed out elsewhere,[24] much of the language of Luke's preface is found in the (albeit much longer) prefaces of Josephus to his history of the *Jewish War*, his *Antiquities*, and his *Against Apion*, and much of it also appears in the more straightfoward historical *Roman Antiquities* of Dionysius of Halicarnassus. Lucian would surely have been even more dismissive of Luke–Acts than he was of Callimorphus. But I do not think our gathering would have been all that surprised or puzzled by the kind of material that followed the preface: that preface would not have channelled their expectations all that precisely (though they would have realized they were not then likely to hear a poem, a letter or a speech).

Septuagintal and Commonplace Greek
They might well have been not all that shocked when Luke did not maintain the somewhat pretentious language of his first sentence. But it does leave me with a question for which I have not found a satisfactory answer (and do not feel well equipped to attempt one). The narrative that follows is not even in the 'street-corner' talk that Lucian disparaged; it is, as everyone notes, in the archaic 'dialect' of the Septuagint. There seems to be little if anything in any way analogous to this mixture. Lucian himself writes his *De Dea Syriae* in what we are told is dialect, and other writers sometimes quote brief utterances in local speech. One can only assume (with E. Plümacher)[25] that Luke's Septuagintal archaism would be expected to reinforce the anchorage of the narrative in a Jewish antiquity known to the hearers, and accepted by them as a validating ancient tradition (on which more again, later).

---

24. Downing, 'Redaction Criticism'.
25. E. Plümacher, *Lukas als hellenistischer Schriftsteller* (Göttingen: Vandenhoeck & Ruprecht, 1972), pp. 72-74.

A bios?

It has taken us much longer to get past the preface than it would Theophilus's first reader. We now need to move on a little, and rather faster. It is worth asking again what sort of genre appraisal might be forming in people's minds as they listened. According to the recent study by Richard Burridge, the Gospel would clearly—and swiftly—emerge as a *bios*, a character portrait (a 'character-sketch' might seem as suitable) as we saw in Chapter 5 above. *Bioi*, Lives, share together in varying degrees a large number of features, and this sharing is strong enough to afford a 'family resemblance' (L. Wittgenstein) which is different from simple identity, but still genuinely recognizable.[26] The most important common feature Burridge discovered may seem on reflection rather obvious. In works classified as Lives a single named person predominates among references in the nominative, as the subject of verbs, and as the utterer of verbs in speech. Even leading figures in histories do not figure as prominently.[27] I shall not try to summarize again the remainder of Burridge's criteria for an ancient Life, but would note that I am not alone among reviewers in finding his case overall convincing.

Apologetic Historiography?

Some of Burridge's own conclusions, however, would lead us to expect that Theophilus would then be somewhat surprised later on when he heard Acts read, now clearly linked by its preface as the sequel in a two-part work. Another recent monograph, Gregory E. Sterling's *Historiography and Self-Definition*, discerns a genre for the two volumes taken together: that of 'apologetic history' in the tradition of (though not directly influenced by) Josephus's *Antiquities*, and works by Berossus, Manetho, Eupolemos and others.[28] Perhaps the distinction between 'genre' and 'mode' that Burridge takes from A. Fowler is also relevant here: Luke–Acts shares many of the features of an apologetic 'mode', even if the evidence does not warrant the positing of a distinctive genre or sub-genre.[29] It would seem still more appropriate, however, to stress

26. Burridge, *What are the Gospels?*, p. 39 *et passim*; Wittgenstein, *Philosophical Investigations*, pp. 31-32, for 'family resemblance'.

27. Burridge, *What are the Gospels?*, pp. 134-38, 195-97.

28. G.E. Sterling, *Historiography and Self-Definition: Josephus, Luke–Acts and Apologetic Historiography* (Leiden: E.J. Brill, 1992).

29. Burridge, *What are the Gospels?*, pp. 41-42, referring to Fowler, 'The Life and Death of Literary Forms'.

the flexibility of and overlap between all the genres we or the ancients discern.[30] Loveday Alexander finds in Acts' outline of Paul's life and character, elements of a narrative pattern that has much in common with sketches of eminent philosophers (as in Diogenes Laertius).[31] In fact Plutarch in his *Parallel Lives* treats such characters as Romulus, Numa, Publicola and Camillus in a manner very similar to their treatment by Dionysius in his *Roman Antiquities*; and we may compare Joseph and Moses in Philo and in Josephus, respectively. Josephus himself refers us to his *Jewish War* for his own *Life*'s continuation (*Life* 413). Thus we can read Luke's Gospel on its own as a Life of Jesus, or Luke–Acts as a two-part apologetic history of the Christian people and their movement and their leaders; but we can also read them for much the same kind of entertainment as we might gain from a romance, as I shall further argue, shortly (with R. Pervo).

So, Theophilus and his party soon realize they are hearing the content of the tradition they have learned here presented—performed—as a Life, a character-sketch, of Jesus. Yet when, later—maybe a lot later— they then hear Acts, or if they hear both volumes read together, it is still quite easy for them to take the whole as an effective reaffirmation of the validity of their lived tradition within the Graeco-Roman world, apologetic historiography in that sense.

Sacred Tradition and Divine Ordering
Luke begins his narrative not only in a 'hieratic' language, but in an ancient and sacred enclosure, where tradition is respected, and where humans are most open to divine intervention (and it is often noted how emphatically the ongoing story returns to Jerusalem and the Temple). There is to be no arbitrary human interruption of the safe providential ordering of things; if anything new or startling happens, it will be by divine necessity. This latter motif is amply illustrated from pagan and from Jewish sources by J.T. Squires, *The Plan of God in Luke–Acts*: 'epiphanies of divine messengers and their oracular pronouncements indicate that God is to be at work in the events which follow, while a hint of the necessity of ensuing events is also given'. The interrelation of providence, fate and the various means of divination (portents,

---

30. Cf. D.W. Palmer, 'Acts and the Ancient Historical Monograph', in Winter and Clarke (eds.), *The Book of Acts*, pp. 1-29; Downing, 'A Genre for Q and a Social-Cultural Context for Q', Chapter 5 above.
    31. L. Alexander, 'Acts and Ancient Intellectual Biography'.

dreams and oracles) is evident in the Hellenistic historians, while Josephus demonstrates how this Hellenistic perspective is congenial with the scriptural perspective of the Hebrew people. Luke's inter-weaving of the strands thus makes sense because they were already understood to be related to one another.[32]

Order and Law

What needs to be added to Squires's case here is a note of the close connection between this strand and issues of custom, law, law-abiding, and the avoidance of 'innovation', any threat of anarchy. There has seemed to many to be a puzzling tension in Luke between instances (as here, in the early chapters of the Gospel) where sacred tradition is (at least in the intention of the text) faithfully observed, and others (as in Peter's vision in Acts 10) where sacred tradition is decisively abrogated. Discussions in the 1980s tended to ignore contemporary Hellenistic debates about law, custom and tradition, and so (I would argue) failed to recognize the fairly conventional stance Luke is affirming. I quote a conclusion for which I have argued elsewhere:

> The observance of the actual ancestral practices themselves (whether codified or not, whether written or not) was commended on all sides, save only for any that could clearly be shown to harm human flourishing, *eudaimonia* ... The observance of ancestral custom is part of a concern for cosmic order, but also for civic order.[33]

And so, for instance, Jesus' parents are very soon shown complying at some cost with (supposed) Roman taxation law. What Luke will go on to reassert, to Theophilus's and his friends renewed relief, is that God himself has insisted that the most obnoxious and exclusive and notorious Jewish customs do not have to be imposed on non-Jews: male circumcision, the most troublesome food laws and any strict Sabbatarianism. Yet other roots in ancient Jewish piety remain—the Christian movement is no arbitrary innovation, and so presents no threat of social disruption.[34] As we listen we can say to ourselves, 'this tells our story:

32. J.T. Squires, *The Plan of God in Luke–Acts* (SNTSMS, 76; Cambridge: Cambridge University Press, 1993), pp. 188-89.

33. F.G. Downing, 'Law and Custom: Luke–Acts and Late Hellenism', in B. Lindars (ed.), *Law and Religion* (Cambridge: James Clarke, 1988), pp. 144-58 (152); contra: Esler, *Community*, pp. 110-30; though compare his pp. 214-17 on 'ancestral tradition'.

34. It is of course entirely plausible that Luke is *also* trying to reassure both

we are an interesting, admirable, patient and law-abiding group who maintain an inheritance of ancient piety with pleasure and joy, while by divinely commanded selectivity we avoid any demeaning or craven ("superstitious") restrictions'. (This previously argued conclusion of mine then tallies well with the analysis of 'apologetic historiography' presented since then by Sterling, *Historiography*.)

Revolt or Propriety?

Just how law-abiding in other respects does the Christian movement appear in Luke's narrative? Mary's song sounds quite revolutionary, and even the two mission charges propose clothing that would have betokened a Cynic assault on convention if adopted by figures in the public eye in Corinth or Athens. I have argued in various places that much of the 'Q' material Luke uses would on its own sound startlingly Cynic (as it did to many later Christian commentators).[35] But at 22.35-36 Luke has Jesus make it quite clear that the Cynic-sounding period is over, 'now' things are different, purses and satchels and swords (!) are the order of the day.[36] Even the realized ideal of 'friends having all in common' (Acts 2.44; 4.32) happens only at the start of the next phase, in the holy city; there is no suggestion of its recurring later.[37] And though Paul does voluntarily work for a living, he is clearly presented as someone entirely acceptable to many people of middle eminence and good will. Christianity as it spreads is led by a decent man who can appeal to decent people who retain their social propriety.[38]

Entertainment: Romance and Emotion

Those in the first-century Mediterranean world who put words together for others to listen to seem to have been well aware of the need to work hard to hold their hearers' attention.[39] You had to give them a lot of

present and potential Jewish Christians: see D. Marguerat, 'Juifs et chrétiens selon Luc–Actes: Surmonter le conflit des lectures', *Bib* 75 (1994), pp. 126-46.

35. Most recently, Downing, *Cynics and Christian Origins,* esp. ch. 5, pp. 115-42, in the light of the second half of the book; but also *Christ and the Cynics*, pp. 9-87.

36. That this marked a change from Cynic-style poverty is noted by John Chrysostom, *Homily on 1 Corinthians* 9.

37. Cf. A.C. Mitchell, 'The Social Function of Friendship in Acts 2.44-47 and 4.32-37', *JBL* 111 (1992), pp. 255-72.

38. Cf. J.H. Neyrey and B. Malina, 'Conflict in Luke–Acts', in Neyrey (ed.), *The Social World of Luke–Acts*, pp. 97-122.

39. Cf. D. Litfin, *St Paul's Theology of Proclamation: 1 Corinthians 1–4 and*

what they wanted—they were, in a very real sense, your masters. You had to feed back to them, attractively, convictions they already held, and that could be difficult enough (though sometimes financially very rewarding). And even if you wanted people to change at some point, your proposal had to be shown to be consistent with their most deeply held convictions. And all the time, you had to entertain.

It is no coincidence that there is considerable overlap, not only in such works as Philostratus's *Life of Apollonius*[40] but also in high-brow historians, between history and romance.[41] There seems to be still more in common with contemporary romances in Luke–Acts, as demonstrated by Richard Pervo.[42] In particular we should note the prominence of the travel motif, as discussed by Loveday Alexander.[43] It hardly figures at all in histories (or in most Lives, save the later *Life of Apollonius of Tyana*) but provides the basic structure for ancient novels. Its importance in Acts is obvious, and in Luke 9–19. But earlier still in the Gospel Jesus is already a travelling man. Jesus travels to a trial and death presumably already well known to the hearers, and the journey does not need extra perils to maintain interest (and, anyway, the main incidents are also already known). But Paul's journeys through prisons and lynchings and shipwreck in particular are very much the stuff of the novels, even if (as Richard Bauckham points out)[44] the mission in mind is clearly different—the spread of the gospel, not the ultimate reunion of fraught lovers.

Of course Luke–Acts does not have a prominent heroine to share the story line (and provide more or less explicit erotic interest—only in the picaresque satires are men on their own sex-objects!); that development among Christians has to wait for the writing of *The Acts of Paul and Thecla*. But the histories certainly give space to female characters—as

Greco-Roman Rhetoric (SNTSMS, 79; Cambridge: Cambridge University Press, 1994), pp. 105-106; Palmer, 'Acts and the Ancient Historical Monograph'; Pervo, *Profit with Delight*; and Dionysius of Halicarnassus, *Roman Antiquities* 1.8.3.

40. Cf. R. Bauckham, 'The *Acts of Paul* as a Sequel to Acts', in Winter and Clarke (eds.), *The Book of Acts*, pp. 105-52.

41. As acknowledged by, e.g., Palmer, 'Acts and the Ancient Historical Monograph', p. 29. On the romances see now Hock, Chance and Perkins (eds.), *Ancient Fiction*.

42. Pervo, *Profit with Delight*.

43. L. Alexander, 'Voyaging in Luke–Acts', in Tuckett (ed.), *Luke's Literary Achievement*, pp. 17-49.

44. Bauckham, 'The *Acts of Paul* as a Sequel to Acts', p. 137.

erotic figures, and as tragic pleaders and victims; and just occasionally as taking some unexpected initiative. Josephus responds to these motifs in models such as Dionysius's *Roman Antiquities* by imaginative elaborations of incidents in the Jewish Scriptures. Luke, as is often noted, gives more space than do either Mark or Matthew to women in the story, with the prologue centring on Mary. Luke's sinful woman wiping Jesus' feet with her hair is subtly but powerfully erotic in a first-century context; Martha's sister Mary is the ideal 'docile' disciple.[45] Priscilla and Lydia display more enterprizing initiative.

Hints of sexuality connect with other emotional issues, obviously present in the romances, but also in the histories. Josephus adds notes of joy, exaltation, sorrow; and Luke has similar notes where none such appear in Mark (cf. D. Marguerat's discussion of the pathos of Luke's dramatic narrative, Acts 5.1-11[46]). It is also clear that repentance (with overtones of contrition) is a dominant theme in Luke's theology. Dionysius remarks on the efficacy of the acknowledgment of fault and the craving of pardon, and assures his hearers that the gods are disposed to forgive, and are easily reconciled (*eudialaktos, Roman Antiquities* 11.12.3 and 8.50.4). Josephus quotes the latter assertion at *War* 5.416, and stresses in a number of the speeches he composes both repentance and the availability of forgiveness. The drama of someone changing from one entrenched commitment to another makes for good listening—and so the 'conversions' of Peter and of Paul are each repeated three times in Acts.[47] In the romances characters are constantly having to change their attitudes and confess and be reconciled. The ass tales of Lucius of Patras, Lucian (possibly) and Apuleius in particular celebrate conversion.

Yet another gripping motif, as we know from our own television screens, is the courtroom drama. Some of the novels include such scenes, and they are given considerable space by Josephus and by Dionysius before him. In the histories they allow issues to be debated, and especially do they allow awkward charges to be voiced and answered, rather than risk seeming to gloss over them. So Luke has

45. See n. 14 above.

46. Cf. D. Marguerat, 'La mort d'Ananias et Saphira (Ac 5.1-11) dans la stratégie narrative de Luc', *NTS* 39 (1993), pp. 209-26 (209).

47. On which see D. Marguerat, 'Saul's Conversion (Acts 9, 22, 26) and the Multiplication of Narrative in Acts', in Tuckett (ed.), *Luke's Literary Achievement*, pp. 120-48.

obviously false charges levelled against Jesus (23.2; the charges have been rebutted in advance, and Pilate rejects them), and against the Jerusalem Christians, and Paul. The Christians around Theophilus are reassured, whatever the rumours and popular gossip, no one can validly suspect them of being a threat to society—but neither are they boring.

However, the critics of Pervo are almost certainly right when they insist that the presence of romantic features does not constitute Acts or Luke–Acts as 'a romance' as such.[48] It is *bios*-come-history in apologetic and romantic mode.

The Social World: The Village and the Town
Once again we return to the start of the performance. We have been entertained as we would have been by Josephus or by Dionysius with scenes from an enchanted world full of holy people and divine powers and wondrous births and a precocious child for whom much is promised. And then we are brought up sharp in the 'real world' of Tiberius, Pilate, Herod and the rest. And it now becomes a world with which we are much more familiar, as Harold Moxnes has explained for us. It is not exactly 'our' world, because 'we' are the townspeople found in Acts. But it is the world of the villages around us, with which we have more or less friendly links. It is a world of top-heavy power structures, centred in the towns, and weighing heavily on the village people. Among themselves villagers can usually expect solidarity—their slightly less impoverished neighbours recognize their 'patronal' responsibilities, both to share their wealth for festivities, and to act as 'brokers' between the village community and the absentee urban landlords and administrators.

> Thus Luke describes the world of Jesus in Palestine, but in such a way that his readers would recognise it. It was partly an unfamilar world, but partly also a familiar one. Luke's redactional comments serve to make this world more relevant and familiar.[49]

Moxnes notes some of the differences between the social setting of the followers of Jesus in the Gospel from the setting suggested in Acts. Pressing the evidence rather further than he chooses to, I would urge again that the idealized village ethos of the Gospel is abandoned for a

48. E.g. Palmer, 'Acts and the Ancient Historical Monograph', pp. 3 and 29; Baukham, 'The *Acts of Paul as a Sequel to Acts*', pp. 140-41.
49. Moxnes, *The Economy of the Kingdom*, pp. 62, 74 and 162.

much more conventional patronal ethos in Acts. No one in Acts imitates the birds or the flowers, as Jesus bade in the Gospel. Friends share all in common only in Jerusalem.[50] Paul works for a living or relies on patrons, but his patrons do not take on clients wholesale into their households or for indefinite support. There are no penitent and extravagantly generous tax-collectors. Theophilus can breathe easy. However, he is not entirely let off the hook, if Richard Rohrbaugh is right in suggesting that the city has invaded the countryside in Luke 14's version of the Great Supper, becoming contaminated, to some degree, by its ethos. The host is shamed by those he considered his equals, and must now expect guests only from among those he considers his inferiors, drawn from among the poorest inhabitants and the outcasts on the fringes.[51] Perhaps this actually is Theophilus, together with his new friends, listening to the first performance of the Gospel?

Some aspects of a first-century Mediterranean ethos are, we thus see, more pervasive throughout both books—especially for one important but not all-important example, concern for honour and shame. Roman soldiers are worthy in both (and one acknowledges that Jesus was *dikaios* ['in the right']). The shame of Jesus' crucifixion is reversed by his ascended glory (and it had all been a mistake); the shame of Paul's flogging is reversed by the humble apologies of the magistrates, and so on.[52] For all the stress on repentance and change, and emotion, Luke sees people socially, and in terms of status rather than of personal relationships.[53] You convert to a new group and its ethos and beliefs; any effect on your personality is left unstated.

50. Mitchell, 'The Social Function of Friendship in Acts'.

51. R.L. Rohrbaugh, 'The Pre-Industrial City in Luke–Acts', in Neyrey (ed.), *The Social World of Luke–Acts*, pp. 125-49.

52. B.J. Malina and J.H. Neyrey, 'Honour and Shame in Luke–Acts: Pivotal Values of the Mediterranean World', in Neyrey (ed.), *The Social World of Luke–Acts*, pp. 25-65; and for a careful assessment of this strand as not all-important, see F.G. Downing, '"Honor" among Exegetes', *CBQ* 61.1 (1999), pp. 53-73; repr. in *idem*, *Making Sense*, ch 1.

53. B.J. Malina and J.H. Neyrey, 'First-Century Personality: Dyadic, not Individualistic', in Neyrey (ed.), *The Social World of Luke–Acts*, pp. 67-96. But on this theme in a wider setting, see F.G. Downing, 'Persons in Relation', ch. 2 of *idem*, *Making Sense*.

Theology-Ideology

The remainder of this chapter is a sketch of how the overtly announced ideas, the theology-ideology of Luke, especially as set out in the speeches in Acts, might have appeared to Theophilus and his friends.

In my 'Ethical Pagan Theism and the Speeches in Acts' I adduced evidence that seemed to indicate a fairly general common 'recipe' employed by Josephus, Dionysius of Halicarnassus and Luke, in composing speeches. Many of the speeches I suppose might well have been categorized as 'deliberative', as long as that does not suggest any strict or exclusive adherence to formula. In broadest outline the recipe runs:

1. God is powerful.
2. We must therefore be virtuous, keeping the ancient rules.
3. We shall then enjoy the good life.
4. And avoid the unpleasant alternatives.

The speeches can, however, be analysed in much more detail, to support many more common sub-headings (in Dionysius 'God' may be *theos*, *theioi* or *to theion*).

1. (a) God has and exercises foresight, as all-seeing, present, powerful, righteous.
    (b) God shares this foresight in prophecy and omens; his presence may be felt.
    (c) God also makes known his regular demands: there is law.
    (d) God is gracious, and kind to the good, forgiving to the penitent.
2. (a) We must respond with virtue, piety, righteousness, be worthy (or penitent).
    (b) We must bear in mind the divine commands given in law, custom, conscience.
    (c) We must put them into practice
        (i)   in cultic ritual properly understood
        (ii) in submission to hierarchic authority
        (iii) in maintaining family and tribal custom; in solidarity with 'our' people
        (iv) in natural human kindliness, forgiveness, magnanimity.
3. (a) The Good Life will be our reward, now.
    (b) We can have confidence, be hopeful.
    (c) We shall be remembered; we shall live with God after death.

4. (a)   Failures (small ones) will be forgiven those who repent.

    (b)   Serious and terminal failure is a real possibility, we must be aware.

    (c)   And punishment is bound to follow; bad conscience, illness, destruction, slavery, contumely and eternal loss.

Taking for an example Acts 13.16-47 as a single speech (like Josephus, Luke often breaks his speeches into two uneven parts), we find it is a *logos parakleseōs*. The opening address leads into a narrative (vv. 17-25) that prepares for the statement of the thesis (v. 26), 'to us has been sent the message of this salvation'. The narrative is resumed (vv. 27-31) and the thesis restated (v. 32). Proofs from Scripture (vv. 33-37) follow, and the conclusion is stated (vv. 38-39). There is then a negative exhortation with a further proof (vv. 40-41), followed by a peroration (the brief second part of the speech, vv. 46-47). It certainly has enough of the look of a deliberative speech to have been recognized as such by Theophilus and his dinner-party guests.

Yet the content would also be recognizable to anyone used to the kind of things that historians put in the mouths of their protagonists— and presumably to those used to the kinds of appeals to publicly approved sentiments that would be trotted out in popular assemblies. We Christians, Luke is reminding his hearers, have a very creditable variant of the beliefs and attitudes that are approved by the best and most prestigious writers and speakers in our society—not only the best of Judaism, but the best of non-Jewish ideas and attitudes.[54] Reading Acts today we may take it Luke will have been convinced that it was not just a good variant, but the best—and true. But it was important that its validity could be demonstrated in terms of the beliefs and attitudes of 'enlightened' contemporaries, woven from much the same threads, part of the same intertexture.

Here is a sketch of the detail of our chosen example, the speech of Acts 13, in context:

1. (a)   God...chose...led...brought...raised.

    (b)   prophet...testified...promise fulfilled...prophets.

    (c)   law of Moses...'a man who will do my will'.

---

54. Marguerat, 'Juifs et chrétiens', p. 146, notes Luke's concern to preserve 'ce que le judaïsme a de meilleur': but this is also (as in Josephus) very closely akin to 'the best of "paganism"'.

(d)   God bore with the wilderness generation...salvation...[grace of God (v. 43)].[55]

2. (a)   'you that fear God'; David, 'a man after my own heart'; worthy/unworthy; [the devout (v. 43, again)].

   (b)   the whole passage is a reminder; the utterances of the prophets read every Sabbath...

   (c)   (i) baptism, sepulchral burial, synagogue liturgy.

   (ii)   The introductory narrative sketch is about divinely delegated authority (Josephus takes the Saul–David sequence as a signal example of this theme). John acknowledges Jesus' authority; rulers acted in ignorance, not malice.

   (iii) the people...fathers...sons of the family of Abraham...us their children.

   (iv)   David is a man after God's heart; rulers' ignorance, not malice (again); [those already devout (v. 43, again)].

3. (a)   Canaan as inheritance; saviour, salvation, announcement of good news.

   (b)   promise fulfilled to us; every believer is justified/forgiven; Paul and Barnabas speak out boldly.

   (c)   God raised Jesus [v. 48, eternal life is made explicit].

4. (a)   God bore with the fathers; baptism of repentance; forgiveness of sins.

   (b)   Saul rejected (implicit); condemnation under Mosaic law; 'beware', 'you judge yourselves unworthy'.

   (c)   Destruction of the Canaanites; 'corruption'; 'perish'; 'unworthy of eternal life'.

Verse 39 imports a Pauline-sounding word (in a non-Pauline sense), and the whole contains many explicit and also implicit Septuagintal allusions, to which trait we have already referred above. But the themes, the motifs, are from the familiar stock common to Dionysius and Josephus.

The sequel to the article just summarized is entitled 'Common Ground with Paganism in Luke and in Josephus', and discusses the 'prayer' at Acts 4.24-30, the speech at Lystra, Acts 14.8-18 and that before the

---

55. 1 (a) and (b) are now massively supported by Squires's monograph, *The Plan of God in Luke–Acts*, in which he acknowledges my essay, p. 63 n. 136.

Areopagus, Acts 17.22-31, and the similar structure of some prayers in Josephus (and one in Philo).[56]

I would actually draw a slightly different conclusion now: I would take as a more important motive for Luke's writing, that of reassuring the hearers of the intellectual and moral—and social—respectability of their group and its beliefs and ethos; and, while still affirming the concern to entertain, I would not now suppose Luke expected to have his work bought by or read to complete outsiders. He is entertaining and reassuring Theophilus and his Christian friends, not least reassuring them that their faith is both entertaining and eminently respectable. His friends may well have found Theophilus's dinner party enjoyable and comforting—and, very likely, encouraging.

56. Downing, 'Common Ground', pp. 546-59.

Chapter 11

SHIFTING SANDS

Conflicting Certainties

Reconstructions of Christian origins continue to proliferate, some confidently according much of the original impetus to Jesus, and ascribing to him most if not all of what is told of him in the Gospels (with or without other sources), while others, exhibiting, it seems, equal if not still greater conviction, credit most of the work evidenced in most of the accepted source material to those who saw themselves as his followers. The foundations for either certainty (or any in between) seem on inspection more than a little shaky, a house built on sand.

Most if not all engaged in these reconstructions would seem to accept that the Gospels (as our traditional main source material) along with the rest of the canonical and other potential sources are 'intentional' documents, and as such are primarily evidence for what those responsible for them wanted believed. As it is with such historians that this essay is concerned, we may begin there. On the basis of the intentionality of the documents (with or without recourse to the 'impossibility' of the miracles recounted) one might, then, attempt to construct a scenario in which the figure of Jesus was entirely fictional. This (re-)construction would be aided, of course, (like all the others) by very little external evidence. We might allow that by the early second century (Tacitus), and maybe as early as Nero, Roman intelligence sources accepted (unwarrantedly, we would be arguing) that this Jesus had actually lived and been crucified in Palestine under Pontius Pilate, and that was what these deluded Christians believed; and we would have to give some account of this development from fiction to 'fact'. In this we would have to account for the history of the manuscripts of the gospels and of other supposedly near contemporary Christian writings and their relationships with other Christian documents perhaps more surely datable in the second century, and try to show how all our more immediate data fitted in with what we can glean of the culture and social structures and wider history of the time, allowing both for apparent independence and interdependence, within some arguable timescale: a wide range of the intertexture. All of this might be done (and perhaps has been, without my being aware of it); and let us suppose it coherent and comprehensive. What certainty could it warrantably claim? There are external controls in what we can tell of cultural forms and norms and technical skills and suchlike; but there is, we agreed from the start, practically no external evidence for the early Christian movement(s), and certainly none that demands this interpretation which we have (hypothetically) advanced. The argument is almost entirely internal, a matter of coherence (not 'correspondence'). If our historian intended certainty, he or she would have to show that she or he had included all the pieces that were arguably relevant *and that there was no other way of arranging them coherently*. Since it is clear that such a demonstration is necessarily impossible, there could be no certainty. Pieces can always be arranged differently (as they are, constantly, even for much better evidenced movements and series of events). History is constantly rewritten.

For the time being, of course, various protagonists have their many varying ways of arranging their particular selections of the pieces, and there is no agreement even as to what constitutes the complete set of relevant data needing to be arranged. In brief, the argument as a whole is inescapably circular, since our decision as to what is relevant shapes our reconstruction, but cannot be justified until we have completed it, even though scholars (or at least their publishers' blurb writers) keep offering us their accounts of Christian origins as definitive: 'The first comprehensive determination of who Jesus was, what he did, what he said'; or 'What Did Jesus Really Say?' followed by, '...And what Jesus Really Said and Did'.[1]

---

1. From the dustjacket of Crossan, *The Historical Jesus*; and R.W. Funk and R.W. Hoover (eds.), and The Jesus Seminar, *The Five Gospels: The Search for the Authentic Words of Jesus* (San Francisco: HarperSan Francisco, 1993); and G. Lüdemann, *The Great Deception, and What Jesus Really Said and Did* (ET; London: SCM Press, 1998). W. Arnal, 'Major Episodes in the Biography of Jesus: An Assessment of the Historicity of the Narrative Tradition', *TJT* 13.2 (1997), pp. 201-26 (202), affirms, 'it makes more sense to begin with a mass of secure data and use it to generate conclusions than it does to use preconceptions about Jesus to determine what data are relevant' (p. 202). The latter is discussed below; here I

Critiques of Criteria

In the early rounds of 'the new quest of the historical Jesus', around 30, 35 years ago, some scholars took to explaining and attempting to formalize and some to reflecting critically on their 'criteria', their recurrent patterns of argument and assessment. There was for a while a debate, one to which I offered a contribution, my 1968 volume, *The Church and Jesus*.[2] It is noticeable that more recently authors have again taken to explaining their shared criteria for according some piece of tradition to Jesus or to later followers, and have felt it worth explaining the proper application of each; yet agreed criteria still do not in practice lead to agreed results.[3] However, there is no intention to offer here a revised critique and response to other criticisms, refinements and defences since offered. What is reasserted here, with illustrations from recent work of others, is a critique of the failure to examine the underlying presuppositions of the search for a definitive account of Christian origins, despite the inevitable limitations, given the extreme paucity of genuinely independent data.

One survey has been provided recently by G. Theissen. Many New Testament scholars, as he notes, place most stress still on a 'criterion of dissimilarity' (to wit, only what differs from the beliefs and practices of contemporary Jews or of the early Christians is what has clearly not been brought into the record from either source) but then follow this insistence with the apparently contradictory one, that matter ascribed to Jesus must fit in with what we know of the Palestine of his day. Theissen insists instead that first and foremost, 'all that we attribute to Jesus must be imaginable in the historical context of his life...in the

---

simply note the happy trust that a mass of secure data might be forthcoming before reconstruction gets under way.

2.   Downing, *The Church and Jesus; A Study in History, Philosophy and Theology* (SBT 2.10; London, SCM Press, 1968). My impression of the 'bunching' of interest in questions about criteria is supported by G. Theissen, 'Historical Scepticism and the Criteria of Jesus Research', *SJT* 49.2 (1996), pp. 147-76 (151) n. 5.

3.   See the survey by D. Polkow, 'Methods and Criteria for Historical Jesus Research', SBLSP 28 (1989) pp. 336-56, and his concluding comments, p. 356. Ten years on there is still no wide agreement, with Theissen, for instance, taking a very different line on the relative importance of 'contextual coherence' and 'dissimilarity'; see next note.

context of local circumstances and in the contexts of Jewish traditions and mentality' (while allowing that 'our knowledge of Judaism is necessarily limited').[4] As it stands this seems to make good sense. Jesus might have differed very little from fellow Jews, and his many unreflective or thought-out agreements with others might have constituted most of what mattered to him. We do not know this to be true or false before we begin. If we commence with a criterion of dissimilarity it predetermines and may well distort our focus (as others also have pointed out),[5] and even if a 'criterion of coherence' allows further matter in, it comes in with this distinctive colouring. And, of course, another Dead Sea cave might provide evidence that removed some or all of our remaining dissimilarities. So, incomplete though our picture will be, as Theissen notes,[6] let's start where every individual life starts, let's begin with what we can piece together of the socio-cultural context itself.

Yet Theissen's 'criterion of contextual correspondence' also predetermines our conclusions. The cultural context with which his Jesus is to be interlinked is to be provided by a particular reconstruction of Judaism at the time, drawn 'above all' from non-Christian Jewish sources. Pagan sources and inscriptions can merely substantiate for us such figures as Pilate. In practice this will a priori *exclude*, for instance, the suggestion made by various recent commentators, including myself, that there could have been an influential Cynic component in Jesus' Galilean context. The notion that some of the matter ascribed to Jesus indicates precisely the possible availability, around Jesus' time and in Jesus' (still Jewish) circle, of Cynic ways of thinking and behaving is effectively excluded by Theissen before we begin. Although he admits, as noted, that our knowledge of first-century Judaism is limited, and 'all our knowledge of Jesus is more or less hypothetical', he 'knows' this

---

4. Theissen, 'Historical Scepticism', pp. 165-69; see also G. Theissen and A. Metz, *The Historical Jesus: A Comprehensive Guide* (London: SCM Press, 1998), pp. 114-18; and see the Select Index to the volume, under 'plausibility'. Among other terms discussed along with 'dissimilarity' are 'embarrassment', 'contradiction' and 'discontinuity' (with various distinctions among them)'.

5. Downing, *The Church and Jesus*, p. 116; and, e.g., J.P. Meier, *A Marginal Jew*. I. *The Roots of the Problem and the Person: Rethinking the Historical Jesus* (ABRL; New York: Doubleday, 1991), p. 173, and n. 23.

6. Theissen, 'Historical Scepticism', p. 163.

about Jesus' Galilee without further argument.[7]

This is not to insist that a Cynic component must be included in every reconstruction. Once fully noted, compared and contrasted, it is still possible to insist that even the most striking similarities between Cynic and Jesus traditions are coincidental. But there is no objective base for excluding them from the start and in principle from a thorough consideration.

In much the same way E.P. Sanders can dismiss Jesus' declaration (Mk 7.15) that all foods are clean as 'too revolutionary to have been said by Jesus himself'.[8] Or Maurice Casey can insist that Jesus the Jew could not have invited his friends to drink his blood, the suggestion is 'viciously unhistorical'.[9] Given a particular picture of Jesus bound by a particular reconstruction of his Jewish context, such conclusions will follow. But they are part of the hypothesis, not data given before the hypothesis is advanced and elaborated.

What Sanders and Casey and Theissen (and more recently Theissen and Metz) and many others in fact do is begin with a hypothetical reconstruction in mind, one that already very properly includes a reconstructed context, and then set about showing how large a number of chosen pieces can be fitted together in detail in their design. This is, of course, the only way to go about the task undertaken. But its limitations need to be much clearer both to authors and to readers.[10] Obviously,

7.   Theissen, 'Historical Scepticism', pp. 147-48, though he himself makes a similar point about reliance on the *Gospel of Thomas*: do that and 'you must arrive at...a non-apocalyptic Jesus' (p. 159). In Theissen and Metz, *The Historical Jesus*, p. 216, an argument from a stereotypic impression of Cynic 'uniform' first advanced by Theissen years ago, parrotted by others, but never, it seems, reassessed against the evidence, is offered to show 'So Jesus is not a Jewish Cynic' because his disciples do not dress accordingly. Cynics were individualists, and are on record as diverging widely in dress; but Theissen's Jesus (allowed individuality in other directions, 'Historical Scepticism', pp. 168-70) is not also allowed it here. When the decision has been made in advance, an argument as weak as that offered may well seem sufficient.

8.   E.P. Sanders, *Jewish Law from Jesus to the Mishnah: Five Studies* (London: SCM Press, 1990), p. 28; cited by Meier, *A Marginal Jew*, p. 173.

9.   M. Casey, 'No Cannibals at Passover', *Theology* 96.771 (1993), pp. 199-205, citing p. 203; for a fuller statement of his particular reconstruction, *idem, From Jewish Prophet to Gentile God* (Cambridge: James Clarke, 1991).

10.   Compare, for instance, the discussion on framing adequate hypotheses in Wright, *The New Testament*, pp. 98-109. Although Wright can allow for 'several quite plausible hypotheses about Jesus' (p. 106), he is quite sure he can exclude

every worthwhile reconstruction of Christian origins entails a reconstructed context, and one's account of it has to begin somewhere. But that one's Jesus then fits the context one discerns for him fairly well only shows how effectively one has worked on the total reconstruction, not the trustworthiness of each part on its own; one can demonstrate coherence in the end product, but not the objective validity of individual elements of the reconstruction considered one by one, and outside of one's framing hyopothesis.[11]

Relative to a particular reconstruction there may be a fair degree of certainty in detail.[12] For instance, once I have allowed that the authors of the documents I have included in my reconstruction share pluriform but determinate oral and oral-literary conventions of their day, then certain hypothetically possible interrelationships among the documents are, in that reconstruction, clearly ruled out, and others are plausible if not certain. But even if 'my' account of the culture of the day is accepted, another historian is free to place 'his' authors in a cultural ghetto, and grant them sufficiently pressing reasons to invent literary procedures of their own.[13]

To offer another example, W. Arnal begins by excluding the story of Jesus' baptism from the early tradition because some items are 'theologically tendentious' and half are also 'supernatural'. On the other hand, many philosophically literate people would allow that all experience is 'experience as', and that entails the possibility that in some cultures any event *might* be experienced in what some of us in our day might only be able to see as theologically tendentious and unreal supernatural terms, and therefore that an event so interpretatively experienced could well enter an oral tradition in such terms in its early days: such terms are not automatically late constructs (though they still may have been). Arnal's modern rationalism, rather than argued evidence,

others on the basis of a position established apart from them.

11. Cf. F.G. Downing, 'Deeper Reflections on the Jewish Cynic Jesus', *JBL* 117.1 (1998), pp. 97-104 (102-104); repr. as ch. 6 of Downing, *Making Sense in (and of) the First Christian Century*; and a fuller statement in *idem*, 'The Jewish Cynic Jesus'. The trust that 'individual data' may be 'verified' is expressed by Meier, *A Marginal Jew*, p. 170.

12. Argued already in Downing, *The Church and Jesus*, p. 189; and *idem*, 'The Social Contexts of Jesus the Teacher', pp. 439-51.

13. See Downing, 'Compositional Conventions and the Synoptic Problem', Chapter 8 above; and 'A Paradigm Perplex: Luke, Matthew and Mark', Chapter 9 above.

determines his view of what is and is not possible in first-century 'experience as'.

'It Can't Have Been Invented'

The authors I read seem unwilling to accept such relativity in their detailed findings, and assume that they can from within their more or less formed position reach piecemeal conclusions that should surely be recognized by everyone else, universally assured individual results, fixed points with equal force whatever the reconstruction being proposed. Just such a claim is often made, for instance, for the story of Jesus being baptized by John. As Arnal, now, has recently reminded readers, 'Günter Bornkamm is typical in claiming that "the fact that Jesus let himself be baptized by John belongs to the data of his life which cannot be doubted"'.[14] This episode also figures in E.P. Sanders's list of 'eight indisputable facts' relating to Jesus and his first followers, and J.D. Crossan as a further example claims that 'Jesus' baptism by John is one of the surest things we know about them both'.[15] In this instance a great many writers do indeed agree, Gerd Theissen also among them (despite his reservations concerning 'the criterion of dissimilarity').[16] 'The reasons offered for this confidence', concedes Arnal,

> are not unimpressive. It is frequently noted that the baptism is theologically embarrassing to early Christians in its implication that Jesus was both sinful and subordinate to John. This account, so the reasoning goes, would thus hardly have been invented by early Christians and consequently must be regarded as accurate.

14. G. Bornkamm, *Jesus of Nazareth* (ET; New York: Harper & Row, 1960), p. 49, quoted by Arnal, 'Major Episodes', p. 202, with Arnal's added emphasis.

15. Sanders, *Jesus and Judaism*, p. 11; Crossan, *The Historical Jesus*, p. 234. These are also cited in Arnal, 'Major Episodes', pp. 201-202.

16. Arnal, 'Major Episodes', conveniently lists a variety of scholars who reach the same conclusion, pp. 217-18 n. 9. I add, Theissen, 'Historical Scepticism', p. 160; cf. Theissen and Metz, *The Historical Jesus*, pp. 117, 196. Meier, *A Marginal Jew*, pp. 167, 169, although initially talking of 'probabilities' finds a churchly creation of the story 'highly unlikely'. N.T. Wright, *Christian Origins and the Question of God*. II. *Jesus and the Victory of God* (London: SPCK, 1996): 'All agree that Jesus began his public work in the context of John's baptism' (p. 160); cf. pp. 162 and 131-33.

However, Arnal later cogently concludes, 'The theological embarrassment argument, despite its apparent strength, is...unconvincing. Invok-
ing this argument assumes a relatively fixed and exalted christology
among the early followers of Jesus from the very beginning', and assumes that John could never have been seen as a figure superior to or at
least senior to Jesus, or even that the encounter with the better-known
John could have been invented in the first place to legitimate Jesus.[17]
As I myself argued a decade or so ago,

> It would be quite reasonable to suggest an hypothesis that included a
> stage in the life of the tradition where Jesus, like every first-century
> teacher, had to be found a predecessor (there is plenty of evidence for
> such a demand being likely to be felt). John may be seen as the sole
> available contemporary candidate (see Josephus), despite the contrast in
> their views acknowledged in the tradition. Only a little while later does
> this become embarrassing (with which compare the unease of Cynic tra-
> dition at Diogenes' connection with Antisthenes, itself very likely origi-
> nally an invention).[18]

This I argued purely hypothetically, to make the case that rather than
there being some fixed points such as this (albeit some or much of the
rest insecure), nothing is fixed, all is relative.

However, it is worth pursuing this particular example further. Arnal
cites, in provisional agreement with 'the argument from embarrassment', Luke's making John disclaim messiahship (Lk. 3.15-16) and
John's talk in Mark of a 'stronger one' coming after him (these in
addition to Q/Lk. 7.28, 'less than the least'; John's demurral in Mt.
3.14-15; and, we might add, the fourth evangelist's omission of any
baptism of Jesus as such at all). But this now seems incoherent. The
more inferior one makes the John of Mark and of Luke, surely the more
strange it might seem for Jesus in either work to have him as a predecessor, let alone accept baptism from him. Mark certainly has the
baptizer say he is not worthy to stoop and untie the sandal thong of the
one coming after him, but Mark himself shows no embarrassment at all
at Jesus having accepted the unworthy one's sousing; in fact John and
his baptism can be very positively compared with Jesus' own activity
(Mk 11.27-33); and Mark is contentedly followed by Luke (Lk. 20.1-

17. Arnal, 'Major Episodes', pp. 204-205, citing a much smaller number of
scholars making this or a similar point.

18. Downing, *Jesus and the Threat of Freedom*, p. 154, arguing with Sanders,
Jesus and Judaism.

8). We seem to be being asked to acknowledge at least one more twist in some streams of the tradition.

And then Arnal offers us yet further turns in its growth. Originally, he suggests, there was no link between John and Jesus in any of the tradition, (nor in Jesus' own life, it seems), but a need came to be felt (as just suggested) for a precursor or perhaps for this precursor, and so 'the coming one' (Q/Lk. 3.16 and Mk 1.8) and the mixed quotation of Mal. 3.1 and Exod. 23.20, 'Behold I send my messenger before your face, who will prepare your way...', were related to John (whether validly or not is not stated; Q/Lk. 7.27, Mk 1.2) and taken as pointing to Jesus. This is then later elaborated in Q with the rest of Q/Lk. 7.24-28, 31-35, and to John himself is ascribed a summary of Q's message, Q/Lk. 3.7-9, 16-17. The link is then 'narrativized' by Mark in the baptism story, and he also uses elements of the scene he has created to structure his narrative as a whole.[19]

Assuming (with no argument offered to the contrary) some 'Q-teacher' or teachers with followers in Galilee or a little further north, we are thus being invited to imagine some(one) at some time unspecified, deciding it would be fitting to find Jesus a predecessor in John; although no one remembers it for a fact, it seems appropriate, and no one sees fit to insist it never was so. Are we where no one knows this? Or is it just where no one cares? Once in the tradition, however, this item is stuck. Jesus is 'the coming one', and John his precursor, and these notes, multiply attested (being in Q and in Mark), suggest 'a firmer place in the tradition and a longer history than the baptism narrative itself, although without prejudice to their probable inauthenticity'.[20] This tradition reaches Mark, who builds on it (around 75? or earlier?). Already Mark (or someone) finds John himself embarrassing (as Arnal has himself reminded us, John is not worthy to untie Jesus' sandal thong); but instead of quietly dropping him, Mark makes him a major player in the story, and invents an account of Jesus actually accepting baptism at his unfit hands. That's an intriguing reconstruction of the mind-set of Mark and friends.

Those responsible for Q seem, however, at some point to have to respond to doubts whether Jesus *is* to be seen as the one John expected (Q/Lk. 7.20). These doubts are not only articulated but somewhat oddly placed on the lips of the claimed predecessor himself, without his ever

19. Arnal, 'Major Episodes', pp. 205-206 and notes, quoting from p. 206.
20. Arnal, 'Major Episodes', p. 206.

being allowed to confess himself persuaded, curiously undermining his ascribed role, and that even though at around the same time (or not that long before or later) a summary of the whole message of the Q collection to date is placed on his lips. Perhaps it is influential later followers of John who are very unsure, and the Q people feel they have to include this doubt and respond to it (but apparently without these followers of the baptizer also protesting that in actual fact John and Jesus had nothing to do with each other at all). The Q people at some point then totally downgrade the predecessor they (or their predecessors) had invented, he is now 'less than the least in the kingdom of God' (Q/Lk. 7.28)—but still do not drop him; rather they leave him to summarize the entire message of the collection.

When Matthew and Luke read Mark they find the baptism or at least the baptizer difficult, but they retain both, even though this is the first they have heard of the awkward baptism (it can't be in their prior tradition, because Mark invented it).

It may well be that Arnal can produce or even has produced an account of the early Christian communities that would make sense of these odd procedures, the inventing of matter with considerable freedom, yet with an inability to drop it once incorporated, however embarrassing it later becomes, and however awkward the necessity of adding further matter to counter the embarrassment. My first point is simply to note how easily a perceptive and widely read scholar can discern the inadequacy in the picture of the early Christians presupposed by others' 'arguments from embarrassment', and yet fail to see any need to explain, let alone defend, the incoherent picture of the early Christians entailed by his own account. (Yes, of course, groups and individuals can entertain incoherent beliefs, that cannot be ruled out a priori, either. But if that is the picture adopted, one has precluded any argued reconstruction.)

It would certainly be difficult to find other examples of authors in late east Mediterranean antiquity so bound by their own or others' recent inventions as to be unable to excise them in response to later unease or dissatisfaction, and thus left with the sole option of adding counters to their own or their immediate predecessors' recent constructs. Josephus can leave inconvenient bits out in his 'accurate' retelling of Scripture. Only sacred texts and canonical law codes themselves are fairly safe from major excisions, and that because of their antiquity; but they are also as safe from major revisionary additions to the text. Matthew and

Luke are both much freer than this with Q in many contexts, and freer still with Mark (on most versions of this part of the hypothesis in question). An inventive group like Arnal's Q lot could surely be expected to manage things better.

It is also difficult to imagine 'the Q people' engaged in so many twists and turns in quite so short a space of time (30 years?) and taking followers along with them through every fresh twist. However, perhaps a coherent and cohesive and inclusive account can be built around the proposals presented.

No Escape from the Circle

My point is that it is only within such a comprehensive reconstruction that proposals such as Arnal's could make sense, yet Arnal, no more than most contemporary scholars, finds any need even to sketch a comprehensive context for his detailed arguments. And as they stand they have no *necessary* implications for any alternative reconstructions: they do not in themselves make other readings any less plausible. At best they can be offered in the market to anyone who feels they might fit or be made to fit, be given a scenario in which they had a coherent part to play.

It also seems significant that Arnal can rely on 'the known tendencies of the tradition', and on the ways apothegms are formed (and so can assure us that 'in Q's expansion of the Beelzebul Accusation' 'we actually have a saying in the process of giving birth to a narrative'.)[21] As a further example, D. Polkow, in agreement with others in an assessment of 'criteria', can be sure that the 'mustard seed' could not begin life in the tradition with an exaggeration and then be rationalized by tradents; nor could its author have issued it in different forms.[22] Such complexities can be safely ignored in the light of agreed tacit presuppositions left unexamined even in a helpfully critical survey. Yet we have in fact only secured our generalizations when we have completed

21. Arnal, 'Major Episodes', pp. 207, 216 (despite being aware, n. 89, of studies by V.K. Robbins and B.L. Mack that show how narratives do [better, may] generate sayings). Note also the earlier work of E.P. Sanders, *The Tendencies of the Synoptic Tradition* (SNTSMS, 9; Cambridge: Cambridge University Press, 1969).

22. Polkow, 'Methods and Criteria', pp. 345-47. Against any such certainty that we just know how people in the ancient east Mediterranean world could or could not use words, see 'Words and Meanings', Chapter 3 above.

our reconstructions. We do not have independent dated records of expansions or contractions, additions or excisions in gospel material. Such supposed developments are part of a hypothesis, not independent and prior foundations for it.

In agreement with Arnal and others, it should be entirely obvious that 'the criterion of embarrassment', 'of dissimilarity', could only work absolutely if we had independent evidence for the beliefs and attitudes of the tradents over the entire period of the oral tradition, for the formation of the texts (and of their copying), and for the Christian movement itself, however variegated or uniform, disjointed or interconnected it was (or the movements were) for, say the first hundred years. But we have not. As I (with one or two others) argued some 30 years ago now, until we know what to ascribe to Jesus we do not *know* what his early followers added or altered; but until we know that, we don't know what to ascribe to Jesus.[23] The circle remains. We can try to conceal parts of the circle with criteria that seem objective—but they in fact remain within the same ring. Or we can show the weaknesses in others' suggestions, and then parade our own onto the arena from which we have thus driven the opposition, as though ours were the only viable alternatives. And all these arguments will as much be set in a circle as any other set, mostly propped up by unseen presuppositions whose invisibility (and that alone) may allow what does appear to seem able to stand independently.

Seeking Wider Coherence

There is some hope. The larger the circle, the more the sources integrated into the total picture, the less room seems to be left for special pleading, and the more cogent may be the result. For instance, if I can link notes of formal prosections of Christians in Revelation, *1 Clement*, 1 Peter and Ignatius with Pliny the Younger's inability, noted in *Letter* 10.96, to find any precedent in his own or neighbouring provinces, we

---

23. D. Mealand, 'The Dissimilarity Test', *SJT* 31.1 (1978), pp. 41-50 (45-46), is unusual in taking this issue seriously, but still supposes we have enough independent information about the Christian groups from whom emerged the sources we claim for Jesus to allow us to get started. Yet even on the law, Mealand's example, Paul on circumcision and commensuality has nothing to help illuminate Matthew who deals with neither. See further, below.

seem to be able to place the Christian sources a little more securely.[24] Yet, of course, mine is still part of a total reconstruction of Christian origins, and others have reasons within theirs that presumably render irrelevant or ineffective those that figure in mine. Nonetheless it remains true that the smaller the selection of source material, the easier it is to produce a result that suits one's own preferences, as Richard Hays illustrates in a review of *The Five Gospels*, quoting Thomas Jefferson,

> Among the sayings and discourses imputed to Him [Jesus] by His biographers, I find many passages of fine imagination, correct morality, and of the most lovely benevolence; and others, again, of so much ignorance, so much absurdity, so much untruth, charlatanism, and imposture, as to pronounce it impossible that such contradictions should have proceded from the same being. I separate, therefore, the gold from the dross; restore to him the former, and leave the latter to the stupidity of others...[25]

Most scholars discussing criteria do in fact spread their nets wider by including 'multiple attestation', and so *The Five Gospels* claims merit for paying considerable attention in particular to the *Gospel of Thomas*. It also takes for granted Markan priority and the source Q. But, as others again would insist, none of this is universally accepted.[26] Some still hold to Matthaean priority, with Mark conflating and abbreviating Matthew and Luke; others have Matthew use Mark, and Luke both of them. The inclusion or exclusion of matter from John's Gospel obviously has a major effect on any resultant sketch of Jesus, but arguments either way already presuppose the result.

Reading various critical reviews of *The Five Gospels* leaves me not a little puzzled and disappointed. Critics readily point out the announced but undefended presuppositions (the 'seven pillars' displayed early on, pp. 2-5), and then also point to other unadmitted ones they discern besides.[27] What I have not found is any awareness of how spurious is

---

24. See F.G. Downing, 'Pliny's Prosecutions of Christians: Revelation and 1 Peter', *JSNT* 34 (1988), pp. 105-23: prosecutions of Christians in the east must be dated during or after Pliny's governorship.

25. R.B. Hays, 'The Corrected Jesus', *First Things* 43 (1994), pp. 43-48 (but without source details for Jefferson).

26. E.g. R.W. Yarbrough, 'The Gospel according to the Jesus Seminar', *Presybterion* 20.1 (1994), pp. 12-13.

27. Reviews by M. Davies, *ExpTim* 105.10 (1994), pp. 308-309; D. Catchpole, *Theology* 97.780 (1994), pp. 457-60; C.M. Tuckett, *JTS* NS 46.1 (1995), pp. 250-53; Yarbrough, 'The Gospel'; Hays, 'The Corrected Jesus'.

the 'multiple attestation' by 74 scholars, 'self-selected', but nonetheless disagreeing and needing a complexly weighted voting system. If it were, as claimed in positivist style, a matter of 'empirical, factual evidence—evidence open to confirmation by independent, neutral observers—[as] the controlling factor in historical judgments' (p. 34), then a simple 'unweighted' vote should have been enough. All (or a very large majority) would have agreed at least on what was beyond doubt 'in' (red) and what was beyond doubt 'out' (black). 'Maybe in, maybe out' would be harder to quantify; but if it were 'a matter of empirical, factual evidence' there should be no great need for pinks and greys, whether academics do or do not 'like simple choices' (p. 36). Indeed actual voting figures might have been quite interesting.[28] But the insistence on four choices, weighted, shows clearly that it was never a matter 'open to confirmation by independent neutral observers' (or else that the participants were none such).[29]

As reviewers of *The Five Gospels* do observe, the 'criterion of dissimilarity' is frequently deployed in the notes that attempt to summarize the winning conclusions. But scholars who differ this much, even using that criterion, must be starting with different pictures of the development of the tradition and of the community(-ies) involved. So, even if they agree 'in' or agree 'out' (or 'maybe'), it is for more or less different underlying reasons, and the agreement is purely formal, little better than chance coincidence, a lottery, and meaningless. To repeat, if they really had the same reasons for their decisions, their decisions themselves should have been the same, and the voting could have been simple.

More than 90 years ago Albert Schweitzer, writing of the problematic transition from Jesus to church, insisted that 'Modern historical theology...until at least it has described the popular Christianity of the first three generations...must concede to all hypotheses which fairly face

---

28. Quantitative comparisons are not readily available, but J.D. Crossan's earlier and simpler distinction between 'from Jesus' and 'from the later Jesus tradition', with around 80 'complexes' in the former group seems to give us far more than the Seminar's red and rather less than the red and pink together; Crossan, *The Historical Jesus*, pp. 434-50.

29. With the foregoing, compare the criticisms levelled by N.T. Wright, 'Five Gospels but no Jesus', in W.R. Farmer (ed.), *Crisis in Christology* (Livonia, MI: Dove, 1995), pp. 115-57, especially pp. 123-27.

this problem and endeavour to solve it their formal right of existence'.[30] Some 40 years ago E. Käsemann insisted,

> we are still short of one essential requisite for the identification of the authentic Jesus material, namely, a conspectus of the very earliest stage of primitive Christian history; and there is also an almost complete lack of satisfactory and water-tight criteria for this material.[31]

Still no such agreed account has been forthcoming, nor is it likely, for we have to accept that we only have at best single attestations of our sources for the various Christian communities with which our evangelists were most closely associated. Although Paul may well be aware of versions of the synoptic tradition, for instance,[32] he quotes none of it as it stands, and ignores altogether large swathes of it. We have therefore no external source to help to validate our construction of Matthaean, Markan, Johannine, Q or other 'communities',[33] no 'hard' evidence that such was what any evangelist-in-context was bound to be doing with the traditions transmitted. We are left to construct hypotheses and fill them out in ways others may or may not find persuasive (and which may be near or far from 'the truth'—but we will not know).[34] A house built on shifting sands needs a 'raft' foundation if it is to survive intact. Individual foundation stones are very insecure.

This pressure for multiple self-consistent, coherent hypotheses does not, however, imply that 'anything goes'. It was argued to the contrary, above. The more the pieces that are included, and interconnected, the more coherent the links with a still wider hypothesis and agreed (or agree-able) fixed points in the wider world, the less subjective is the

---

30. A. Schweitzer, *The Quest of the Historical Jesus* (ET of *Von Reimarus zu Wrede*; London: A. & C. Black, 3rd edn, 1954 [1905]), p. 314.

31. E. Käsemann, *Essays on New Testament Themes* (ET of *Exegetische Versuche und Besinnungen*, I; Gottingen: Vandenhoeck & Ruprecht, 1960; London: SCM Press, 1964), p. 36.

32. See D. Wenham, *Paul: Follower of Jesus or Founder of Christianity?* (Grand Rapids: Eerdmans, 1995).

33. Contra D.L. Mealand, 'The Dissimilarity Test', p. 46, 'we know rather more about earliest Christianity than can be gleaned from the gospels'. For arguments against taking these as evidence for 'communities', anyway, R. Bauckham (ed.), *The Gospel for All Christians: Rethinking the Gospel Audiences* (Edinburgh: T. & T. Clark, 1998).

34. See, now, John S. Kloppenborg Verbin's fine *Excavating Q*, p. 54, '*Hypothesis are all that we have and all we will ever have*' (original emphasis).

result likely to seem, the more persuasive is it likely to appear.[35] And not a few of the scholars critically appraised above propose approaches that in themselves go quite a long way towards meeting this requirement. Crossan, Theissen, Wright in particular try in their own ways to explain their approaches, and make them widely inclusive. They are open to internal criticism, of course, but more importantly still, it has been argued here, they have on the basis of each one's own grand reconstruction no warrants for excluding items from other competing inclusive reconstructions. Such attempts at premature exclusion are not only ill-founded, but may distract from the more needful task of building firm internal links within their own grand hypotheses, and expanding these to include further available data whose relevance for the work in question they may within that work effectively argue.

My own work (represented in this selection, and in *Making Sense in (and of) the First Christian Century*) has attempted to share in setting Christian origins more clearly in the cultural context, the intertexture, to which the early documents seem to belong.

35. Wright, *The New Testament*, pp. 104-109, argues as though one could test one's hypothesis against wider evidence, whereas all one can do is expand one's hypothesis to include more data, fitting partial hypotheses into a larger whole. His criterion of 'simplicity' is too subjective to be useful, and certainly cannot be used to exclude others' proposals set in other contexts. (Wright's own efforts look very complex to me, but I would only attempt to criticize them on the basis of internal claims; see, e.g., my 'Exile in First-Century Judaism', ch. 8 in *Making Sense*.)

CONCLUDING UNSCIENTIFIC POSTSCRIPT

It is hoped that the attentive and critical reader will by now have (if only marginally) an enriched awareness of some of the ways in which people 'did things with words' in the first Christian century.

Those who can, do; those who can't, criticize (with acknowledgments to George Bernard Shaw). In advance of a 'tu quoque?' perhaps I may append a very brief autobiographical note. After publishing *The Church and Jesus* (1968) I began a very limited study of speeches in Josephus, which led to a much more painstaking examination, and then that led to Philo and then to a wide range of writings from the Graeco-Roman world, mainly from the first century BCE to the second CE. Out of that came a source book, *Strangely Familiar*, attempting to illustrate a very wide range of attitudes and beliefs and practices in the ancient world, much wider than the usual 'philosophy and myth' or 'quaint but cunning artefacts' approaches. (Initially the book was accepted by a publisher who then backed out; is still available from me.) Out of the awareness represented by that collection stemmed another source book, *Christ and the Cynics*, and some 40 articles in various journals over the last 20 years (some included, along with new matter, in this volume and its companion), two major studies (*Cynics and Christian Origins*, and *Cynics, Paul and the Pauline Churches*), as well as theological reflections and an attempt to present some conclusions in a more accessible form, *Jesus and the Threat of Freedom*. In all this work I have been attempting, usually explicitly, to present my conclusions as part of one plausible hypothesis, disputing others' work only within their own terms of reference, and trying at least to remember to allow that some other as yet unformed hypothesis might still afford a home to any conclusion I have sought to show ill-founded on its own terms.[1]

---

1. *Strangely Familiar: An Introductory Reader to the First Century* (Manchester: Downing, 1985) obtainable from the author (address in SNTS and SBL member lists); *Christ and the Cynics*; *Cynics and Christian Origins*; *Cynics, Paul and the Pauline Churches*; *Jesus and the Threat of Freedom*.

In most of my longer publications I have included at least a brief personal theological reflection, setting my conclusions within the context of my commitment as an Anglican Christian (ordained), and a fairly ineffective Christian socialist, because readers need at least some clue that may help them discern underlying pressures. My reflections now are simply a suggestion for any who approached this volume in terms of present, past or incipient Christian believing. I would urge that it is worth considering these sorts of exploring and elaborating of hypotheses about Christian origins (and ongoing Christian history) as an updated form of the kind of biblical meditation proposed by Ignatius Loyola. But, with this present procedure, rather than jumping straight to imagining gospel events in their imagined physical context, one tries to envisage the whole process, working back from more or less secure texts and other data, through possible transmission, to original events (whether original events in Jesus' life, or original inventions among early storytellers or original embroidery or pruning by early 'editors'), and then forward again, making as many interconnections as possible, on the largest scale which each can sustain. The process may be valid not only as historiography but also as spiritual formation.[2]

---

2. The issue of faith and certainty is clearly important to some (e.g. Theissen, 'Historical Scepticism', p. 147, 'faith is absolute certainty', and 'personal certainty in dealing with the historical Jesus' is still there at the end (p. 175). I argued against any need for 'certainty' in faith (though words may be being used differently) in my *Has Christianity a Revelation?* (London: SCM Press, 1964), and responded to some criticisms of that book in 'Revelation, Disagreement and Obscurity', *Religious Studies* 21 (1986), pp. 219-30.

BIBLIOGRAPHY

Achtemeier, P.J., '*Omne verbum sonat*: The New Testament and the Oral Environment of Late Western Antiquity', *JBL* 109.1 (1990), pp. 3-27.

Adams, E., 'Historical Crisis and Cosmic Crisis in Mark 13 and Lucan's *Civil War*', *TynBul* 48.2 (1997), pp. 329-44.

Aletti, J.-N., *Comment Dieu est-il juste? Clefs pour interpréter l'épître aux Romains* (Paris: Seuil, 1991).

—'La *Dispositio* rhétorique dans les épîtres pauliniens: Proposition de méthode', *NTS* 38.4 (1992), pp. 385-401.

—'La présence d'un modèle rhétorique en Romains: Son rôle et son importance', *Bib* 71.1 (1990), pp. 1-14.

Alexander, L., 'Acts and Ancient Intellectual Biography', in Winter and Clark (eds.), *The Book of Acts*, pp. 31-64.

—'The Living Voice: Scepticism towards the Written Word in Early Christian and in Graeco-Roman Texts', in D.J.A. Clines, S.E. Fowl and S.E. Porter (eds.), *The Bible in Three Dimensions* (Sheffield: JSOT Press, 1990), pp. 221-47.

—'Luke's Preface in the Context of Greek Preface Writing', *NovT* 38.1 (1986), pp. 48-74.

—*The Preface to Luke's Gospel* (SNTSMS, 78; Cambridge: Cambridge University Press, 1993).

—'Sisters in Adversity: Re-telling Martha's Story', in Brooke (ed.), *Women in the Biblical Tradition*, pp. 167-86.

—'Voyaging in Luke–Acts', in Tuckett (ed.), *Luke's Literary Achievement*, pp. 17-49.

Alexander, P.S., 'Midrash and the Gospels', in Tuckett (ed.), *Synoptic Studies*, pp. 1-18.

—'Rabbinic Biography and the Biography of Jesus: A Survey of the Evidence', in Tuckett (ed.), *Synoptic Studies*, pp. 19-50.

Anderson, G., *Ancient Fiction: The Novel in the Graeco-Roman World* (London: Croom Helm, 1984).

—'The *Pepaideumenos* in action: sophists and their outlook in the Early Empire', *ANRW* II.33.1 (1989), pp. 79-208.

Arnal, W., 'Major Episodes in the Biography of Jesus: An Assessment of the Historicity of the Narrative Tradition', *TJT* 13.2 (1997), pp. 201-26.

Ascough, R.S., *What Are They Saying About the Formation of the Pauline Churches?* (New York: Paulist Press, 1998).

Atherton, C., *The Stoics on Ambiguity* (Cambridge: Cambridge University Press, 1993).

Attridge, H.W., 'Reflection on Research into Q', *Semeia* 55 (1992), pp. 223-34.

Aune, D. '*Septem Sapientem Convivium*', in Betz (ed.), *Plutarch's Ethical Writings*, pp. 51-105.

Austin, J.L., *How to do things with Words* (Oxford: Clarendon Press, 1962).

—*Philosophical Papers* (ed. J.O. Urmson and G.J. Warnock; Oxford: Clarendon Press, 1961).

Avery-Peck, A.J., 'Rhetorical Argumentation in Early Rabbinic Pronouncement Stories', *Semeia* 64 (1993/94), pp. 49-72.

Bailey, K.E., 'Middle Eastern Oral Tradition and the Gospels', *ExpTim* 106.12 (1995), pp. 363-67.

Balsdon, J.P.V.D., *Life and Leisure in Ancient Rome* (London: Bodley Head; New York: McGraw–Hill, 1969).

Barnett, P., 'Polemical Parallelism: Some Further Reflections on the Apocalypse', *JSNT* 35 (1989), pp. 111-20.

Bauckham, R., 'The *Acts of Paul* as a Sequel to Acts', in Winter and Clarke (eds.), *The Book of Acts*, pp. 105-52.

—'The Rich Man and Lazarus: The Parable and the Parallels', *NTS* 37.2 (1991), pp. 225-46.

Bauckham, R. (ed.), *The Gospel for All Christians: Rethinking the Gospel Audiences* (Edinburgh: T. & T. Clark, 1998).

Beavis, M.A., *Mark's Audience: The Literary and Social Setting of Mark 4.11-12* (JSNTSup, 33; Sheffield: JSOT Press, 1989).

Bellinzoni, A.J., Jr (ed.), *The Two-Source Hypothesis: A Critical Appraisal* (Macon, GA: Mercer University Press, 1985).

Berger, K., *Formgeschichte des Neuen Testaments* (Heidelberg: Quelle & Meyer, 1984).

—'Hellenistischer Gattungen im Neuen Testament', *ANRW* II.25.2 (1984), pp. 1031-1462.

Best, E., *Mark: The Gospel as Story* (Edinburgh: T. & T. Clark, 1983).

Betz, H.D. *Galatians* (Hermeneia; Philadelphia: Fortress Press, 1979).

—*Plutarch's Theological Writings and Early Christian Literature* (Leiden: E.J. Brill, 1975).

Betz, H.D. (ed.), *Plutarch's Ethical Writings and Early Christian Literature* (Leiden: E.J. Brill, 1972).

Blackburn, B., *Theios Anêr and the Markan Miracle Traditions* (WUNT 2.40; Tübingen: J.C.B. Mohr, 1991).

Boismard, M.-E., 'Commentaire', in P. Benoit and M.-E. Boismard, *Synopse de quatre évangiles*, II (Paris: Cerf, 1972).

Bolt, P.G., 'Mark 16.1-8: The Empty Tomb of a Hero?', *TynBul* 47.1 (1993), pp. 27-37.

Bonner, S.F., *Education in Ancient Rome from the Elder Pliny to the Younger Cato* (London: Methuen, 1977).

Borgen, P., 'Philo of Alexandria: Reviewing and Rewriting Biblical Material', *StudPhilAnn* 9 (1997), pp. 37-53.

Bornkamm, G., *Jesus of Nazareth* (ET; New York: Harper & Row, 1960).

Botha, P.J.J., 'Greco-Roman Literacy as Setting for New Testament Writings', *Neot* 26.1 (1992), pp. 195-215.

—'Mark's Story of Jesus and the Search for Virtue', in Porter and Olbricht (eds.), *The Rhetorical Analysis of Scripture*, pp. 156-84.

—'The Verbal Art of the Pauline Letters', in S.E. Porter and T.H. Olbricht (eds.), *Rhetoric and the New Testament* (JSNTSup, 90; Sheffield: JSOT Press, 1993), pp. 409-59.

Bowerstock, G.W., *Greek Sophists in the Roman Empire* (Oxford: Clarendon Press, 1969).

Branham, R.B., 'Diogenes' Rhetoric and the Invention of Cynicism', in Goulet-Cazé and Goulet (eds.), *Le cynisme ancien et ses prolongements*, pp. 445-73.

Braun, W., *Feasting and Social Rhetoric in Luke 14* (SNTSMS, 85; Cambridge: Cambridge University Press, 1995).

Brent, A., 'John as Theologos: The Imperial Mysteries and the Apocalypse', *JSNT* 75 (1999), pp. 103-14.

Brett, M.G., 'Motives and Intentions in Genesis 1', *JTS* NS 42.1 (1991), pp. 1-16.

Brown, R.E., *The Death of the Messiah* (2 vols.; London: Geoffrey Chapman, 1994).

Brooke, G.J., *Exegesis at Qumran* (JSOTSup, 29; Sheffield: JSOT Press, 1985).

—*Women in the Biblical Tradition* (Lewiston, NY: Edwin Mellen Press, 1992).

Brooke, G.J. (ed.), *Narrativity and the Bible* (Leuven: Peeters, forthcoming).

Bryan, C., *A Preface to Mark: Notes on the Gospel in its Literary and Cultural Settings* (New York: Oxford University Press, 1993).

Bultmann, R., *Die Geschichte der synoptischen Tradition* (Göttingen: Vendenhoeck & Ruprecht, 1957).

—*History of the Synoptic Tradition* (ET; Oxford: Basil Blackwell, 1972).

Burnyeat, M.F., 'Wittgenstein and Augustine *De Magistro*', *AristSocSup* 61 (1987), pp. 1-24.

Burridge, R.A., *What are the Gospels? A Comparison with Graeco-Roman Biography* (SNTSMS, 70; Cambridge: Cambridge University Press, 1992).

Cancik, H., 'Bios and Logos: Formgeschichtliche Untersuchungen zu Lukians "Leben des Demonax" ', in *idem* (ed.), *Markus-philologie*, pp. 115-30.

—*Markus-philologie* (WUNT, 33; Tübingen: J.C.B. Mohr, 1984).

Carcopino, J., *Daily Life in Ancient Rome* (ET; Harmondsworth: Penguin Books, 1956 [1941]).

Carruth, S., and A. Garsky, *Documenta Q* (Leuven: Peeters, 1996–).

Casey, M., *From Jewish Prophet to Gentile God* (Cambridge: James Clarke, 1991).

—'No Cannibals at Passover', *Theology* 96.771 (1993), pp. 199-205.

Catchpole, D.R., 'The Beginning of Q: A Proposal', *NTS* NS 38.2 (1992), pp. 205-21; repr. in *idem*, *The Quest for Q*, pp. 60-78.

—'Q, Prayer and the Kingdom: A Rejoinder', *JTS* NS 40.2 (1989), pp. 377-88; repr. in *idem*, *The Quest for Q* (Edinburgh: T. & T. Clark, 1993), pp. 201-28.

—Review of R.W. Funk *et al.*, *The Five Gospels, Theology* 97.780 (1994), pp. 457-60.

Charlton, W., *Aesthetics* (London: Hutchinson, 1970).

Clark, D.L., *Rhetoric in Greco-Roman Education* (New York: Columbia University Press, 1957).

Clark, G., *Augustine: The Confessions* (Cambridge: Cambridge University Press, 1992).

Clarke, M.L., *Higher Education in the Ancient World* (London: Routledge, 1971).

Classen, C.J., 'Paulus und die antike Rhetorik', *ZNW* 82 (1991), pp. 1-33.

Cohen, R. (ed.), *New Directions in Literary History* (London: Routledge, 1974).

Collins, A.Y., 'Finding Meaning in the Death of Jesus', *JR* 78 (1998), pp. 173-92.

—'From Noble Death to Crucified Messiah', *NTS* 40.4 (1994), pp. 481-86.

—'The Genre of the Passion Narrative', *ST* 47 (1993), pp. 3-28.

—'The Significance of Mark 10.45 among Gentile Christians', *HTR* 90.4 (1997), pp. 371-82.

Corley, K.E., *Private Women, Public Meals: Social Conflict in the Synoptic Tradition* (Peabody, MA: Hendrickson, 1993).

Crossan, J.D., *The Historical Jesus: The Life of a Mediterranean Jewish Peasant* (San Francisco: HarperSanFrancisco, 1991).

Davidson, D., *Essays on Actions and Events* (Oxford: Clarendon Press, 1980).

Davies, M., Review of R.W. Funk *et al.*, *The Five Gospels, ExpTim* 105.10 (1994), pp. 308-309.

Dewey, J. (ed.), *Orality and Textuality* (Semeia, 65; Atlanta: Scholars Press, 1995).

Dill, S., *Roman Society from Nero to Marcus Aurelius* (London: Macmillan, 1905; repr. New York: Meridian, 1956).

Dodds, E.R., *Pagan and Christian in an Age of Anxiety* (Cambridge: Cambridge University Press, 1965).

Dormeyer, D., *The New Testament among the Writings of Antiquity* (ET; Sheffield: Sheffield Academic Press, 1998 [1993]).

Downing, F.G., Article/review of M. Sato, *Q und Prophetie*, *Bib* 72.1 (1991), pp. 127-32.

—*Christ and the Cynics* (JSOT Manuals, 4; Sheffield: JSOT Press, 1988).

—*The Church and Jesus: A Study in History, Philosophy and Theology* (SBT, 2.10; London: SCM Press, 1968).

—'Common Ground with Paganism in Luke and in Josephus', *NTS* 28 (1982), pp. 546-59.

—'Common Strands in Pagan, Jewish and Christian Eschatologies in the First Century', *TZ* 51.3 (1995), pp. 196-211; repr. in *idem*, *Making Sense*, ch. 9.

—'Compositional Conventions and the Synoptic Problem', *JBL* 107.1 (1988), pp. 69-85.

—'Contemporary Analogies to the Gospels and Acts: Genres or Motifs?', in Tuckett (ed.), *Synoptic Studies*, pp. 51-65.

—'Cosmic Eschatology in the First Century: Pagan, Jewish and Christian', *AC* 64 (1995), pp. 99-109.

—*Cynics and Christian Origins* (Edinburgh: T. & T. Clark, 1992).

—*Cynics, Paul and the Pauline Churches* (London: Routledge, 1998).

—'Deeper Reflections on the Jewish Cynic Jesus', *JBL* 117.1 (1998), pp. 97-104; repr. in *idem*, *Making Sense*, ch. 6.

—'Ears to Hear', in A.E. Harvey (ed.), *Alternative Approaches to New Testament Study* (London: SPCK, 1985), pp. 97-121.

—'Ethical Pagan Theism and the Speeches in Acts', *NTS* 27 (1981), pp. 544-63.

—*Has Christianity a Revelation?* (London: SCM Press, 1964).

—' "Honor" among Exegetes', *CBQ* 61.1 (1999), pp. 53-73; repr. in *idem*, *Making Sense*, ch. 1.

—'Interpretation and the Culture Gap', *SJT* 40 (1987), 161-71; repr. in *idem*, *Making Sense in (and of) The First Christian Century* (JSNTSup, 197; Sheffield: Sheffield Academic Press, 2000), ch. 12.

—*Jesus and the Threat of Freedom* (London: SCM Press, 1987).

—'The Jewish Cynic Jesus', in A. Schmidt and M. Labahn (ed.), *The Historical Jesus in New Research* (JSNTSup; Sheffield: Sheffield Academic Press, forthcoming).

—'Law and Custom: Luke–Acts and Late Hellenism', in B. Lindars (ed.), *Law and Religion* (Cambridge: James Clarke, 1988), pp. 144-58.

—'Meanings', in M. Hooker and C.J. Hickling (eds.), *What about the New Testament? Essays in Honour of Christopher Evans* (London: SCM Press, 1975), pp. 127-42.

—'Pliny's Prosecutions of Christians: Revelation and 1 Peter', *JSNT* 34 (1988), pp. 105-23.

—'Quite like Q: A Genre for Q: The "Lives" of Cynic Philosophers', *Bib* 69.2 (1988), pp. 196-225, repr. in *idem*, *Cynics and Christian Origins*, pp. 115-42.

—'Redaction Criticism: Josephus' *Antiquities* and the Synoptic Gospels', I: *JSNT* 8 (1980), pp. 46-65; and II: *JSNT* 9 (1980), pp. 29-48; repr. S.E. Porter and C.A. Evans (eds.), *New Testament Interpretation and Methods* (BibSem, 45; Sheffield: Sheffield Academic Press, 1997), pp. 161-99.

—'Revelation, Disagreement and Obscurity', *Religious Studies* 21 (1986), pp. 219-30.

—'The Social Contexts of Jesus the Teacher: Construction or Reconstruction?', *NTS* 33 (1987), pp. 439-51.

—*Strangely Familiar: An Introductory Reader to the First Century* (Manchester: Downing, 1985)

—*The Theologian's Craft* (Unsworth, Lancs: Downing), 1974.

—'Theophilus' First Reading of Luke–Acts', in Tuckett (ed.), *Luke's Literary Achievement*, pp. 91-109; repr. in *idem*, *Making Sense*, ch. 10.

—'Towards the Rehabilitation of Q', *NTS* 11 (1965), pp. 169-81; repr. in Bellinzoni Jr (ed.), *The Two-Source Hypothesis*, pp. 269-86.

—'Ways of Deriving "Ought" from "Is" ', *PhilQ* 22.88 (1972), pp. 234-47.

—'The Woman from Syrophoenicia and her Doggedness', in Brooke (ed.), *Women in the Biblical Tradition*, repr. in *idem*, *Making Sense*, ch. 5.

Downing, J., 'Jesus and Martyrdom', *JTS* NS 14.2 (1963), pp. 279-93.

Drury, J., *Tradition and Design in Luke's Gospel* (London: Darton, Longman & Todd, 1976).

Duckworth, G.E. (ed.), *The Complete Roman Drama* (2 vols.; New York: Random House, 1942).

Duff, P.B., 'The March of the Divine Warrior and the Advent of the Greco-Roman King: Mark's Account of Jesus' Entry into Jerusalem', *JBL* 111.1 (1992), pp. 55-71.

Dunn, J.D.G., 'Prolegomena to a Theology of Paul', *NTS* 40 (1994), pp. 407-32.

Du Plessis, G., 'Speech-Act Theory and New Testament Interpretation with Special Reference to G.N. Leech's Pragmatic Principles', in P.J. Hartin and J.H. Petzer (eds.), *Text and Interpretation: New Approaches in the Criticism of the New Testament* (Leiden: E.J. Brill, 1991), pp. 129-42.

Ebeling G., *An Introduction to a Theological Theory of Language* (ET; London: Collins, 1973).

Edwards, J.R., 'Markan Sandwiches: The Significance of Interpolations in Markan Narratives', *NovT* 31.3 (1989), pp. 193-216.

Edwards, R.A., *A Theology of Q* (Philadelphia: Fortress Press, 1976).

Esler, P.F., *Community and Gospel in Luke–Acts* (SNTSMS, 58; Cambridge: Cambridge University Press, 1987).

Evans, D., *The Logic of Self-Involvement* (London: SCM Press, 1963).

Evason, S. (ed.), *Companions to Ancient Thought*. III. *Language* (Cambridge: Cambridge University Press, 1994).

—'Epicurus on Mind and Language', in *idem* (ed.), *Language*, pp. 91-99.

Farmer, W.R., *The Synoptic Problem* (New York: Macmillan, 1964).

Farmer, W.R. (ed.), *Crisis in Christology* (Livonia, MI: Dove, 1995).

Ferguson, E., *Backgrounds of Early Christianity* (Grand Rapids: Eerdmans, 1987).

Fischel, H.A., *Rabbinic Literature and Greco-Roman Philosophy* (Leiden: E.J. Brill, 1973).

Fowler, A., 'The Life and Death of Literary Forms', in R. Cohen (ed.), *New Directions in Literary History* (London: Routledge & Kegan Paul, 1974), pp. 77-94.

Fuentes González, P.P., *Les Diatribes de Télès* (Histoire des doctrines de l'antiquité-classique, 23; Paris: Vrin, 1998).

Funk, R.W., and R.W. Hoover (eds.), and The Jesus Seminar, *The Five Gospels: The Search for the Authentic Words of Jesus* (San Francisco: HarperSanFrancisco, 1993).

Furnish, V.P., 'On Putting Paul in his Place', *JBL* 113.1 (1994), pp. 3-17.

Gempf, P., 'Public Speaking and Published Accounts', in Winter and Clarke (eds.), *The Book of Acts*, pp. 259-304.

Georgi, D., 'Who is the True Prophet?', in G.W.E. Nickelsburg and G.W. MacRae (eds.), *Christians among Jews and Gentiles: Essays in Honor of Krister Stendahl* (Philadelphia: Fortress Press, 1986), pp. 100-126.

Gerhardsson, B., *Memory and Manuscript* (ET; Lund: C.W.K. Gleerup, 1961).

Gilliard, F.D., 'More Silent Reading in Antiquity: *non omne verbum sonabat*', *JBL* 112.4 (1993), pp. 689-94.

Goodman, M., *State and Society in Roman Galilee AD 132–212* (Totowa, NJ: Rowman & Allanhead, 1983).

Goulder, M.D., *Luke: A New Paradigm* (JSNTSup, 20; Sheffield: JSOT Press, 1989).

—'Luke's Compositional Options', *NTS* 39 (1993) pp. 150-52.

—*Midrash and Lection in Matthew* (London: SPCK, 1974).

Goulet-Cazé, M.-O., *L'ascèse cynique* (Paris: Vrin, 1986).

—'Le Livre Six de Diogène Laërce', *ANRW* II.36.6 (1992), pp. 3880-4048.

Goulett-Cazé, M.-O., and R. Goulet (eds.), *Le cynisme ancien et ses prolongements* (Paris: Presses Universitaires de France, 1993).

Greenlee, J.H., *Scribes, Scrolls and Scripture* (Grand Rapids: Eerdmans, 1985).

Grice, H.P., 'Logic and Conversation', in P. Cole and J.L. Morgan (eds.), *Syntax and Semantics*. III. *Speech Acts* (New York: Academic Press, 1975), pp. 41-58.

Guenther, H.O., 'The Sayings Gospel Q and the Quest for Aramaic Sources: Rethinking Christian Origins', *Semeia* 55 (1992), pp. 41-76.

Gundry, R.H., *Mark: A Commentary on his Apology for the Cross* (Grand Rapids: Eerdmans, 1993).

Hacker, P.M.S., 'Davidson on Intentionality', *Philosophy* 73.286 (1998), pp. 539-52.

Hägg, T., *The Novel in Antiquity* (ET of *Den Antika Romanen* [Uppsala: Bokförlaget, 1980]; Oxford: Basil Blackwell, 1983).

Halliday, W.R., *The Pagan Background of Early Christianity* (London: Hodder & Stoughton, 1925).

Hanfling, O., *Wittgenstein's Later Philosophy* (Basingstoke: Macmillan, 1989).

Hankinson, R.J., 'Usage and Abusage: Galen on Language', in Evason (ed.), *Language*, pp. 166-87.

Hanson, A.E., 'Papyri of Medical Content' (YCS, 28; Cambridge: Cambridge University Press, 1985).

Hanson, P.D. (ed.), *Visionaries and their Apocalypses* (London: SPCK, 1983).

Harris, J.R., *The Diatessaron of Tatian* (Cambridge: Cambridge University Press, 1898).

Harvey, A.E., *Jesus and the Constraints of History* (London: Gerald Duckworth, 1982).

Hays, R.B., 'The Corrected Jesus', *First Things* 43 (1994), pp. 43-48.

Hedrick, C., 'Representing Prayer in Mark and in Chariton's *Chaereas and Callirhoe*', *PRS* 22.3 (1995), pp. 239-57.

Henaut, B.W., *Oral Tradition and the Gospels: The Problem of Mark 4* (JSNTSup, 82; JSOT Press, 1993).

Hendrickx, H., *The Passion Narratives of the Synoptic Gospels* (London: Geoffrey Chapman, 1977).

Hengel, M., 'Aufgaben der neutestamentlichen Wissenschaft', *NTS* 40.3 (1994), pp. 311-57.

—*The 'Hellenization' of Judaea in the First Century after Christ* (ET; London: SCM Press, 1989).

—*Judaism and Hellenism* (2 vols.; ET; London: SCM Press, 1974).

Hock, R.F., *The Social Context of Paul's Ministry* (Philadelphia: Fortress Press, 1980).

Hock, R.F., and E.N. O'Neil (trans. and eds.), *The Chreia in Ancient Rhetoric*. I. *The Progymnasmata* (Atlanta: Scholars Press, 1986).

Hock, R.F., J.B. Chance and J. Perkins (eds.), *Ancient Fiction and Early Christian Narrative* (Atlanta: Scholars Press, 1998).

Hogg, H.W., *The Diatessaron of Tatian* (*ANF*; Edinburgh: T. & T. Clark, 1897).

Holmberg, B., *Sociology and the New Testament* (Minneapolis: Fortress Press, 1990).

Hornblower, J., *Hieronymus of Cardia* (London: Oxford University Press, 1981).

Horst, P.W. van der, *Aelius Aristides and the New Testament* (Leiden: E.J. Brill, 1980).

—'Can a Book End with ? A Note on Mark XVI. 8', *JTS* NS 23 (1972), pp. 121-24.

—*Hellenism–Judaism–Christianity* (Kampen: Kok, 1994).

—'Hellenistic Parallels to the Acts of the Apostles', *ZNW* 74 (1983), pp. 17-26; repr. *JSNT* 25 (1985), pp. 49-60.

—'Macrobius and the New Testament', *NovT* 15 (1973), pp. 220-32.

Houston, W., 'What Did the Prophets Think They Were Doing?', *BibInt* 1.2 (1993), pp. 167-88.

Hughes, F.W., *Early Christian Rhetoric and 2 Thessalonians* (JSNTSup, 30; Sheffield: JSOT Press, 1989).

Hurtado, L., 'Greco-Roman Textuality and the Gospel of Mark: A Critical Assessment of Werner Kelber's *The Oral and the Written Gospel*', *BibRes* 7 (1997), pp. 91-106.

Iersel, B. van, *Mark: A Reader-Response Commentary* (JSNTSup, 164; Sheffield: Sheffield Academic Press, 1998).

—'The Sun, Moon and Stars of Mark 13.24-25 in a Greco-Roman Reading', *Bib* 77.1 (1996), pp. 84-92.

Jackson, H.M., 'Why the Youth Shed his Cloak and Fled Naked: The Meaning and Purpose of Mark 14.51-52', *JBL* 116.2 (1997), pp. 273-89.

Jacobson, A.D., *The First Gospel* (Sonoma, CA: Polebridge Press, 1992).

—'The Literary Unity of Q', *JBL* 101 (1982), pp. 365-89.

—'Wisdom Christology in Q' (PhD dissertation, Claremont Graduate School, California, 1978).

Jones, C.P., 'Cynisme et "sagesse barbare": Le cas de Pérégrinus Proteus', in Goulet-Cazé and Goulet (eds.), *Le cynisme ancien*, pp. 305-18.

—'The Early Christians as a Scholastic Community', *JRH* 1 (1960), pp. 4-15.

Judge, E.A., 'St. Paul and Classical Society', *JAC* 15 (1972), pp. 19-36.

—'St. Paul the Sophist', *JRH* 3 (1963), pp. 125-37.

—*The Social Pattern of Christian Groups in the First Century* (London: Tyndale Press, 1960).

Käsemann, E., *Essays on New Testament Themes* (ET of *Exegetische Versuche und Besinnungen*; London: SCM Press, 1964 [1960]).

Kelber, W.H., *The Oral and the Written Gospel* (Philadelphia: Fortress Press, 1983).

Kennedy, G.A., *New Testament Interpretation through Rhetorical Criticism* (Chapel Hill: University of North Carolina Press, 1984).

Kermode, F., *The Genesis of Secrecy* (Cambridge, MA: Harvard University Press, 1979).

Kerr, F., *Theology after Wittgenstein* (London: SPCK, 2nd edn, 1997 [1986]).

Kindstrand, J.F., 'Diogenes Laertius and the Chreia Tradition', *Elenchos* 7 (1986), pp. 219-43.

Kirk, A., *The Composition of the Sayings Source: Genre, Synchrony and Wisdom Redaction in Q* (NovTSup, 91; Leiden: E.J. Brill, 1998).

Kirwan, C., 'Augustine on the Nature of Speech', in Evason (ed.), *Language*, pp. 188-211.

Kloppenborg, J.S., 'City and Wasteland: Narrative World and the Beginning of the Sayings Gospel Q', *Semeia* 52 (1991), pp. 145-60.

—*The Formation of Q* (Philadelphia: Fortress Press, 1987).

—'Literary Convention, Self-Evidence and the Social History of the Q People', *Semeia* 55 (1992), pp. 77-102.

—*Q Parallels: Synopsis, Critical Notes and Concordance* (Sonoma, CA: Polebridge Press, 1988).

Kloppenborg Verbin, J.S., *Excavating Q: The History and Setting of the Sayings Gospel* (Edinburgh: T. & T. Clark, 2000).

Kloppenborg, J.S. (ed.), *The Shape of Q* (Philadelphia: Fortress Press, 1994).

Kloppenborg, J.S., and L.E. Vaage, 'Early Christianity, Q and Jesus: The Sayings Gospel and Method in the Study of Christian Origins', *Semeia* 55 (1992), pp. 1-14.

Kloppenborg, J.S., and S.G. Wilson, *Voluntary Associations in the Graeco-Roman World* (New York: Routledge, 1996).

Knox, W.L., 'The Ending of Mark's Gospel', *HTR* 35 (1942), pp. 13-25.

Koester, H., *Introduction to the New Testament* (ET; 2 vols.; Berlin: W. de Gruyter, 1982).

—'Jesus the Victim', *JBL* 111.1 (1992), pp. 3-15.

—'The Memory of Jesus' Death and the Worship of the Risen Lord', *HTR* 91.4 (1998), pp. 335-50.

Kraeling, C.H., *A Greek Fragment from Tatian's Diatessaron* (London: Christophers, 1935).

Leech, G.N., *Principles of Pragmatics* (London: Longman, 1983).

Lentz, J.C., *Luke's Portrait of Paul* (SNTSMS, 77; Cambridge: Cambridge University Press, 1994).

Levi, M.A., 'I Flavi', *ANRW* II.2 (1975), p. 192.

Levinson, S., *Pragmatics* (Cambridge: Cambridge University Press, 1983).

Litfin, D., *St Paul's Theology of Proclamation: 1 Corinthians 1–4 and Greco-Roman Rhetoric* (SNTSMS, 79; Cambridge: Cambridge University Press, 1994).

Long, A.A. (ed.), 'Allegory in Philo and Etymology in Stoicism', *StudPhilAnn* 9 (1997), pp. 198-210.

—*Hellenistic Philosophy* (London: Gerald Duckworth, 1974).

—*Problems in Stoicism* (London: Athlone Press, 1971).

Longstaff, T.W.R., *Evidence of Conflation in Mark* (Missoula, MT: Scholars Press, 1977).

Luce, T.J., *Livy* (Princeton, NJ: Princeton University Press, 1977).

Lüdemann, G., *The Great Deception, and What Jesus Really Said and Did* (ET; London: SCM Press, 1998).

Lührmann, D., 'Q in the History of Early Christianity', in Kloppenborg (ed.), *The Shape of Q*, pp. 59-73 (first pub. as 'Q in der Geschichte des Urchristentums', in *idem*, *Die Redaktion der Logienquelle* [WMANT, 33; Neukirchen–Vluyn: Neukirchener Verlag, 1969], pp. 88-104).

Luz, M., 'Oenomaus and Talmudic Anecdote', *JSJ* 23.1 (1991), pp. 42-80.

MacDonald, D.R., 'Secrecy and Recognition in the Odyssey and Mark: Where Wrede went Wrong', in Hock *et al.* (eds.), *Ancient Fiction*, pp. 139-53.

Mack, B.L., *A Myth of Innocence: Mark and Christian Origins* (Philadelphia: Fortress Press, 1988), pp. 322-23.

—*The Lost Gospel: The Book of Q and Christian Origins* (Shaftesbury: Element, 1993).

Mack, B.L., and V.K. Robbins, *Patterns of Persuasion in the Gospels* (Sonoma, CA: Polebridge Press, 1989).

MacMullen, R., *Paganism in the Roman Empire* (New Haven: Yale University Press, 1981).

—'Peasants during the Principate', *ANRW* II.1 (1975), pp. 245-73.

—*Roman Social Relations, 50 BC to AD 284* (New Haven: Yale University Press, 1974).

Magness, J.L., *Sense and Absence: Structure and Suspension in the End of Mark's Gospel* (Atlanta: Scholars Press, 1986).

Malherbe, A.J., 'Herakles', *RAC* 14 (1988), pp. 569-70.

—*Social Aspects of Early Christianity* (Philadelphia: Fortress Press, 2nd edn, 1983).

Malherbe, A.J. (ed.), *The Cynic Epistles* (SBLSBS, 12; Missoula, MT: Scholars Press, 1977).

Malina, B.J., and J.H. Neyrey, 'First-Century Personality: Dyadic, not Individualistic', in Neyrey (ed.), *The Social World of Luke–Acts*, pp. 67-96.

—'Honour and Shame in Luke–Acts: Pivotal Values of the Mediterranean World', in Neyrey (ed.), *The Social World of Luke–Acts*, pp. 25-65.

Marguerat, D., 'Juifs et chrétiens selon Luc–Actes: Surmonter le conflit des lectures', *Bib* 75 (1994), pp. 126-46.

—'La mort d'Ananias et Saphira (Ac 5.1-11) dans la stratégie narrative de Luc', *NTS* 39 (1993), pp. 209-26.

—'Saul's Conversion (Acts 9, 22, 26) and the Multiplication of Narrative in Acts', in Tuckett (ed.), *Luke's Literary Achievement*, pp. 120-48.

Marrou, H., *A History of Education in Antiquity* (ET; London: Sheed & Ward, 1956).

Mattila, S.L., 'A Question Too Often Neglected', *NTS* 41.2 (1995), pp. 199-217.

Mealand, D., 'The Dissimilarity Test', *SJT* 31.1 (1978), pp. 41-50.

Meeks, W.A., *The First Urban Christians* (New Haven: Yale University Press, 1983).

Meggitt, J., *Paul, Poverty and Survival* (Edinburgh: T. & T. Clark, 1998).

Meier, J.P., *A Marginal Jew*. I. *The Roots of the Problem and the Person: Rethinking the Historical Jesus* (ABRL; New York: Doubleday, 1991).

Merritt, R.L., 'Jesus Barabbas and the Paschal Pardon', *JBL* 104.1 (1985), pp. 57-68.

Millar, F., *A Study of Cassius Dio* (London: Oxford University Press, 1964).

Mitchell, A.C., 'The Social Function of Friendship in Acts 2.44-47 and 4.32-37', *JBL* 111 (1992), pp. 255-72.

Mitchell, M.M., *Paul and the Rhetoric of Reconciliation: An Exegetical Investigation of the Language and Composition of I Corinthians* (Tübingen: J.C.B. Mohr; Louisville, KY: Westminster/John Knox Press, 1992).

Moxnes, H., *The Economy of the Kingdom: Social Conflict and Economic Interaction in Luke's Gospel* (Philadelphia: Fortress Press, 1988).

—'Patron–Client Relations and the New Community in Luke–Acts', in Neyrey (ed.), *The Social World of Luke–Acts*, pp. 241-68.

Muckensturm, C., 'Les Gymnosophistes étaient-ils des Cyniques modèles?', in Goulet-Cazé and Goulet (eds.), *Le cynisme ancien*, pp. 225-40.

Murphy-O'Connor, J., *Saint Paul's Corinth* (Wilmington, DE: Michael Glazier, 1983), pp. 94-96.

Musirillo, H.A., *The Acts of the Pagan Martyrs* (Oxford: Clarendon Press, 1954).

Mussies, G., *Dio Chrysostom and the New Testament* (Leiden: E.J. Brill, 1972).

Myers, C., *Binding the Strong Man: A Political Reading of Mark's Story of Jesus* (Maryknoll, NY: Orbis Books, 1988).

Neirynck, F., *Duality in Mark: Contributions to the Study of the Markan Redaction* (BETL, 31; Leuven: Peeters, 1972).

—'The Sayings of Jesus', in *idem*, *Evangelica II: Collected Essays* (BETL, 99; Leuven: Peeters, 1991), pp. 409-568.

Neusner, J., *Midrash in Context* (Philadelphia: Fortress Press, 1983).

Neyrey, J.H. (ed.), *The Social World of Luke–Acts* (Peabody, MA: Hendrickson, 1991).

—*What is Midrash?* (Philadelphia: Fortress Press, 1987).

Neyrey, J.H., and B.J. Malina, 'Conflict in Luke–Acts', in Neyrey (ed.), *The Social World of Luke–Acts*, pp. 97-122.

Nock, A.D., *Essays on Religion in the Ancient World* (ed. Z. Stuart; London: Oxford University Press, 1972).

Norden, E., *Agnostos Theos* (repr. Stuttgart: Teubner, 1956 [1912]).

Nussbaum, O., 'Geleit', *RAC* 9 (1969), pp. 963-78.

O'Neill, J.C., 'The Lost Written Records', *JTS* NS 42 (1991), pp. 483-504.

—*Paul's Letter to the Romans* (Harmondsworth: Penguin Books, 1975).

Oyen, G. van, 'Intercalation and Irony in the Gospel of Mark', in van Segbroeck *et al.* (eds.), *The Four Gospels*, pp. 949-74.

Palmer, D.W., 'Acts and the Ancient Historical Monograph', in Winter and Clark (eds.), *The Book of Acts*, pp. 1-29.

Palmer, H., *The Logic of Gospel Criticism* (New York: Macmillan, 1968).

Paquet, L., *Les cyniques grecs: Fragments et témoinages* (Ottowa: Les Presses de l'Université d'Ottowa, 2nd edn, 1988).

Patte, D., (ed.), *Kingdom and Children: Aphorism, Chreia, Structure* (Semeia, 29; Atlanta: Scholars Press, 1983).

Pelletier, A., *Flavius Josèphe, adapteur de la lettre d'Aristée* (Paris: Cerf, 1962).

Pelling, C.B.R., 'Plutarch's Adaptation of his Source Material', *JHS* 100 (1980), pp. 127-40.

—'Plutarch's Method of Work in the Roman Lives', *JHS* 99 (1979), pp. 74-96.

Person, A.F., 'The Ancient Israelite Scribe as Performer', *JBL* 117.4 (1998), pp. 601-609.

Pervo, R., 'A Nihilist Fabula: Introducing the *Life of Aesop*', in Hock *et al.*, *Ancient Fiction*, pp. 77-120.

—*Profit with Delight* (Philadelphia: Fortress Press, 1987).

Pinborg, J., 'Classical Antiquity: Greece', in *Current Trends in Linguistics* 13: *Historiography of Linguistics* (The Hague: Mouton, 1975), pp. 69-126.

Piper, R.A. (ed.), *The Gospel behind the Gospels: Current Studies on Q* (NovTSup, 75; Leiden: E.J. Brill, 1995).

Plümacher, E., *Lukas als hellenistischer Schriftsteller* (Göttingen: Vandenhoeck & Ruprecht, 1972).

Polkow, D., 'Methods and Criteria for Historical Jesus Research', in D.J. Lull (ed.), *Society of Biblical Literature 1989 Seminar Papers* (SBLSP, 28; Altanta: Scholars Press, 1989), pp. 336-56.

Porter, S.E., 'Literary Approaches to the New Testament: From Formalism to Deconstruction and Back', in S.E. Porter and D. Tombs (eds.), *Approaches to New Testament Study* (JSNTSup, 120; Sheffield: Sheffield Academic Press, 1995), pp. 77-129.

Porter, S.E., and T.H. Olbricht (eds.), *The Rhetorical Analysis of Scripture* (JSNTSup, 146; Sheffield: Sheffield Academic Press, 1997).

Quinn, K., 'The Poet and his Audience in the Augustan Age', *ANRW* II.30.1 (1982), pp. 75-180.

Quine, W.V.O., *From a Logical Point of View* (Cambridge, MA: Harvard University Press, 1953).

—*Word and Object* (Cambridge, MA: MIT Press, 1960).

Radford, C., 'The Power of Words', *Philosophy* 68.265 (1993), pp. 325-42.

Räisänen, H., *Paul and the Law* (ET; Philadelphia: Fortress Press, 1986).

Rajak, T., *Josephus* (London: Gerald Duckworth, 1983).

Reardon, B.P. (ed.), *Collected Ancient Greek Novels* (Berkeley: University of California Press, 1989).

Reed, J.T., 'Modern Linguistics and the New Testament: A Basic Guide to Theory, Terminology and Literature', in Porter and Tombs (eds.), *Approaches to New Testament Study*, pp. 222-65.

Rhoads, D., and D. Michie, *Mark as Story: An Introduction to the Narrative of a Gospel* (Philadelphia: Fortress Press, 1982).

Riesenfeld, H., *The Gospel Tradition* (ET; Philadelphia: Fortress Press, 1970).

Robbins, V.K., *Exploring the Texture of Texts: A Guide to Socio-Rhetorical Interpretation* (Valley Forge, PA: Trinity Press International, 1996).

—*Jesus the Teacher: A Socio-Historical Interpretation of Mark* (Philadelphia: Fortress Press, 1984).

—'Pronouncement Stories and Jesus' Blessing of the Children, in *SBLSP 1982* (ed. K.H. Richards; Chico, CA: Scholars Press, 1982), pp. 407-30.

—'The Reversed Contextualisation of Psalm 22 in the Markan Crucifixion', in van Segbroeck *et al.* (eds.), *The Four Gospels*, pp. 1161-1182.

—'Summons and Outline in Mark: The Three-Step Progression', *NovT* 23.2 (1981), pp. 97-114.

—*The Tapestry of Early Christian Discourse: Rhetoric, Society and Ideology* (London: Routledge, 1996).

—'The Woman who Touched Jesus' Garment', *NTS* 33 (1987).

Roberts, C.A., 'The Role of the Patron in the *Cena Dominica* of Hippolytus' *Apostolic Tradition*', *JTS* NS 44 (1993), pp. 170-84.

Roberts, C.H., 'Books in the Graeco-Roman World and in the New Testament', in P.R. Ackroyd and C.F. Evans (eds.), *Cambridge History of the Bible*, I (Cambridge: Cambridge University Press, 1970), pp. 53-56.

Robinson, J.M., and H. Koester, *Trajectories through Early Christianity* (Philadelphia: Fortress Press, 1971).

Rohrbaugh, R.L., 'The Pre-Industrial City in Luke–Acts', in Neyrey (ed.), *The Social World of Luke–Acts*, pp. 125-49.

—' "Social Location of Thought" as a Heuristic Construct in New Testament Study', *JSNT* 30 (1987), pp. 103-19.

Runia, D., 'Naming And Knowing: Themes in Philonic Theology, with special reference to the *De mutatione nominum*', in R. van den Broek *et al.* (eds.), *Knowledge of God in the Graeco-Roman World* (EPRO, 112; Leiden: E.J. Brill, 1988), pp. 48-75; repr. D. Runia, *Exegesis and Philosophy: Studies on Philo of Alexandria* (Aldershot: Variorum, 1990).

Russell, D.S., 'Plutarch's Life of Coriolanus', *JRS* 53 (1963), pp. 17-35.

Sanday, W. (ed.), *Studies in the Synoptic Problem* (Oxford: Clarendon Press, 1911).

Sanders, E.P., *Jesus and Judaism* (London: SCM Press, 1985).

—*Jewish Law from Jesus to the Mishnah: Five Studies* (London: SCM Press, 1990).

—*The Tendencies of the Synoptic Tradition* (SNTSMS, 9; Cambridge: Cambridge University Press, 1969).

Sanders, E.P., and M. Davies, *Studying the Synoptic Gospels* (London: SCM Press; Philadelphia: Trinity Press International, 1989).

Sato, M., *Q und Prophetie: Studien zur Galtungs-und Traditionsges Chichtlichte der Quelle Q* (WUNT, 2.29; Tübingen: J.C.B. Mohr, 1988).

Schmidt, K.L., 'Die Stellung der Evangelien in der allgemeinen Literaturgeschichte', in H. Schmidt (ed.), *EUXARISTHRION: Studien zur Religion und Literatur des Alten und Neuen Testaments* (Göttingen: Vandenhoeck & Ruprecht, 1923), pp. 50-134.

Schramm, T., *Der Markus-Stoff bei Lukas* (Cambridge: Cambridge University Press, 1971).

Schweitzer, A., *The Quest of the Historical Jesus* (ET of *Von Reimarus zu Wrede*, 3rd edn, 1906; London: A. & C. Black, 1954).

Searle, J.R., *Intentionality* (Cambridge: Cambridge University Press, 1983).

—*Speech Acts* (Cambridge: Cambridge University Press, 1969).

Seeley, D., *Deconstructing the New Testament* (Leiden: E.J. Brill, 1994).

—'Jesus' Death in Q', *NTS* 38.2 (1992), pp. 222-34.

Segbroeck, F. van, *et al.* (eds.), *The Four Gospels 1992: Festschrift Frans Neirynck* (3 vols.; BETL, 100; Leuven: Peeters, 1992).

Shepherd, T., *The Definition and Function of Markan Intercalation as Illustrated in a Narrative Analysis of Six Passages* (PhD dissertation, Andrews University, 1991).

—'The Narrative Function of Markan Intercalation', *NTS* 41.4 (1995) pp. 522-40.

Shiner, W.T., 'Creating Plot in Episodic Narratives: *The Life of Aesop* and the Gospel of Mark', in Hock *et al.* (eds.), *Ancient Fiction*, pp. 163-92.

—*Follow Me! Disciples in Markan Rhetoric* (SBLDS, 145; Atlanta: Scholars Press, 1995).

Shuler, P.L., *A Genre for the Gospels* (Philadephia: Fortress Press, 1982).

Simpson, R.T., 'The Major Agreements of Matthew and Luke against Mark', *NTS* 12 (1965/66), pp. 273-84; repr. in Bellinzoni (ed.), *The Two-Source Hypothesis*, pp. 382-95.

Smith, D.E., 'Table Fellowship as a Literary Motif in the Gospel of Luke', *JBL* 106 (1987), pp. 613-38.

Smith, J.Z., 'Wisdom and Apocalyptic', in Hanson (ed.), *Visionaries and their Apocalypses*, pp. 101-20 (repr. from B.A. Pearson [ed.], *Religious Syncretism in Antiquity* [Missoula, MT: Scholars Press, 1975]).

Smith, M., *Jesus the Magician* (San Francisco: Harper & Row, 1978).

Spencer, F.S., 'Acts and Modern Literary Approaches', in Winter and Clarke (eds.), *The Book of Acts*, pp. 381-414.

Squires, J.T., *The Plan of God in Luke–Acts* (SNTSMS, 76; Cambridge: Cambridge University Press, 1993).

Steck, O.H., *Israel und der gewaltsame Geschick der Propheten* (WMANT, 23; Neukirchen–Vluyn: Neukirchener Verlag, 1967).

Sterling, G.E., *Historiography and Self-definition: Josephos, Luke–Acts and Apologetic Historiography* (NovTSup, 64; Leiden: E.J. Brill, 1992).

Stirewalt, M.L., *Studies in Ancient Greek Epistolography* (Atlanta: Scholars Press, 1993).

Stock, B., *Augustine the Reader* (Cambridge, MA: Belknap, 1966).

Stone, M.E., 'New Light on the Third Century', and *idem*, 'Enoch and Apocalyptic Origins', in Hanson (ed.), *Visionaries*, pp. 85-91 and 92-100 (repr. from M.E. Stone, *Scriptures, Sects and Visions* [Philadelphia: Fortress Press, 1980]).

Stowers, S.K., 'Social Status, Public Speaking and Private Teaching: The Circumstances of Paul's Preaching Activity', *NovT* 26.1 (1984), pp. 59-82.

Streeter, B.H., *The Four Gospels: A Study of Origins* (London: Macmillan, 1924).

Talbert, C.H., *What is a Gospel?* (Philadelphia: Fortress Press, 1977).

Tannehill, R.C. (ed.), *Pronouncement Stories* (Semeia, 20; Atlanta: Scholars Press, 1981).

Telford, W., *The Barren Temple and the Withered Tree* (JSNTSup, 1; Sheffield: JSOT Press, 1980).

Theissen, G., 'Historical Scepticism and the Criteria of Jesus Research', *SJT* 49.2 (1996), pp. 147-76.

—*The Social Setting of Pauline Christianity* (ET; Philadelphia: Fortress Press, 1982).

—*Urchristliche Wundergeschichten* (Gütersloh: Gerd Mohn, 1974); ET: *The Miracle Stories of the Early Christian Tradition* (trans. F. McDonagh; Edinburgh: T. & T. Clark, 1983).

Theissen, G., and A. Metz, *The Historical Jesus: A Comprehensive Guide* (ET; London: SCM Press, 1998).

Tödt, H.E., *The Son of Man in the Synoptic Tradition* (ET; London: SCM Press, 1965).

Tuckett, C.M., 'A Cynic Q?', *Bib* 70.3 (1989), pp. 349-76.

—'On the Stratification of Q: A Response', *Semeia* 55 (1992), pp. 213-22.

—*Q and the History of Early Christianity: Studies on Q* (Edinburgh: T. & T. Clark, 1996).

—'Q, Prayer, and the Kingdom', *JTS* NS 40.2 (1989), pp. 367-76, repr. as part of ch. 4 of his *Q and the History of Early Christianity* (Edinburgh: T. & T. Clark, 1996), pp. 107-138.

—*Reading the New Testament* (London: SPCK, 1987).

—Review of R.W. Funk *et al.*, *The Five Gospels*, *JTS* NS 46.1 (1995), pp. 250-53.

—*The Revival of the Griesbach Hypothesis* (Cambridge: Cambridge University Press, 1983).

Tuckett, C.M. (ed.), *Luke's Literary Achievement* (JSNTSup, 116; Sheffield: Sheffield Academic Press, 1995).

—*Synoptic Studies: The Ampleforth Conference of 1982 and 1983* (JSNTSup, 7; Sheffield: JSOT Press, 1984).

Turner, E.G., *Greek Manuscripts of the Ancient World* (Oxford: Clarendon Press, 1971).

—*Greek Papyri* (Oxford: Clarendon Press, 1968).

Tyson, J.B., 'The Implied Reader in Luke–Acts', in *idem*, *Images of Judaism in Luke–Acts* (Columbia: University of South Carolina Press, 1992), pp. 17-41.

—'The Two-Source Hypothesis: A Critical Appraisal', in Bellinzoni Jr (ed.), *The Two-Source Hypothesis*, pp. 437-52.

Voelz, J.W., 'The Language of the New Testament', *ANRW* II.25.2 (1984), pp. 920-51.

Votaw, C.W., *The Gospels and Contemporary Biographies in the Greco-Roman World* (repr. Philadelphia: Fortress, 1970 [1915]).

Welborn, L.L., 'On the Discord in Corinth: 1 Corinthians 1–4 and Ancient Politics', *JBL* 106.1 (1987), pp. 85-111.

Wenham, D., *Paul: Follower of Jesus or Founder of Christianity?* (Grand Rapids: Eerdmans, 1995).

White, H.C. (ed.), *Speech-Act Theory and Biblical Criticism* (Semeia, 41; Atlanta: Scholars Press, 1988).

White, J.L., *Light from Ancient Letters* (Philadelphia: Fortress Press, 1986).

Williams, B., 'Cratylus' Theory of Names and its Refutation', in Evason (ed.), *Language*, pp. 23-36.

Winter, B.W., and A.D. Clarke (eds.), *The Book of Acts in its First-Century Setting*. I. *The Book of Acts in its Ancient Literary Setting* (Grand Rapids: Eerdmans, 1993; Exeter: Paternoster Press, 1994).

Winton, A.P., *The Proverbs of Jesus* (JSNTSup, 35; Sheffield: JSOT Press, 1990).

Wittgenstein, L., *On Certainty* (Oxford: Basil Blackwell, 1969).

—*Philosophical Investigations* (Oxford: Basil Blackwell, 1953).

Wright, N.T., *Christian Origins and the Question of God*. I. *The New Testament and the People of God* (London: SPCK, 1992).

—*Christian Origins and the Question of God*. II. *Jesus and the Victory of God* (London: SPCK, 1996).

—'Five Gospels but no Jesus', in W.R. Farmer (ed.), *Crisis in Christology* (Livonia, MI: Dove, 1995), pp. 115-57.

Yarbrough, R.W., 'The Gospel according to the Jesus Seminar', *Presybterion* 20.1 (1994), pp. 12-13.

Zeller, D., 'Redactional Process and Changing Settings', in Kloppenborg (ed.), *The Shape of Q*, pp. 128-29 (first pub. as 'Redaktionsprozesse und wechselnder "Sitz im Leben" beim Q-Material', in J. Delobel [ed.], *Les paroles de Jésus* [BETL, 59; Leuven: Peeters, 1982], pp. 395-409).

INDEXES

INDEX OF REFERENCES

OLD TESTAMENT

NEW TESTAMENT

CLASSICAL AUTHORS

OTHER ANCIENT REFERENCES

INDEX OF ANCIENT AUTHORS

INDEX OF CONTENTS

(see also the Indexes of Authors and Index of References)

JOURNAL FOR THE STUDY OF THE NEW TESTAMENT
SUPPLEMENT SERIES